HARDCORE
"IRON MIKE"

HARDCORE "IRON MIKE"

Conqueror of Iwo Jima

Gregg Stoner

iUniverse®

Hardcore "Iron Mike"
Conqueror of Iwo Jima

iUniverse books may be ordered through booksellers or by contacting:

iUniverse
1663 Liberty Drive
Bloomington, IN 47403
www.iuniverse.com
1-800-Authors (1-800-288-4677)

ISBN: 978-1-4917-6507-4 (sc)
ISBN: 978-1-4917-6508-1 (hc)
ISBN: 978-1-4917-6506-7 (e)

Library of Congress Control Number: 2015905738

Print information available on the last page.

iUniverse rev. date: 10/06/2015

TABLE OF CONTENTS

Sergeant Major 'Iron Mike' Mervosh

Dedication

To brother Milan Mervosh who was killed in action in Korea serving 'I' Company, Third Battalion, Seventh Regiment, First Marine Division, and all my foxhole comrades that fought and won the "battle of all battles".

FOREWORD

This is a glorious record of the Fourth Marine Division for the Marines of that division. As such, it will mean something that it cannot possibly mean to anyone else. By that I mean nobody quite understands a battle unless he was in it. There is a great deal of camaraderie in battle that cannot be comprehended by those who did not participate in the fighting. The memories of the battles may rest upon something that seemed minor at the time: the flash of a flame thrower at a critical moment; the mixed smell of gunpowder; sweat; decaying flesh; or the dry taste of cheese in a K-ration just before the jump-off. These are things that cannot be adequately described to someone who was not there.

Therefore, this proud history of the Fourth Marine Division will be something that in all probability can be shared only by the officers and Marines of the outfit. To anyone else a picture may be just a picture; a paragraph may be just a paragraph about the war. To the Marines who were involved the word "Roi" means something else besides "king" in French; Hills '382' and '362' were not just numbers—they were hell!

There is no doubt in my mind that the historians will decide when the final returns are in, that the Central Pacific was the main stroke against Japan. This was the campaign where the 'Fighting Fourth' Marine Division fought all its battles: Roi-Namur, Marshall Islands, Saipan, Tinian, and Iwo Jima. They fought the battles as magnificent and heroic as Marines ever fought.

Countless acts of bravery and heroism under fire with courage and determination and a keen sense of duty under fire went unrewarded because they were "all in a day's work", or unwitnessed by any officer or Marines who lived to tell about it. Many of those acts lie buried beneath the beach and volcanic ash.

The Japanese staged their only organized night counterattack of the battle the night of 8-9 March against our lines. From 1800 to 2000 hours the rockets, mortars, grenades, rifle, and machine guns fell along our lines followed by systematic infiltration. Waves of Japanese hammered our lines and some even broke through to the command posts. Many enemy soldiers carrying land mines strapped to their chests came at us in attempts to blow us up in their suicidal charges. Others, seeing their charges were failures, simply killed themselves with their grenades. Hand-to-hand fighting took place up and down our lines. We killed the majority of the enemy that day in our foxholes as we blasted every moving object. The next morning seven hundred eighty-four enemy bodies were counted.

The 'end of the battle all battles' however, was in sight. At 1500 hours the tenth patrol reached at the coast without encountering opposition. By the next day the division front had heavy opposition in the wild terrain. The 25th Marines were still meeting a packet of heavy resistance when the enemy chose to make their last stand. Finally, during the night of 15-16 March, a party of over sixty of the enemy tried to break out of the pocket, and failing to do so they slunk back in their caves and bunkers, which the Marines cleared out by 1000 on the 16th of March.

The commanding general announced on 16 March that Iwo Jima was secure. However, fighting continued for another ten days in the far side of the island. The 4th Marine Division Cemetery was dedicated on that date and naval support units sailed away.

The 23rd and 25th Regiments had returned to their ships by 17 and 18 March respectively, and the 24th Regiment, and most of the division sailed away on the 20th of March. The division's combat efficiency was rated at thirty-five percent.

Iwo Jima played a significant role in the final days of World War II. It became a way station for upwards of 2,200 B-29 bombers and their crews numbering some 25,000. The proximity of the island would end up saving the lives of the pilots and crews by allowing them a jumping off point for bombing runs to Japan—a place where they could also return to when done with their missions.

In all the battles that were fought and won, never before, and never after, would equal the fighting on Iwo Jima, which is recorded as the most demanding, toughest, and bloodiest battle in adding to the illustrious chapters to our history and heritage of our country. What is least known by many, and is never shown in the history books, or shown on film clips, is that the "battle of all battles" was a perfect battle on a perfect battlefield and was a defender's dream. The landscape resembled the moon with is lunar appearance from the bombed out craters with a ghostlike earthquake appearance in the northern part of the island. There were crazy ridges, crevices, and gorges with washboard terrain. What I mean by 'perfect battle on a perfect battlefield' is that there wasn't any collateral damage—not one single structure above the ground, nor any civilians. It was strictly fighting man against fighting man; the true words were "kill or be killed". It was one-of-a-kind in the history of the Marine Corps, our country, and possibly the world. God bless our Marines who accomplished that mission.

Those WWII veterans will always be respected and remembered as the epitome and truism of the Greatest Generation, and that hopefully results in a most thankful generation. All those Greatest Generation fighting men saved this nation, our democracy, our civilization, and also saved the world by knowing how to fight and win battles, and then proceeding to rebuild the nation during the post-war years.

The Fighting Fourth returned to its training base at Camp Maui to replenish equipment and Marines, and to initiate a rigorous training program preparatory to the planned invasion of the Japanese homeland. However, two atom bombs were dropped on Nagasaki and Hiroshima and the rest is history.

Don't ever let anyone tell you—not ever—that it wasn't tough. According to figures the Fourth Marine Division was in combat a little over sixty days in World War II. But, in those sixty-odd days the division saw more action than many other divisions in *six hundred days*. Their action was with a keen sense of duty, with courage and determination as fierce as any Marine ever saw. The price the Fourth Division had to pay was extremely heavy, as it must be on vital targets. This price amounted to about seventy-five percent casualties. It takes real Marines to have the guts to stand such losses and still come up with the determination to accomplish their missions.

I was a privileged Marine to be with the Fourth by participating in all its battles. Many were buried out there—they were Marines who fought for their country and Corps. I hope the readers of this book will forever know what it meant.

INTRODUCTION

Sergeant Major "Iron Mike" D. Mervosh is an icon Marine who served thirty-five years in the Marine Corps and ultimately became the most senior enlisted man in all the armed services. When Iron Mike enters a room he instantly becomes the center of attention, as younger Marines crowd around him to listen to his stories and have their photos taken with him.

What makes Iron Mike such a draw? Well, for one thing, he is a man who spent his early Marine Corps years landing on the beaches of such places as Roi-Namur, Saipan, Tinian, the Marshal Islands, and of course, Iwo Jima. The fact that he landed on Iwo Jima and is still around to talk about it is legendary in itself. He is one of few men today that can say he was on the beach at Iwo Jima when the flag was raised on Mount Suribachi. But he went on to serve in Korea during the Korean War, and then had two tours of duty fighting in the Vietnam War. This Marine has seen more action on more war fronts than just about anybody alive—that might explain why he is a magnate for younger Marines.

My first exposure to Iron Mike was at a West Coast Drill Instructor Association annual reunion at Marine Corps Recruit Depot (MCRD), San Diego. Marines around me started to buzz, "There's Iron Mike!" There was an immediate crowd that went up to him as he arrived, and he was never alone from that moment forward. I have to plead some ignorance: I didn't know who he was, but I would soon find out!

I learned that he had been the subject of chapters in several books, and the one I was first familiar with was a chapter in *The Few and the Proud* by Larry Smith. The author had dedicated a chapter to Iron Mike and in it he told of his career in the Marine Corps—a career that included two tours as a drill instructor at Parris Island. His chapter was titled "Iron Mike Mervosh" and was the second chapter in the book. I obtained a copy of the book and read it from cover-to-cover, but I found Iron Mike's story to be the most compelling of all the chapters that were dedicated to other Marine icons. On our next occasion to run into each other I had that book with me and I asked him to autograph it. He wrote: "To Gregg with highest regards, Iron Mike Mervosh." I was thrilled to have his autograph.

Iron Mike Mervosh is someone who is constantly being asked to be a guest speaker at a variety of events. He does not plan his speeches—he simply gets up and starts talking. A general once requested Iron Mike to speak at a large event and the general had his secretary call Iron Mike to find out what he would be talking about. Iron Mike told the secretary that he doesn't prepare a speech. The secretary was perplexed and she told him that the general had to know what he was going to say. Iron Mike declined the engagement immediately, as he insists on being natural at the podium. The secretary relayed the message to the general and it was not long after that the general accepted his independent manner of doing things.

The sergeant major is almost ninety-two years of age at the time of this writing, but to talk with him one would guess he is much younger. He is still sharp as a tack and has a fantastic memory recall of his Marine Corps experiences that occurred over seventy-two years ago. He has also remained fit and trim, and there is no doubt that he still fits into his dress blues uniform when he needs to.

There are Marines that wear more decorations than Iron Mike—most of his fighting years were done when fewer medals were awarded—he still feels that under today's award standards that every Marine that landed on Iwo Jima would be awarded our top medals of valor. Iron Mike doesn't talk about his Bronze Star with combat "V" or his three Purple Hearts for wounds he received in battles in different wars—he is not about bragging or showing off. He is the real deal. In fact, he will proudly proclaim that he has five precious awards he is proud of having: two arms, two legs, and his head.

Iron Mike Mervosh held every enlisted rank that the Marine Corps offered as he came up through the ranks, ultimately becoming a sergeant major—he held that rank for nineteen and one-half years before he retired as the most senior enlisted man in all of our military services. But what really motivated the man was his desire to fight and to lead his men. He wanted no part of desk jobs or being in the rear. His idea of leading is to lead from the front with his rifle at fixed bayonet and at-the-ready.

He has appeared as a guest speaker at over one hundred events, and the number is continually increasing each year. People love to hear Iron Mike talk about his experiences. He doesn't care about being politically correct—he simply says it like it is. In fact, he is about as far from being politically correct as one can get, and he doesn't care one iota. His stories mesmerize audiences because of his colorful manner of describing things. He speaks at schools too, and young boys and girls look up to him the way a real hero should be viewed.

In preparation for writing this book many hours were spent interviewing Iron Mike, most of which occurred at his home in his den that would best be described as a museum—it is filled with artifacts that fill every square inch of the many shelves and wall space in the room. Just to look around the room was a fascinating trip—he has photos of himself with president Gerald Ford, and movies stars such as Hugh O'Brian, Charlton Heston, Lee Marvin, and others. He proudly points out that President Jimmy Carter invited him to the inauguration ceremony and parade, White House reception, and the inauguration banquet. In addition, President Gerald Ford invited him to a wreath laying ceremony on the U.S.S. Arizona in Pearl Harbor. I had the impression that it was the people in those pictures that were in awe of the sergeant major and not the other way around.

Although he was an active duty Marine for thirty-five years, and held his sergeant major rank for nineteen and one-half years, his most cherished memories stem from his time spent growing up in the Great Depression and those times in the Fourth Marine Division during World War II. Even though those memories are well over seventy years old, his recollection of them is like they just occurred yesterday.

This book was written with a combination of stories quoted by Iron Mike in the first person, and also by using commentary and background information from the author. I wanted the readers to be able to appreciate the way Iron Mike speaks and how he just says it like it is. There are not many people today that will say exactly what they mean—Iron Mike does.

The book is structured in a chronological manner, starting with Iron Mike's early years growing up in Pittsburgh in the Great Depression, and then getting involved with the Marine Corps when the Japanese invaded Pearl Harbor. The combat years were the real highlights of this storied Marine, and once those wars were over Iron Mike was relegated to senior staffing positions, something that he really was not fond of, as he felt most comfortable leading a group of Marine grunts on a combat mission with a rifle at the ready. But Iron Mike is not just a combat warrior—he is a leader and has always used his extraordinary leadership skills in his assignments.

When it came time to decide on a title for this book I asked Iron Mike what he felt the title should be. Without so much a second of hesitation he confidently said: "Let's call it *Hardcore Iron Mike.* People always said I was hardcore and it pretty much defines what I am all about." Hardcore Iron Mike it is.

He doesn't like to talk about it much, but one of his greatest accomplishments was caring for his ailing wife Maggie who was diagnosed with cancer. Iron Mike stayed by here side throughout her long illness, caring for her every need twenty-four hours per day, seven days per week. He did everything he could to comfort her and continue to maintain the household. Maggie finally lost her battle to her disease, and although it has been several years since, Iron Mike is still in grief over the loss of his wife of 63 years. I let him quietly keep his memories to himself and never pressed for more information—I respected his continuous strong feelings about her.

Sergeant Major Iron Mike Mervosh is more than just a warrior—he has a heart of gold too. Several times he asked me questions about my service number and other personal pertinent Marine data. Later I came back to his home for a continuation of our interviews and he presented me with an official looking Marine Corps warrant promoting me to honorary gunnery sergeant! It was signed by Iron Mike and was done so on the Marine Corps birthday. He just wanted to give me something special for helping him tell his story in the book. I hold that gift special and it will remain in my Marine Corps room forever.

This book is his story as told by the man himself.

Chapter 1

GROWING UP IN THE GREAT DEPRESSION

My parents were Serbian immigrants and in our household we spoke the Serbian language. In those days babies were not normally born in hospitals—it was the midwives who delivered the kids at home. In the Serbian tradition the midwife got to choose the names of the newborns. The payment for a delivery was normally a bottle of booze. I was named "Dush". I never liked that name, and would later change it to "Mike". But I would later learn that in the Serbian language "Dush" means "leader", so I guess the midwife knew something about me right away.

I was told I cried a lot when I was a baby. We lived in an old house, and one night I started to cry in the middle of the night. My mother woke up and realized immediately that she smelled gas from a gas leak somewhere in the house. She opened the windows to bring fresh air in, and then ran to my crib and picked me up and told me to keep crying so that I could breath the fresh air. I guess my crying probably saved us. My life would be like that.

Times were always tough for us. My dad worked in the steel mills, and work was never a constant thing. When the mills had no work the men were laid off, and that meant more financial hardships. I recall seeing his pay for two week's work—it was $24.00. My dad was a hardworking man like all the men back then and he never complained. He was very easygoing and never got rattled. We lived in a placed called "Larkin's Alley" and the row houses were built close together with about two inches between them. One time my mom screamed, "Fire!" and raced down to my dad who was sitting on the porch. He just told her not to worry, that the fire department would take care of it. Mom was still excited, so Dad just said again that he had insurance and they would take care of any damage. He was like that—nothing got to him. The fire damaged a couple of the rooms and we ended up having to sleep on the kitchen floors for a couple of months while the burned areas were repaired. In those days families adapted to whatever came their way.

My mother did catering for weddings, funerals, and other special occasions. She made a little money from that. She was great cook and we always looked forward to her returning from those events because she often brought home leftovers for us. She was always able to put a meal on our table and we never went hungry. The depression caused people to learn to live within their means, and often that meant just eking by with little or nothing.

I was the oldest child in my family and had a sister named Anna who was two years younger, and another brother Milan who was six years my junior. The youngest was twelve years younger than me—his name was Sam. We took baths once a week, and it was always on Saturday. We used a washtub that was kept in the kitchen. Since I was the eldest I was given the first bath in clean water. My two younger brothers had to use the same water. Because Anna was a girl she was given clean water for her bath. That was the way everyone did things back in those days. Many of the homes didn't have a bath and some of the neighbors would come over to our house to use ours. Dad had the bath installed when the house was built and all the neighbors envied us.

As Serbians we celebrated Saint Nicholas Day, and it was the biggest Serbian day of celebration. We all got together for a special meal. We put extra leafs in the dining room table, and also set up a smaller table in the kitchen. The kids had to eat in the kitchen. It was a real family oriented day for us. My dad always had his homemade beer and wine, and he even had some homemade whiskey. He put the beer in jars and bottles that were handy, but never he had any beer bottles. The beer was always warm since we had no way to cool it down. He never made anything to sell, as it was just for personal consumption. Whiskey has a very strong aroma when it is being made and one day a cop came by the house and told my dad that he could smell it very easily. My dad said it was for private consumption and then gave the cop some whiskey in a jar to take home. We never heard any more about it after that.

Mom would buy chickens from the butcher shop to cook, but they were not like the ones in the stores today: they still had the feathers on and we had to remove them before cooking. My sister, brother Milan, and I had to pluck the feathers off the chickens and Mom used to make us save the feathers. The feathers were then used for making new pillows. My brothers and I used to get in pillow fights, and one time I hit my brother with the pillow and the pillow split open causing the feathers to fly everywhere! My mom was really upset about the mess.

We were very careful not to waste anything. We learned to be very frugal with everything we did. I remain that way to this day—I can't stand to waste anything. I think most people from that era are pretty much the same way.

I was seven years old when I started the first grade. By the time I was in third grade they realized I was pretty smart and I was meritoriously promoted to the fifth grade. I was so nervous the first day of school that I forgot to shave. *(Note: this a joke that Iron Mike loves to tell people and he waits until it sinks in before he smiles and then laughs with the listener!)*

Pittsburgh was primarily a steel mill town, and there was heavy black smoke that belched from the smoke stacks at the mills. The smoke was so thick that the sky was often dark until noon when the winds would start to clear the skies a little. And when it snowed out the snow turned black from the ash falling from the smoke. The factories would dump their wastes and sewage into the river making it very contaminated. We swam in the river anyway, as it was our only source of water to swim in. We didn't worry about the contamination, as it wasn't an issue then.

The schools would offer oatmeal to the students one day each week. I remember how I loved that stuff and looked forward to that special day every week. We always had a meal to eat, but nobody got fat. Fresh bread was ten cents a loaf in those days, but stale bread more than a day old was sold for five cents—we always bought the stale bread. We didn't have a coffee percolator, so we just dumped the coffee grounds into the boiling water. We would then dunk our stale bread into the coffee and it tasted really good. We also broke the stale bread into crumbs and mixed it with milk. In the cold winters we would have two bottles of milk delivered every day. The milk was much richer back then, as the cream was not removed like it is today. The cream was always on the top, and when it froze the cream would swell outside the bottle and we would all fight about who would get to eat the "ice cream".

Charles Lindbergh flew across the Atlantic in 1927 when I was just four years old. He was my hero when I was a boy and I wanted to be just like him. Lindbergh wore a pair of boots, so at my first opportunity I got a pair of boots like his. The boots came with a jackknife as part of the deal, but my dad took the knife away because he was afraid I might get in fights at school and hurt somebody. I didn't get the knife back until I turned seventeen years old.

The kids in our neighborhood played a lot of ball in the streets. We had maybe three baseball gloves for the whole team—we shared the gloves we had. We didn't have any catcher masks or pads, so the catcher often got a ball slammed into his face or chest. We always had fun as kids. Kids today don't know how to have fun like we used to—today they stay inside and play video and computer games instead of going outside and getting some real exercise at the same time.

The Great Depression . . . what the hell was great about it? The times continued to get bleaker for everyone, my family included. In those days the markets and retailers were run mostly Jewish immigrants. I always admired those shop owners because they kept accurate records of their accounts. We didn't always have cash to spend and they would put our charges on the account. My mom got concerned when the bill reached $60, but the Jewish owner told her not to worry, that my dad would be back to work some day and she could pay then. Those merchants were very generous with credit to those who couldn't pay. The whole system was different then. People paid their bills when they could, but they always paid.

My dad was very accomplished at dealing with electrical things, as well as being good at carpentry. He was always fixing things or building things for the house. Most men were very capable in that era, and there wasn't much my dad couldn't make or fix. I don't know where he learned those things, but it sure came in handy at times. I would watch him while he fixed things and I was always awed by what he could do.

When I was young I had to financially help out at home. To help my family I held a variety of jobs. One of them was selling Serbian daily newspapers. I would buy them for one cent and sell them for three cents. I could make $1 each time and I did that two times each week. I always contributed my money to the family—we all pitched in to make things work. Another job I had was shoveling coal. All the homes in my neighborhood used coal to heat their homes. We would hop onto a slow train with coal cars and then start tossing the pieces of coal onto the ground. We later loaded those pieces from the ground into bushels and would sell them to the needy for ten cents per barrel. After the coal was burned up we had to remove the ashes and haul them away and we charged another ten cents per bushel. During mild weather it was much easier than in the winter when the ashes became frozen and we had to dig it out of the barrel and have it dumped at the various ash sites. Our family had coal delivered and my job was to shovel the coal into the cellar. Some of the neighbors also had coal delivered and I would sometimes shovel their coal into their cellars and they would give me money—generally it was ten cents, but sometimes if I got lucky I received twenty-five cents. Sometimes it was just an IOU.

In my early teens I had a job working for a huckster. Hucksters were vendors that sold fruits and vegetables off a wagon or out of the back of a pickup. I had to walk five miles with the horse and wagon to get the goods we sold. One of my jobs was to shovel the poop off the road when the horse dropped it. I never cared for that part, but one time a man stopped me and told me I didn't need to do that since the birds would come and eat the poop. The streets had horse troughs at the curbs for the horses to drink from, and we thought nothing of taking a drink from the same trough. We could make $1.50 for working eight hours of hard work, and sometimes it was as much as $2.00 on a really good day. I gave my earnings to my family to help with the cost of living. That is how things were done in the depression days.

Sometimes we would go to the golf course and caddy for the golfers. They would tip us twenty-five cents sometimes. We would go into the rough to retrieve the balls that the golfers shot there. Once a golfer hit into the rough and we could not find his ball—the balls all had special markings on them so you could tell what type of ball you had, and we just could not find this golfer's ball. I found another one and tossed it onto the green—he shot that ball from that point.

Another job I had was working in a bowling alley. They didn't have automatic pinsetters back then. All the pins had to be reset by a pin man. I set pins and received three cents per bowling line, and if I could set up ninety bowling lines I could earn up to $2.70. Sometimes the pins would be hit so hard by the bowling balls that they would spin out of control and fly into us and it hurt like hell. It was pretty dangerous at times. If the bowler won his game he would sometimes toss a quarter down the lane for us.

My mom bought our clothes at the Little Mills Store—the store would extend credit and that made it a convenient store when we had no money. In addition, bargains were offered and those bargains were needed to make ends meet. That store was for people that worked in the mills. We only got things we absolutely needed. Most of my clothes were handed down to my younger brothers when I outgrew them.

Illnesses were treated at home because nobody went to doctors. If a person got scarlet fever or the measles they would tack a sign on the door to warn people. Everyone had his or her own home remedies for sickness. When someone died the mortuaries prepped the body, but funerals were not conducted in funeral parlors—they were done in the person's home. The body would be put in the living room and the wake was held, and then the body was carried off to the graveyard for burial.

Times got tougher and tougher as the Great Depression went deeper into the abyss. It seemed like there would be no end to the terrible times we were in. We had absolutely no frills, as we were getting by having to stretch our meals and other necessities as far as we could. We grew up without extras and that was our normal. Everyone helped each other back then. The thing is, we didn't think of it as a depression. To us it was just the way things were so we just went about our business. We didn't realize how really poor we were, and everyone was in the same boat.

Crime was not a problem, and we never locked our windows or doors. Neighbors would just walk in the door without knocking—we did the same. Everyone was like family to one another. You can't do that today. On hot nights we kept the windows open, and once in a while a stray cat would wander in. I woke up once to a cat walking over me—it was a very startling way to wake up.

One time I was climbing a fence and when I got to the top I fell over the other side. I didn't realize there was a metal picket fence on the opposite side, and it had pointed pickets. I fell head first and with the luck of God my head went right between two pickets. The points went into my neck area and it broke my collarbone. It hurt like hell. Nobody had medical insurance then. After that my mom took out a life insurance policy on my life and it cost her something like ten cents a month. I guess my mom figured I was going to end up killing myself. The insurance guy would come over and collect the small premium every month.

We had street gangs then, but they weren't like today. We were known by the streets we were from: the 10th Street Gang, 13th Street Gang, 26th Street Gang, etc. We didn't have knives or guns like they do today. The only weapons we had were our fists. We were proud of our areas, and if someone crossed into our streets it was time for a good rumble. We only used our fists to fight with. It was all clean stuff. There were anywhere from ten to twenty gang members. Sometimes we even played football or baseball with the other gangs. We were pretty competitive. Today the gangs think that their gang members are their family—to us our gang members were just the guys we hung out with, and we all had our families at home.

We were always horsing around, and once I was slapping and punching another kid in play. A man named Mike Cupon saw me and came over and told me that he thought I had some good moves, and then he offered to train me to be a boxer if I would join his boxing club. The club practiced in a place called Brashear Association, and it was sort of like a YMCA. It was a small gym, but it had a shower and a lot of guys inside were playing checkers and chess. The place kept us off the streets and out of trouble. I was still small then, and my first boxing fight would be as a welterweight. My opponent was a guy named B.B Wright. It was a very close fight, but I lost. Later I learned that B.B. Wright turned pro after thirty fights. I was a good boxer and the bouts were held where the Pittsburgh Pirates played ball. The winner would get $5 and the loser would get $3, and when I won I would give my winning purse to my mom. Boxing matches were known as "smokers" because about ninety percent of the audience smoked cigars and the area was full of heavy cigar smoke.

I learned to like boxing and I worked hard at it when at the gym. My trainer Mike Cupon had long arms like a gorilla, and he could reach down and pick up a basketball with one had. The Pittsburgh

Steelers hired him as a trainer because he had strong hands and could give the players good rubdowns. He continued teaching me how to box and I became very good at it.

In high school I played baseball and football. I played both defense and offense in football, and my position was center. I made "All-city" at center and only weighed one hundred sixty pounds. We never played on grass either—the fields were dirt or hard clay, and often had rocks on the surface. We only played games in the daytime since there were no lights on the field for night games like the schools have today. Once we went to Altoona, Pennsylvania to play a game. Altoona was about a ninety-mile round trip. We arrived and got ready to play but their team didn't show up by game time. Finally, after a very long wait, they showed up. When they got off their bus their faces were all black. We found out that they worked in the coalmines and had to finish their shift before they could play us. They outweighed us by twenty to thirty pounds and they ended up killing us. For them school was secondary—their jobs came first.

Not everyone graduated from high school—a lot guys had to drop out of school so they could get jobs. Many of the young men would find work in the steel mills, but even those jobs were scarce. The depression was just a very tough time for everyone. Most jobs didn't require a higher education anyway; so dropping out of high school was not considered a bad thing. In fact, a high school diploma then was probably the equivalent of a college degree today.

One thing that I can say upon looking back on that era—the Great Depression was the foundation that created the "Greatest Generation". The sacrifices that were made by every man and woman, and the hard work that was required just to survive made people very tough. It was this group of men and women that would end up taking on the enemies in World War II and come out victorious. I am extremely proud to be from that generation of Americans.

Chapter 2

THE SHOCK OF PEARL HARBOR

America was ambivalent to the war that was developing in Europe. Nobody wanted the United States to enter the war. We were doing just fine supplying war goods to our allies as a neutral country. The United States had stopped supplying oil and steel to Japan because of their imperialistic ways in the South Pacific. Despite Japan's aggressions we remained distant and wanted no part of that situation.

Japan had other ideas. Japan needed our oil in order to accomplish their goals, so they needed to bring our country to the negotiating table. We were a mighty power at the time, but we had weaknesses too. Japanese leaders decided that the best way to bring America to it's knees was to take out our Pacific fleet—that would cripple our ability to fight in the Pacific, and that was what they were counting on to bring us to the point of opening up our fuel supplies to them. It would also prevent us from interfering in Japan's determination of taking over South Pacific territories controlled by Great Britain, the United States, and the Netherlands.

Just before 0800 on 7 December 1941 the Japanese initiated a surprise attack on Pearl Harbor and two other Pacific islands that we had naval bases on. Their attack was extremely fierce and caught our sleeping forces by complete surprise. The onslaught was without mercy as their planes dropped bombs and torpedoes that destroyed or severely damaged our ships. Planes on the ground were destroyed before they could be scrambled. Our forces were not prepared for such an attack. When it was over, the harbor was full of sunken and damaged ships and the carnage that goes with such an attack. Thousands of our men and civilians were killed or wounded. It was the first foreign invasion on American soil.

There was no television in those days, and the reports of the raid had to be relayed by radio to the mainland. It would be hours before communications could be set up to announce the attack to the American citizens. President Franklin Roosevelt made the announcement—it was very somber and still sticks in my mind to this day.

I remember I was at the pool hall with my buddies. Some were playing pool; others were playing the pinball machines. I didn't have any money, so I was just hanging out with them. Suddenly someone turned the radio up as a news flash was being announced. They said the Japs had attacked Pearl Harbor and killed thousands of Americans. We were shocked—just like all of America was. It was something that seemed inconceivable to all of us. We were outraged. It just didn't seem real.

I had no idea where Pearl Harbor was. None of us did. I later learned it was in the Hawaiian Islands, but that was far away. It was a territory of the United States, but was not a state at the time. All of us decided we needed to do something. We decided to go down join the service and fight the Japs—we wanted to seek revenge for their cowardly attack on Pearl Harbor.

The United States declared war on Japan the following day. That prompted Germany and Italy to declare war on us, an act that we reciprocated. The U.S. became instantly involved in the World War II.

The next day following the attack my buddies and I all went down to the recruiting office. The recruiting office had all the military services in its one office in Pittsburgh, and there were long lines of young guys like us, and all of them had the same idea as we did: join the service and kill the Japs—everyone was talking about that while we stood in the long line.

I hadn't graduated from high school yet but I didn't care—I wanted to join the service to get revenge. Revenge was a major factor that all the young men had and it was more like a burning desire. When it was finally my turn to speak to the recruiter I first spoke to the Navy recruiter. He told me that I could travel and see the world. The Army recruiter told me that they would teach me a trade. When I got to the Marine recruiter he didn't try to sell me the Marines. Instead he asked me what I could do for them! I was impressed and decided the Marines were for me. He asked me if I had finished high school yet. I told him I hadn't, and he then told me to finish school first, and come back when I had graduated. He also told me that they had quotas and had already filled the quotas, so they couldn't take any more enlistees anyway. He asked for my phone number so he could call me. I told him we didn't have a phone, so he asked if I could provide a neighbors phone number instead. I told him we were all poor where I lived and nobody had a phone. He took my address and said he would contact me that way.

I was disappointed. I figured I could always finish school when I got back from the war. My dad had a different idea: he wanted to know what the heck I was thinking, as he was very upset with me. I told him that I wanted to go into the Marines—he tried to talk me out of it, but I wasn't going along with him. Then my mother started in on me and told me how important a high school degree was. She finally convinced me to stay in school, so I went back and continued with my classes.

I loved the Marine recruiting posters. One of the best showed a Marine with his rifle and bayonet and under the Marine it said, "First to Fight!" Another one that really grabbed me was a poster that said, "Join the Marines and receive $134 per month for life after 30 years!" That one really made me say, 'Wow', and I was sold. It was all I could think about after I graduated.

I finally graduated in June 1942. Graduating high school was a big thing in those days. A lot of guys had to drop out of school to help support their families due to the Great Depression, so with a high school diploma I stood out. I had promised my mom I would do it, and that was important to me too. Even after graduating I continued to do odd jobs to help my family.

All the young men were either being drafted or were enlisting. They were even drafting older men—the sickly were the only ones exempt. America had two major campaigns taking place on two theaters—the European theater against the Germans and Italians, and the Pacific campaign against the Japanese. It seemed like every available man was being taken for military duty. Women began taking men's places in the factories to replace the men that were going to war. It was a major change to the American ways, but everyone was doing their part.

During the war all the families were given ration books for gasoline—two gallons per week. Cigarettes were rationed too, and although they were just six cents a pack, there was a limit of one carton per week. We also had rationing of meat, butter, lard, nylons, rubber, and other things.

Things were still tough at home after I graduated. My dad had been laid off at the steel mill and I had to do a lot of odd jobs to help at home. I don't think I was making more than about ten bucks a month delivering newspapers and other odd work when I could find it. I knew I had to do more to help out, and I had that burning desire to become a Marine. I was torn between my strong urge to join the Marines or staying home as long as I could to help my family. I kept picturing myself as a rifleman with a bayonet. I wanted to take it to the Japs and make them pay for Pearl Harbor.

As the war campaign ramped up the mills and factories went into high gear to produce war goods. My dad finally was working steadily. They increased the pay at the mill and things were starting to look up for a change.

After war was declared we had blackouts on the east and west coasts. There was a fear that the Japanese would attack our coastal cities so the cities close to the seas upheld the blackout requirements—all houses had to have their windows sealed tightly to prevent interior lights to show through the windows. Streetlights were dark too. Cars had to have special dark-out shades to minimize the light. It wasn't a big problem though because with the gas and tire restrictions there weren't a lot of driving going on anyway, especially at night. Air raid wardens patrolling the streets enforced 'lights out'.

The auto industries had converted to manufacturing tanks, planes, ships and landing crafts. Just about every manufacturing plant was converted to making some form of war equipment. People helped out by donating metal, rubber, and other materials needed. Nobody complained—they just did what they could.

Everyone was gung ho to help with the war effort: most patriotic folks contributed by buying war bonds. They paid $18.75 for the bond ten years later at maturity it was worth $25. Children also chipped in and purchased stamps for ten cents that were placed in a booklet toward the $18.75 bond purchase.

The Marines had engaged the Japanese on Guadalcanal in one of the first offensive actions taken by the allies against the Japanese, and it would the first American victory in the war. Americans were buoyed by the victorious action of the Marines. The only thing that had held me back was my dedication of helping my family through those tough times. I had followed through with my commitment to my mother to finish school and get my high school diploma. I worked at every odd job I could to help out. I couldn't wait to be a part of the action.

It was finally my time!

Chapter 3

JOINING THE MARINES

I finally signed my name on the enlistment papers and started my Marine Corps journey. That was in September 1942. I didn't even know what the pay was—it didn't matter. I later found out it was $30 per month, and that was about a dollar a day, but it also included three squares (meals) and a fart sack (a sack that is put over the bunk mattress), and I didn't need money anyway, so I figured I could send money home to help my family out. Everyone who joined the Marines became reservists, and the enlistment was for the duration of the war plus six more months. At the time I didn't really understand the reserve part—I didn't care though because I was just happy to be in the Marine Corps. There was a doctor that was at the recruiting station and he gave each of us a quick physical examination to make sure we were physically fit for duty—I had no trouble passing that.

The day after enlisting we were all put up for the night at the YMCA in downtown Pittsburgh. In the morning we boarded a train for our trip to Marine Corps' east coast boot camp located at Parris Island, South Carolina. The oldest recruit was placed in charge of everyone, and he was handed our orders for safekeeping. We had no idea what to expect when we got there, so our trip on the train was a nice journey for us. Most of us had never been away from home before, especially on such a long trip. Our lives would soon change dramatically. The train trip took about thirty hours, and our car was full of enlistees. We picked up more enlistees at the various stops along the way. They fed us box lunches and we ate those at our seats. We also had to sleep in the seats, but some of us just slept out on the floors to be more comfortable. We passed the time looking out the windows at the passing scenery, but most often we played cards or joked with each other.

The train finally pulled to a stop in to a place called Yemassee located in South Carolina. Between 1914 and 1964, the Marine

Corps utilized the railroad depot at Yemassee, South Carolina as the gateway to Parris Island Recruit Training Depot. Over nearly half a century, more than 500,000 recruits passed through the train station at Yemassee. Half of those came through during World War II. In 1942, the Marine Corps signed a lease with the Atlantic Coast Line Railroad, for a facility to house incoming recruits. The site even had a barracks to house the recruits, and it still stands today. It is all history now, but back then it was just a railroad stop for us.

Once we started to depart the train Marine troop handlers met us as we stepped down from the train and all hell broke loose. They started swearing and yelling at us to move faster and faster to get into formation. One of them kicked me right in the ass and told me to hurry up—I thought I *was* moving pretty fast, but I guess it wasn't fast enough. And these guys weren't even the drill instructors we would soon be facing—they were just troop handlers. They kept yelling for us to line up, and move it. We couldn't do anything right or fast enough for them. I just remember them yelling, "Move it, move it, move it!" We were all scared to death.

Yemassee is over twenty miles away from Parris Island and the Marines had trucks to take us there. The trucks were towing trailers that were called "cattle cars", and they looked like they were originally designed for transporting cattle. We were crammed into that cattle car like livestock going to market. The trip to Parris Island seemed to last forever as the truck bounced over the road. We were hanging on to the sides of the trailer for dear life as we rolled down the road, and I was jammed somewhere in the middle of that crowded group of enlistees. I think all of us had serious second thoughts about why we joined the Marines as we rode into what seemed like hell.

When the truck rolled to a stop at Parris Island we finally got to meet our drill instructors. Sergeant (Sgt) Fisk was our senior drill instructor (DI) and he ordered us to get out of the truck and form up in platoon formation. We had to jump off the trailer, and everything we did was too slow for him, and a kick in the ass was a quick reward for being too slow. We had no idea what a platoon formation was either. We were finally shoved and cajoled into a formation. He looked at us as he started to yell out, "From now on I am your father, and the junior drill instructor is your mother. You can screw your mother, but you are not going to screw with me!" "Holy cow," I thought to myself—"what the heck is going on here?" They swarmed all over us like flies on stink.

Sgt Fisk was as mean as a seabag full of hand grenades. He was a veteran of the Nicaragua campaign. Our junior drill instructor was Private First Class (PFC) Peters. He was actually meaner than Sgt Fisk! We called him Private (Pvt) Peters, but he was so mean we felt that PFC stood for "Praying for Corporal", and his harsh actions were intended to get him another stripe. PFC Peters was as ugly as two seabags full of rear ends! Our senior DI would sometimes laugh, but the junior DI was a terror man and he never smiled.

The first thing they did was to issue what we called the "bucket issue", which was the initial issue of clothing and things we would need for boot camp training. It also included a metal bucket that we would use for cleaning our clothes and even as a chair to sit on while cleaning our rifles. Everything we needed for our existence was in the bucket issue. We were next issued our bedding gear—two sheets, a pillowcase, a blanket, and a fart sack. Everything was stuffed into our seabag. We were also given our preliminary uniform issue and we had to put all of our civilian gear in boxes to be sent home—we wouldn't need those items anymore. For footwear we were given a set of "boon dockers", a sort of half boot that the Marines used back then.

A Marine named Lou Diamond issued our gear to us. He was a stubborn old salty Marine and he would not salute anyone below the rank of major, and he was so salty that he somehow managed to get away with it.

We were put into a company of twelve platoons. The first few days at Parris Island involved each of us getting a second physical exam by Navy doctors—it was more thorough than the one we had at our recruiting office. It was important that nobody had physical problems that would interfere with training and subsequent duty as a Marine.

Initially we were housed in tents, but Parris Island also had round metal covered buildings called Quonset huts, as well as wooden two-story barracks. The tents had flaps on the sides and we had to roll them up during the day. We swept the floors daily. Our DI kept yelling out, "See asses high, heads low", as we scrubbed the decks with our brushes.

We were constantly scared of what was coming next. Those two DIs were just never satisfied with anything we did. We were never fast enough. We weren't loud enough. Other than a swift kick in the butt our DIs never laid a hand on us. But boy could they chew us out! I saw other platoon DIs hitting recruits, but ours didn't. In those days the DIs had swagger sticks. Swagger sticks are actually dress items, but they make perfect little weapons to crack someone on the knuckles or to measure the front-to-rear distance from one another while in formation.

The chow we ate was the best eating I had ever had. We could eat all we wanted, and we really scarfed it up. We were given water to drink, but we also had juices and coffee if we wanted. In the morning they served scrambled eggs, but they were made from powdered eggs and had a green tint to them, but to me they sure tasted good. Sometimes we got Spam or Vienna sausages. I wasn't really crazy about the Spam back then, but now I love it. They also served SOS (creamed beef on toast but AKA: "Shit on Shingles", hence the "SOS") and I loved that too, although it looked like it had already been eaten when it was placed on the trays. We went to our tables after getting our chow put on the trays, but we had to stand at the tables until the last seat was filled—there were twelve or fourteen-man tables with benches for us to sit on. We could not talk while we ate and we also had to eat all that we took. In addition we had to eat fast and then get out into platoon formation after we were done. The DIs would be waiting for us and would start right in with their hollering and screaming.

I had a hard time sleeping when we first got to Parris Island. In Pittsburgh there was a lot of noise—sirens blaring, horns honking, steel mill whistles blowing and a lot more. I had grown used to the sounds of the city. But at Parris Island it was quiet at night and the lack of noise kept me awake. I found it too eerie. I guess I must have grown used it eventually, but at first it was hard to take.

Each night I would lie in my rack and recite my Marine Rifle Creed and my General Orders. They became etched in my brain and I can still recite them to this day. We were expected to memorize them and I sure didn't want to find out what would happen to me if I didn't have them down pat:

Marines Rifle Creed

"This is my rifle. There are many like it, but this one is mine. My rifle is my best friend. It is my life. I must master it as I master my life. My rifle without me is useless. Without my rifle, I am useless. I must fire my rifle true. I must shoot straighter than my enemy who is trying to kill me. I must shoot him before he shoots me. I will . . . My rifle and myself know that what counts in war is not the rounds we fire, the noise of our burst, nor the smoke we make. We know that it is the hits that count. We will hit . . . My rifle is human, even as I, because it is my life. Thus I will learn it as my brother. I will learn its weakness, its strength, its parts, its accessories, its sights and its barrel. I will ever guard it against the ravages of weather and damage. I will keep my rifle clean and ready, even as I am clean and ready. We will become part of each other. We will . . . Before God I swear this creed. My rifle and myself are the defenders of our country. We are masters of our enemy. We are the saviors of my life. So be it, until there is no enemy, but peace."

General Orders

1. To take charge of this post and all government property in view.
2. To walk my post in a military manner, keeping always on then alert and observing everything that takes place within sight or hearing.
3. To report all violations of orders I am instructed to enforce.
4. To repeat all calls from posts more distant from the guardhouse than my own.
5. To quit my post only when properly relieved.
6. To receive, obey, and pass on the sentry who relieves me, all orders from the commanding officer, officer of the day, and officers and noncommissioned officers of the guard only.
7. To talk to no one except in line of duty.
8. To give the alarm in case of fire or disorder.
9. To call the corporal of the guard in any case not covered by instructions.
10. To salute all officers and all colors and standards not cased.
11. To be especially watchful at night and, during the time for challenging, to challenge all persons on or near my post and to allow no one to pass without proper authority.

After we arrived at MCRD we found making head calls (going to the bathroom) a big shock to most of us—there was literally *no* privacy. All the commodes were lined up side-by-side with no partitions. It took a time for everyone to get over their initial shyness, but after a while we just figured everyone was in the same boat, so we just did our business in front of everyone. We had to take showers in a large room with spigots coming out of the walls. If anyone was shy before they got to boot camp they were over it pretty quickly. There were rows of sinks with mirrors over each sink, and we used those to brush our teeth and to shave.

Sometimes the DIs would light the "smoking lamp"—that was an expression used to authorize smoking. It was about the only privilege we ever got, but I didn't smoke, so it didn't do me any good. Since I was fourteen years old I had chewed tobacco, and chewing was pretty popular back in those days. Nobody could smoke without the DI lighting the smoking lamp. Any recruit caught smoking without authorization was severely punished—usually they had to smoke half a dozen cigarettes at once with a metal bucket over their head. That was enough to cure anyone from smoking again.

The Marine Corps' Commandant at the time was Lieutenant General (LtGen) Holcomb. Right after the attack on Pearl Harbor LtGen Holcomb ordered recruit training shortened to five weeks—three weeks of garrison training, and two weeks of rifle training at the range. But by March 1942 he changed it back to seven weeks. Under the seven-week schedule, recruits spent three weeks in the recruit depot, two weeks at the range, and the rest of boot camp back at the depot. Through more efficient time management, the seven-week schedule was improved in 1942 and 1943 to add 25% more instruction in core subjects. It was important for the Marine Corps to train new Marines in basic subjects.

One of the duties our DIs taught us was the daily barracks cleaning called "field day", and each day we had to make the barracks spic and span! We swabbed (mopped) the decks, dusted all the bulkheads (walls), and we had recruit details whose job was to clean the heads (bathrooms). At home the women did these chores, but we didn't have that choice now. We had to learn how to swab, scrub commodes, and shine the brass pipes. Everyone had an assignment. When we were done the DIs would inspect the barracks, and no matter how hard we had scrubbed and cleaned, those DIs could find some dirt we missed, and that would mean we were punished with duck-walking at high port or some other form of punishing torture they could think up.

We were taught to wash our own clothes. We would soak the clothes in our buckets, and then use our scrub brushes to scrub them clean. After rinsing off the suds we wrung them out and then tied the clothes to the clothesline. A recruit was assigned to guard the drying clothes. We were rapidly learning to be very self-sufficient, and cleanliness was stressed. Taking a hot shower every day was new to some of the recruits, but it was a welcome relief after a day in the hot Parris Island sun and the extreme humidity that was constantly present. We were all pretty grimy at the end of the day anyway. We were constantly sweating under the heat and humidity, especially after we did drill and physical training (PT). The humidity was so high that even after toweling off from our showers we could never really get dry.

We did close order drill (marching) a lot while in boot camp—altogether they had us in for forty-four hours of drill time on the training syllabus. At first they marched us in soft sand. It was tough going, and the sand made it hard to walk—it was very strenuous. After we became fairly efficient we were taken to the paved grinder for the marching drills. I liked the grinder best because it sounded good when we were all in step. But if we messed up we went back to the sand—or worse, we had to march at high port, or duck walk at high port. Those two things were little tortures for us, and very painful after a short while. On the grinder they would yell out, "Heels, heels, heels" in an effort to get us to step down at the same time. The sound of a marching platoon with all the boon dockers hitting the deck at the same time was really something.

The Springfield rifles we carried were heavy, and our arms became very tired after a while of marching at port arms. That was all part of the discipline learning process provided by close order drill—getting us to find out we had limits that were far greater than we believed we had. Drill was also designed to get us to respond instantly to an order—that would really pay off when we got to combat. We had to respond without thinking. Drill was one of my favorite training activities.

One time during drill our drill instructor was teaching us "stack arms" in which we stack three rifles together in a tripod shape. I was learning the "stack man" position in the middle when the three rifles in my stack fell to the deck. My DI called me "Shithead" and ordered me to sleep with those three rifles that night. I was so uncomfortable with those rifles in my rack, inspected by my DI, that I could not sleep a wink. I never let a rifle stack fall again.

Drill instructors in the 1940's could train recruits as they saw fit to make them into Marines. It was not like today where there is a Standard Operating Procedure (SOP) that dictates all the procedures for training. If our DIs felt like getting us up in the middle of the night to march out into the swamps that surrounded the island, then that is what they did. We never knew what to expect from them. We actually believed that "DI" really stood for "Devil's Instrument" because of the crazy things they had us doing to make us as miserable as possible. I would later come to realize just how important it was for us to learn the discipline needed to endure rough treatment—war was not an easy thing to deal with. However, under the circumstances of the moment, we had no idea of a greater meaning that would come—it was just pure misery for us at the time.

The shortened boot camp training cycle was needed to process more men quicker. They needed us to get through boot camp and then on to the front lines as quickly as possible. We all were glad the training was only seven weeks instead of the former twelve weeks—it was hard to imagine another four weeks of the hell we were encountering. Just dealing with the sand fleas, gnats, and mosquitoes was bad enough, but doing the duck walk at high port was over the top. The sand fleas were really unbearable, as they would bite us resulting in making us itch, but Sgt Fisk and PFC Peters would be all over us if we attempted to scratch the itches.

We were given reveille call each morning at 0500 and the DIs expected that we would all hit the deck at the exact same time. The drill instructors were waiting for us every morning and they really got all over us if we were not in unison. Taps was held at 2200 each night. After our evening chow and the extra assignments the DIs had for us we had some free time to write letters home, polish our boots, and clean our rifles. We had to study our handbooks—they weren't referred to as "guidebooks" yet. We were busy just about one hundred percent of the time. I wrote letters home when I could, but there was so much we had to accomplish that other things had priority.

The weather at Parris Island was extremely hot and humid and we sweated all the time and our clothes were always damp. In a way it was good training for us because we would later face the same hot and humid conditions in the South Pacific campaigns we would be sent to in the near future. Duck-walking for 100 yards at high port in that humidity was a hell in itself. There was no air conditioning in those days, and our barracks were almost unbearable with the heavy moisture and high heat. If we weren't so physically exhausted every night sleeping would have been almost impossible.

Parris Island had a private who was a bugle player. His job was to play bugle calls that indicated everything from reveille, chow call, mail call—all the way to Taps. We had calls for every function at the base, and we had to learn each bugle call by heart. They had special calls for reveille, chow, Taps, etc. After we were in boot camp for about a month we heard a bugle call one morning that we had never heard before. None of us knew what to do. Our drill instructors flew into the barracks and started yelling at us for not knowing the call—it turned out to be the pay call! We all lined up to get our first pay. They paid us in cash, and my pay was a twenty-dollar bill. To be honest, I had never seen a twenty-dollar bill before. I couldn't believe my eyes! I had never seen that much money before. Of course they had already taken out the ten dollars to pay for our bucket issue. Our pay was $30 a month, or about a dollar a day. I felt so lucky that I was being paid and also getting three squares and a sack. I sent the $20 home to help my family. I didn't need money anyway. At that point I was totally sold on being a United States Marine.

All Marines are riflemen, and shooting was one of the most important things we got trained in. We learned to shoot our Springfield rifles at the rifle range. Training was two weeks long there. The first week we learned all about the rifle and how to sight in, squeeze the trigger, and adjust the slings. The second week we actually fired the rifles to qualify. Those Springfield's were powerful and their 30.06 rounds gave heavy recoil on our shoulders. The Springfield was a bolt-action rifle that had a five-round clip. Compared to the semi-automatics of today those Springfield's were slow, but we still had to shoot the rifle range requirements of rapid fire in the same time as today's semi-automatics. I liked shooting, and on qualification day I qualified as an expert. I figured if I was going to be a grunt I needed to be a good shot. Very few recruits qualified as experts, and I was really proud of that.

We also had to learn how to do hand-to-hand combat. There was an old colonel who taught the rifle and bayonet training class. He was a tough old guy, and he asked for a recruit to come up on the platform with his rifle. We always kept scabbards on the bayonets to prevent injuries, but the colonel told the recruit to take his scabbard off his bayonet that was attached to the rifle, and then charge at him and try to take his head off. The recruit charged at him and attempted to make a killing blow but the colonel just brushed the rifle aside and disarmed the recruit. We all had become pretty salty after our short time in boot camp, but this guy showed us that we knew *nothing* yet. We still had plenty to learn. We practiced the moves that the colonel taught us, and we got pretty good at it—but we kept our scabbards on just in case.

We had to do guard duty and mess hall duties while we were at boot camp. That gave us a break from regular boot camp training, but mess duty had long hours, and it was a lot of hard work. The mess halls had to be cleaned after each meal, and the cooking chores were ongoing. We had to arrive at the mess hall very early in the morning, and we didn't get back to the barracks until late at night. Guard duty was always at night, and we were assigned specific posts to guard. We had to be on the alert at all times, and sometimes the Officer-of-the-Day (OD) would come by and we had to challenge him properly. He would ask us to cite our General Orders (eleven orders for sentries), and by God we had to know them or we would be in hot water for sure. To this day I can still recite my General Orders by heart.

There were some tests in boot camp to help the Marine Corps determine what our specialty would be. I could tell by the questions where the test was leading and I did my best to flunk the test. I wanted to be a Marine rifleman, and nothing else was going to work for me. My strategy worked too, because I was assigned as a "Spec-600", which meant I was going to be a machine gunner. They had not yet started to use the term "military occupational specialty" (MOS) to indicate a specific field of specialty.

The need for men in the Pacific was so great that experienced NCOs such as the DIs were in great demand on the war front. As such, they often would make graduating recruits into DIs to free up

NCOs. Because I was good at drilling the troops my DI put me in for the duty. I didn't want to be a DI though—I wanted to get into the war and fight the Japs. An officer came to us and those of us nominated for DI duty had to pass a test given by the officer. We were required to march a platoon to see if we had the skills to teach and execute the drill movements. I purposely gave commands on the wrong foot so I would look bad. When it was over my DI was really tight-jawed—actually very furious with me, and he chewed me out for screwing up so bad that I wasn't selected. "Why did you do so poorly?" he demanded to know.

I just said to him, "Well, the officer made me nervous."

"Really? You are not nervous with me. Well, that's too bad." And that was all he said. I knew then that I was still going to be a grunt.

In those days recruits didn't graduate from boot camp—we "out-posted". We were sent to New River, North Carolina for our infantry training. We out-posted on a troop train and the ride to New River took about eight hours. We took all of the gear we had been issued at Parris Island, including our rifles. New River was re-named Camp Lejeune in honor of Lieutenant General (LtGen) John A. Lejeune, the thirteenth Commandant of the Marine Corps. The base was 156,000 acres of land, as well as a stretch of eleven miles of beach that was used for practicing beach landings if needed.

It was during Camp Lejeune training that we learned combat tactics as rifle squads. The configuration of rifles squads changed during the phases of WWII. We were trained for a rifle squad with nine men: the squad leader would a corporal and he was armed with a rifle. He led eight Marines with the rank of private or private first class. They were organized as follows: assistant squad leader, two scouts, two riflemen, one rifle grenadier, one automatic rifleman and one assistant automatic rifleman. This organization of the rifle squad was what was used during the early battles in the South Pacific. We learned basic tactics and how to read topography maps and use the compass to find our location and direction of travel.

The weather at Camp Lejeune was similar to Parris Island, but as time wore on it became colder due to winter setting in. It can get really cold at Camp Lejeune, but I was already used to cold winters having grown up in Pittsburgh. But the wind would cut right through our field jackets and that made it pretty cold and hard to handle as winter progressed.

We had to turn in our Springfield rifles and were re-issued M-1 Garands. The M-1s were semi-automatic rifles and we had to learn how to use them—they were different than the bolt-action Springfield's we had learned to shoot at Parris Island. We had to become proficient in using M-1s. Our infantry training lasted several months. During the training we also had to learn how to perform amphibious landings and the techniique of climbing down a net ladder from the side of a ship. We learned to hold the rope ladders by the vertical ropes, not the horizontal ones—the man coming down above might step on your hands if you held the horizontal ropes, and for sure you would end up falling the rest of the way to the boat below. At first we practiced coming down the rope ladders on dry land, but once we had it down correctly we were put on the ships to practice under more realistic conditions. The ships moved up and down as the ocean swells came by, and that resulted in the ropes swaying back and forth—it made for a difficult departure, especially since we were loaded down with all the gear we carried, plus our rifles.

Because my specialty was being a machine gunner I had to spend an additional six weeks at the Infantry School learning how to shoot all the weapons being used in combat including machine guns, Browning Automatic Rifles (BAR), Johnson automatic rifles, and all the aspects of operating those weapons. We not only had to learn how to shoot the various weapons, but we also had to learn to field strip them and then reassemble them blindfolded. Our final exam required that we fieldstrip the rifles blindfolded. I took fifth place out of thirty-five in that category.

We had frequent inspections that included the junk-on-the-bunk inspection once each month in which we had to lay out all of our issued gear on our bunks, neatly folded and in a specific order. I failed the junk-on-the-bunk inspection my first time because my shoelaces were not pressed. The colonel inspected my belt buckle and failed me on that too: I had polished the outside of the buckle but did not polish the inside. Our shoes were issued brown but we put black shoe polish on them. We also wore white socks. We had a list of things we had to do in order to pass the inspections.

I was promoted to private first class (PFC) by the end of training. When we were done with our training we felt like we knew just about everything there was about what being a Marine grunt was all about—we would soon find out how wrong we were. We were all anxious to get into combat. I ended up teaching the company because I had the skills to do so. I also led the platoon in rifle physical training, and we also did the "bucket drills"—drills that entailed filling buckets with sand and then holding them out to our sides and raising them up and down.

There was a brig-rat (a person in the brig) by the name of Pvt Donald Marston. He was up for a General Court Martial for desertion. Our commanding officer (CO) looked at his records and decided he didn't want to keep the man, but I felt we could use him and I wanted to work with him. I guess I was feeling my new PFC stripes, but I wanted him. Our CO decided to let me proceed, so I spent nights teaching him about machine guns. We took them apart and then put them back together again—over and over until he learned it perfectly. I also gave him every crap detail I could think of and he kept coming back for more. He was a good learner, and after a month of constantly working with him he had turned around in a one-eighty. The CO was so impressed that he authorized a liberty card to be issued to Pvt Marston, but when I offered it to him he didn't want it. He stayed in the barracks studying tactics. He turned out to be a good Marine. His brother was also in the Marines, and later on they were both shot in their bellies and each of them had to wear colostomy bags the rest of their life.

Another Marine stands out in my mind from Camp Lejeune: PFC Livingston. We had been out on a training force-march and had marched about eight to ten miles from our base camp. After a brief rest in the woods we returned. Back at our base he told me that he had forgot his rifle at the rest point and asked me if he could take a Jeep back to pick up the rifle. I told him, "Hell no—get your ass in gear and walk back and get your rifle!" A few hours later he showed up with a rifle and said he had found his rifle at the rest spot. I didn't feel he was telling the truth so I asked him to recite his rifle number—all Marines memorized their rifle numbers back then and he should have been able to rattle it off. However, the number he gave did not match the rifle and I knew he had not gone back at all. I ordered him to get his ass back into the field and told him to either come back with his lost rifle or don't come back at all because I would write him up on charges if he didn't find the rifle. He came back with the correct rifle.

We finished infantry training just before Christmas, and we were all given a ten-day leave. They wouldn't let everyone go at the same time so it was split up into two groups: half got to go in time for Christmas, and the other half had to wait until after Christmas. Since the Serbs celebrate Christmas on 7 January my future brother-in-law and I went with the second group. In those days trains were the only real mode of travel, and I rode the train back to Pittsburgh. With the round-trip travel time of the train I ended up with only about four and one-half days at home. When I arrived everyone was very happy to see me, and I was probably the happiest of all to be back home. Those four days were very special because I knew that it might be the last four days for all of us to be together. After that I would be going off to war. It was hard to leave my family, especially since it might be my last time.

I made the return trip to Camp Lejeune to be reunited with my battalion. I arrived one hour late and my sergeant took me to the captain for disciplinary action. The captain chewed me out real good, but that was all that happened—I thought I was going to lose my PFC stripe.

We had done all of our training as a battalion, and now we were being shipped out as a battalion. Two of our three battalions travelled by troop train to California, and the third was put on a ship and sailed to California through the Panama Canal. I was glad to be going on the train. Once again we would aboard the train with all the gear we had been issued—we were always ready for combat at all times.

After we boarded a troop transport train and we headed west. The troop transports had the right-of-way over all other trains, and if there was a passenger train or freight train in our path they had to move over before we got to their location. Just like my first train trip to Parris Island, we not only sat in the train's seats, but also slept in the same seats. The officers had Pullmans for their use. There was a galley where we would pick up our chow, although the line was long just to get the chow. We took our food back to our seats where we ate. The train had to make periodic stops to pick up water supplies and coal. When the train stopped we usually got out and did exercises to keep in shape. When we reached the deserts of Nevada the train pulled to a stop in Las Vegas. At that time Las Vegas was nothing like it is today—it was just a small town with a reputation of being a western gambling town, and a place where a lot of prostitutes stayed—the men who were building Hoover Dam would come to Las Vegas to find women and spend their money gambling. Everyone had heard about this town so we rolled down our windows and everyone was looking out the windows to see what Las Vegas looked like. We stayed for about one hour and once again they made us get out and do some PT.

We finally made it to California and the train wound it's way over the San Gabriel Mountains and then down to the edge of the Pacific. We rolled into Camp Pendleton and stopped at what is now known as the "24" area, which is located near where the Camp Pendleton Air Station is today, and then we marched up the one lane of Rattlesnake Canyon Road to the "14" area. We were getting closer to our destination in the South Pacific.

Chapter 4

TRAINING AND MORE TRAINING

Camp Pendleton is a base that abuts the Pacific Ocean, and it was a perfect location to practice amphibious landings to prepare us for our future engagements in the Pacific battles we were headed for. Our training was intense and lasted for many months. We practiced landings over and over. We would board ships and go out to sea for days at a time, and then come back toward shore to practice beach landings. We wore full battle gear as we climbed down the rope net ladders that hung over the sides of the ship. Then we dropped down into flat-bottomed boats called "Higgins boats" that would take us in to the beaches. When we hit the beach the front portion of the Higgins boats would drop down to form a ramp for us to charge down and into the cold waters. Once ashore we would drop into position on the sands and form into our groups. Once formed up on the beach we would then charge eastward toward the "enemy" positions. Highway 101 ran through the base on the western edge, and we would have to stop the traffic to make our crossings to the other side where we continued our drills in the hills just east of the ocean.

Training was very intense all the time. They were pushing us to our limits. I figured it was done to get us so mad that we looked forward to going into combat just to get away from the training regimen. The more we trained the more we knew what we didn't know. Training in misery was part of the deal—the more miserable we were the feistier we got.

I had heard stories about the Marine Raiders and they sort of captured my imagination. I told my company commander, Captain H. C. Parks, that I wanted to be a Marine Raider. He looked at me and said, "As a PFC you have more command presence than many sergeants. You want to be a Marine Raider? Forget it!" That ended that.

Camp Pendleton was great place to be stationed for us young Marines. We could go on liberty in San Diego, which was about forty miles south, or we could catch a ride up to Los Angeles, which was about ninety miles north. We just hitched rides, and somebody always stopped to pick us up. Once we were headed to Los Angeles and the man who picked us up was only going as far San Clemente, but he ended up driving us all the way up to LA just because we were Marines. There were great beaches to relax on as well. The weather was much nicer than we had at Parris Island or Camp Lejeune—there was no humidity to deal with, and no sand fleas. Our liberty was always subject to our passing an inspection. We had pack inspections every morning and then on Saturday we had uniform inspections. If we passed inspection we were given liberty from 1200 on Saturday until 0500 Monday. We didn't dare arrive late from liberty. I was in Charlie Company, and all the companies had favorite gathering places—ours was the Victory Inn in Los Angeles. These places had "B" girls (bar girls) who would greet the Marines and get the Marines to buy them drinks. Their drinks were probably just watered down, but the guys were taken in by their charms and they gladly bought them drinks. They danced with the girls, and some made "temporary" dates with them as well. Sometimes the Marines would hang out the upper story windows and drop water balloons on the sailors that walked by below. It was all in fun, but the sailors probably didn't think so. Back then we had to deal with "zoot suiters"—young men that wore those pinstriped zoot suits. They would challenge us to fights and we would tear our belts off, wrap them around our wrists with the buckles out, and then swing the buckles toward them. As Marines we didn't take crap from anybody.

Camp Pendleton also had slop chutes (enlisted clubs), but they only served beer. We often would go to the slop chutes after our training day was over. Sometimes we could go to the base theater and watch movies. On some occasions Jack Benny and Bob Hope would come down and entertain the Marines. There was always something for us to do when we had liberty, even if it was just liberty on base. Just getting away from the rigors of training was enough for most of us.

Following a training mission our commanding officer would get us in formation and appraise our performance. He would usually spend the first five minutes telling us how good we were, and then he would spend the next hour telling us how bad we were doing. The following day we would board a transport ship and we were told we were going to war, but later we would make a landing at Camp Pendleton. We never knew or sure what was going to happen—I never knew why they did that.

My group machine gunners had enormous unit pride. One day they handed out a new issue of shoulder pads to be worn on the outside of our utilities to ease the recoil of the heavy machine guns that weighed over ninety pounds. We flat turned them down—we didn't want to be thought of as sissies who couldn't take the recoil of the machine guns, and besides, we thought they would be a hindrance. We wanted to show everyone how tough we were. We had four ammo men and they all knew how to shoot the gun. The tripod weighed fifty-one pounds and the gun itself weighed another thirty-five pounds. The job was a really tough job and a very dangerous one too—so having a shoulder pad was really out of the question. The machine gunners would always be the first guys the enemy wanted to take out, so it took really macho tough guys to handle this job.

Often when we went out on a training mission on Camp Pendleton the COs would race their units back to our base camp and they wanted to see who could get back the quickest. Our hike sometimes was as long as thirty miles in length, and having to race back just to be first was putting a lot of extra burden on us. But we were a competitive lot, and it became a strong rivalry to see who was best. When we got back to our barracks we were then required to field day the barracks (clean the barracks). Besides our uniform inspections on Saturday there was also a barracks inspection before the CO could grant our liberty. One time we failed the inspection and the CO informed the troops at the formation that they were not getting liberty.

A Marine in the rear of the formation said out loud, "Give me liberty, or give me death!"

The officer was immediately incensed and asked, "Who said that?"

The man at the rear said, "Patrick Henry you dumb shit!" That definitely sealed the *no liberty* part of things.

When liberty was finally granted liberty we first had to get our liberty card from the first sergeant. Once we had our cards we then went to the Duty NCO who would inspect us before logging us out on liberty. Since we had no cars we had to catch a bus to get into town, but the MPs (military police) were at the bus stops to give us another inspection. If the MP failed us on his inspection he would send us back to the Duty NCO.

The area around Camp Pendleton and the surrounding communities were mostly just farmlands. Camp Pendleton was originally a large ranch that was initially leased by the government for use in military exercises, but later the land was purchased and turned into Camp Pendleton. It was an ideal training facility, especially due to the miles of beaches that were ideal for beach landing exercises.

We spent a lot of time training aboard ships. Most of us had never been aboard a ship other than at Camp Lejeune while in our training, and we found the conditions very cramped inside. We had bunks that were three and four layers high with very little space between them. The ships rolled with the sea conditions and the motion caused a lot of guys to get seasick. I wasn't bothered by it, but a lot of guys were. Our chow was good, but the mess halls were small and we had to eat in shifts. We stood in long lines just to get to the chow.

Sometimes we would travel to San Diego and board ships, which then took us out to sea for three or four days at a time. I guess it was to get us used to life aboard the ship, as well as the other duties that Marines are required to do aboard ships. Sometimes we would make a landing at San Clemente Island, which lies about sixty miles northwest of San Diego. The naval guns would really pound that island with everything they had—the noise was tremendous when the big guns went off. It was good practice for us, but not so good for the goats that lived on the island.

On 16 August 1943 we were officially formed into the Fourth Marine Division. Our commanding general was Brigadier General (BGen) James L. Underhill. We had a ceremony to commemorate the occasion. We didn't know it at the time, but we would become the first Marine division to go from the states directly into combat.

Creating a battle-ready division takes a long time, and in the meantime we continued our landing practices. At times we did night landings—nothing was left out. It was very repetitive, but it would later prove to have been an invaluable experience for us when we finally hit the beaches on an enemy infested island.

We also had regular Marine duties when we weren't practicing landings. I was assigned guard duty one night. The Corporal of the

Guard told me my post was to guard a train boxcar that had a sealed door. I was told that under no circumstances was I to let anyone enter the sealed car. I was all by myself, but I carried an M-1 that was fully loaded. I walked that post like my life depended on it and at first nothing happened. Without warning a couple of navy guys drove up in a Jeep—one was a commander and the other was a chief. They started to walk up to the boxcar when I came to port arms at the position of attention and said, "Halt! Who goes there?" The two navy guys didn't take me seriously and continued to walk to the boxcar. The commander told the chief, "Common chief, let's open that car." The chief wanted to leave, but the commander kept going. I raised my rifle to the ready and told the officer if he took another step toward the door I would blow his head off. That got their attention and they went back to their Jeep and took off in a hurry. I could tell the commander was pissed off, and I figured I was going to get in trouble. But later they came back with the OD and the OD told me I did a good job.

While we were going through our training I had continued boxing in the smokers, and I eventually earned the title of "Middle Weight Champion" of the Fourth Marine Division. My trainers thought I was good enough that I could have gone pro. Boxing was a motivating thing for me, and it definitely helped build my mental toughness—later that would be worth its weight in gold while in the line of fire. I continued to work out as a boxer. It was hard work, and I could only do boxing training during after-hours or on weekends. Sometimes when we weren't doing night exercises I would go to the gym and work out on the boxing bag, and then I did some sparring with other Marines. I would usually end my training session with a three or four-mile run.

When I went to the slop chutes I only went to shoot the bull and not to drink. In fact, I would not have my first beer and a cigar until my 25th birthday a few years later. I was a fitness fanatic I guess, and drinking and smoking were not in the cards for me at the time. My only vice was chewing tobacco, a vice I took up in my teens, and I still do to this day. I entered a lot of boxing smokers and I was good enough to win most of them. I never sat between the rounds—I chose to stand and intimidate my opponents instead. It was all about mental toughness in my opinion, and I didn't pay any attention to the crowd. In those days most young men were entering the military and I never knew if my opponents had been professional fighters before they entered the military. There was a strong inter-service rivalry too, and if I were fighting a sailor then the navy crowd would be rooting for their man. But cheering does motivate the fighter, so when the Marines cheered for me it was good to hear. Between the rounds they would slosh water on me and that was pretty refreshing. The winner of the fight we got $5, and the loser only got $3. It doesn't seem like much, but that extra two bucks was a strong motivator to win. In my eight years of boxing I had thirty-four fights and lost only four—eighteen fights were won by knockout.

One of my biggest fights was in the Nimitz Bowl. Inside were about 20,000 men, all of them smoking, or so it seemed to me, as the air was very thick with heavy tobacco smoke. I fought in the middleweight class at 160-pounds, but on that night there were no opponents for me inn my weight class. Another light-heavyweight boxer was on hand and he also had no opponent in his weight class. We were asked if we would fight each other. I agreed even though he was in the 174-pound class and was much bigger than I was. They made our fight the main event. Most of the crowd cheers went for me, and that was probably because I was the underdog. We were pretty even during the entire fight, but at one point I slipped on the padding and at the same time the other guy hit me with a hard right to my head. The judges considered it a knockdown even though I had slipped. Ultimately they scored it a split decision and gave the fight to the larger fighter. The difference in the scoring was the "slip" they ruled as a knockdown.

After many months of training and preparation the new 4th Marine Division was slated to ship out on 1 December 1943, almost two years from the initial Pearl Harbor invasion that brought us into the war. But there were still more delays we encountered: there was a shortage of transports that would take our troops to our destination, so in the meantime we continued our beach landing rehearsals to hone our skills. By the beginning of 1944 we had amassed over 19,000 Marines and were almost set to go. Our last amphibious practice landing was a massive assault on San Clemente Island. Once again the goats were the losers.

The Fourth Marine Division was taken to San Diego where we boarded the USS Dupage, a transport ship that would take us to the front. We were out at sea for about four days before they let us know where were headed, a place referred to in code: "Burlesque and Camouflage". We still had no idea where we were going, but we did know it was somewhere in the South Pacific, and that would put us into the war at last.

Aboard ship our training and duties continued. Once again we had to stand in long lines for the mess hall. We spent our time cleaning our rifles, playing cards, and we kept busy all the time. We got along pretty good with the navy guys. On ship used their loudspeakers to announce everything—it was sort of like our bugle calls. We had many drills aboard the ship as we headed west. We were always preparing for the worst so we would be ready if something occurred.

Within a few days we arrived at the Hawaiian Islands and most of the ships anchored off Maui. We didn't know how long we would be staying, but everyone was anticipating going ashore on liberty—we kept waiting for the word, but all that came out of the loudspeakers was, "Now hear this. There will be *no* liberty . . ." All of us were very disappointed.

We finally boarded troop transport USS Calvert at Maui's Maalea Bay. We sailed into Pearl Harbor and past the hulks of the sunken Navy ships that had been destroyed on 7 December 1941. It was very emotional for everyone, and a lot of men just cried as we sailed slowly past. I vowed to kill every Jap I could.

By 22 January 1944 "C" Company, 1st Battalion, 24th Marines departed Pearl Harbor and headed further west. Within a few days they called everyone together and announced our destination: we were headed for the Marshall Islands where our mission was to make a landing on the islands or Roi and Namur. After all our training drills we were finally headed for the real thing.

The voyage from San Diego to our objective Roi-Namur took a total of eighteen days. It was the longest shore-to-shore amphibious operation in the history of warfare. We travelled approximately 4,300 miles, which also really meant that we were the only division to leave the U.S.A. and go directly into combat. During the long sea voyage we passed the time with constant preparation for battle by doing physical exercises, cleaning our weapons and equipment, and then test firing our weapons. We also had briefings about the enemy's strengths and fortifications, operation maps, and intelligence reports.

Our meals aboard ship weren't bad, but it wasn't four-star either—it's what we had. They served beans at every meal. The mess hall had fresh bread that was baked every day, but a lot of food was dehydrated such as the dried milk, dried eggs, etc. The eggs were always a greenish color, and the milk tasted watered-down. One Marine, Gunnery Sergeant Morrison, was a vegan, and he would pass on the meats being offered while going through the mess line. When I realized that I told him to take the meat and I would take it—I needed the extra protein. He agreed, and after that I always went through the chow line next to him.

While on the ships we had to take showers with salt water. Regular soap didn't work with salt water so they gave us a special soap that did the job. We had a shower every day. We also had to use freshwater discipline on the ships: we could only use the scuttlebutts (drinking fountains) two times a day and that was also when we filled our canteens. I used to drink a lot of water while filling my canteen. If a Marine missed the filling time frame he had to wait for the next one. One thing that most of us had to learn was how to handle the ship's rolling movements. A lot of guys got really sick at first—I was fortunate that I only got sick one time, but after that I had my "sea legs" and just adjusted to the motion. The worst seasickness's occurred in the landing craft because they heaved up and down with the ocean swells and it was much more pronounced.

It had been a long time in the making, but at that point our training was finally over. We were now going into the direct action we had prepared so hard for.

Chapter 5

4TH MARINE DIVISION'S SOUTH PACIFIC CAMPAIGNS

Roi-Namur

The official name of our assignment had been given the code word "Operation Flintlock". When we heard we were going to the Marshall Islands to land on a couple of islands called Roi and Namur, and we had no idea where that was. What we did know was that we were finally going to get a shot at the Japs, and we were all excited about that. In fact, when they said we were going to Roi-Namur we all let out a cheer! We were told that the Japs had held those islands for a long time. We were shown a lot of maps, and a lot of overlays of the area. They showed us exactly where we were going to land. We felt we were ready, especially after all that training we had gone through. All the leaders were given topographical maps showing the objectives and where the enemy was believed to be in fortified positions.

We had been taught about the Japanese, and one thing we knew was that they were not afraid of death, and to them, dying for the emperor was the most honorable way to die. They were believed to be suicidal and fanatical. That is a hard enemy to fight and we wondered what we would be in for. We were told about the Japanese dispositions and their tactics, and all this was followed by our own attack plans.

I was looking forward to going to battle with Japan's finest soldiers of the Japanese Army, as well as the Imperial Marines—Japan's most elite fighters. I wanted to fight their best men, as I would not be satisfied to engage inferior troops. I told my men they needed to strengthen themselves mentally and physically to kill or be killed. We continuously inspected our men to make sure that their gear was battle-ready. Our long ocean trips required that we held our men to a high level of discipline.

We were very proud the Fourth Marine Division would be the first American force that would be sent directly from training to the battlefield. We were making history. The trip to our assignment had taken eighteen days, and that gave us a lot of time to study the objectives and to become familiar with the invasion tactics. We learned that the islands were small islands; neither was over one mile square. Roi had a landing strip on it and was the main island for controlling the area. The two islands were heavily fortified with pillboxes, anti-tank fencing, large defense guns, and more. The Japs were definitely planning to hold their position. We were told that there were over 3,000 enemy Japs lying in wait, and they were planning on fighting to their deaths if needed. But we also knew that we had twice their numbers, and we were Marines!

My men were constantly checking and re-checking their gear to make sure everything was there an in good operating condition. I was continuously inspected the machine gun barrels, ammo belts, rifles and bayonets, canteens, Ka-bars, canteens, helmets, battle dressings—you name it. I inspected it to make sure it was all in good order. One of the main lectures themes I repeated over and over was "always be prepared for the unexpected!" We were going up against an enemy that was treacherous, resourceful, silent in their suffering, and deadly as a snake.

Before we began the landing the navy bombarded the islands with over two and one-half tons of heavy shells from a variety of destroyers, battleships, and cruisers. It didn't seem like anything could survive the pummeling that took place. Then the aircraft dropped 1,000-pound bombs and strafed the island to take out as many of the Jap fighters that they could. My unit would be making our landing on Namur, and the other units would hit Roi.

The 24th Marines were the floating reserve for the 4th Marine Division and would not go ashore on the first assault. We were to standby and stay ready to enter the Amtracs and landing craft whenever we were needed. I was amazed as I looked out at the number of ships that made up the Fifth Fleet Transport and Bombardment Task Force. We had almost six hundred ships in the fleet, and it would be the largest naval force ever assembled for a landing in the Pacific Ocean. D-Day was on 31 January 1944.

I was a machine-gunner and I also was issued a .45 pistol, but I wanted a rifle and bayonet instead. I felt that a rifle and bayonet was better than just having a .45 pistol. I also carried as many grenades and satchel charges as I could. My bayonet had been made as sharp as a razor. I made sure my men had their helmet chin straps tightened down real tight.

When we finally debarked the ship it was really pretty easy. The initial landing forces had taken most of the flack and had already moved inland and set up defenses for what would surely be needed for the anticipated Japanese night assaults. We came in as the reserves. We had trained doing this so many times that it was second nature to us. It just went so smoothly. We came to shore aboard LCVPs (Landing Craft Vehicle Personnel), which are flat-bottomed boats with high sides and a flat nose that is a ramp that folds down when we landed. The boat is also known as a "Higgins boat". It held about thirty-six men inside. They said it could go about nine knots fully loaded. The hardest part was the pitching of the landing craft—a lot of Marines got really seasick as the boats rolled up and down with the ocean's swells. When it hit the beach the front ramp went down and we charged out of the boat and onto the beach. We immediately were under some small arms firing from the Japs, but it wasn't what I had expected.

The assault units got bogged down when the Amtracs couldn't cross the anti-tank ditch. They came under a lot of close-quarters combat, as the Japs wanted to test our ability to fight and to test our will.

A short time after I was on the island I saw a Jap with a rifle and fixed bayonet in the same trench line as me about twenty feet beyond my position. He was raising his rifle up as if to indicate he wanted to do battle with the rifle and bayonet. I said to myself, "That Jap is out of ammo", so I raised my rifle up and shot him right between his eyes. I went over to him, as he lay dead on the ground. I picked his rifle up and he had three rounds in it! I dishonored him—he wanted to fight mano-a-mano. Well, I am here to tell the story and he's not. That was my first enemy kill.

Not long after we landed there was a massive explosion. It was incredibly loud, and frankly, from the way it went off we thought the whole damned island was going to sink! Marines had thrown some satchel charges into what they thought was a Jap pillbox, but it turned out to be their underground ammo dump. When it went off it was like our modern day atomic-bomb blast. I was about fifty or sixty yards from the initial blast. There were large things going high in the sky, and then debris started to fall all over the area, and I had rocks coming down all around me, and some hitting my helmet. Later we looked into the pit formed from the blast and the whole damned thing had filled up with water. We had no idea where the water came from. My hearing was shot for the next several days. The whole experience was a very scary one, and it was something I would never forget. That blast has been written about in numerous articles about the invasions of Roi-Namur, and everyone that witnessed it agreed that it was incredible.

Our battalion commander, Lieutenant Colonel (LtCol) Dyess, was leading a charge of our Marines just a couple of hours before we had secured the island. He was a great leader, but the Japs hit him with a machine gun blast and he was killed instantly. He was posthumously awarded the Medal of Honor, and he was the only person ever to receive both the Medal of Honor and the Carnegie Medal for civilian heroism. It was tough to lose a great leader like LtCol Dyess. It made me realize how vulnerable we are. LtCol Dyess rode us very hard when we trained and he demanded that we did things right. After all of our training sessions he would bring us together and go over with us how he felt we had done. He would always spend a few minutes telling us the good things we did—then he would spend the next thirty-minutes to an hour going over all the bad things we did. Then we would go back and train again. He was a hard man to please, but he got the most out of us. I truly respected that man.

The airfield on Roi would allow our planes the ability to target the nearby islands of Saipan and Tinian. It was a very strategic island for the U.S.

The 24th Battalion stayed on the islands for the next four or five days, but the 25th went back to the ship for the next mission. Eventually we were all en route to our next destination. We had accomplished out mission: we captured the islands.

Camp Maui:

We had boarded the SS Robin Wentley and then sailed to Maui where we disembarked in February 1944 for a rest and resupplying, but we really didn't get any rest because there was more training in store for us. We were trucked to Camp Maui and began training exercises for our next mission that was soon to come.

On that truck ride to Camp Maui I observed the storybook beauty of the great fields of sugar cane, palm trees, the mountains, beaches, and the quaint small villages along the route. For some reason the local population did not accept the Marines warmly.

At Camp Maui we all lived in tents with eight to ten Marines per tent. They told us the camp was originally intended for the Army, but the Army would have nothing to do with it, which made it just the thing for us Marines—the more miserable, the better. The term "rest" at Camp Maui was a misnomer.

We ultimately ended up coming back to Camp Maui after each of our missions. The length of training was up to several months. What we learned from the previous missions in combat would always be utilized in our training the Marine replacements that replaced the casualties we suffered from the previous battles. All of the intensive training was not only good for the replacement Marines, but also for the veterans, as it helped build up the confidence for the purpose of survival and having success on the battlefield by winning those important battles.

The training consisted of long hikes, day and night field problems and exercises, firing exercises, amphibious landings, etc. We had over forty training areas that were ideal for our training missions and for our next objective area to be ready to go to overcome the enemy.

Saipan:

We once again boarded ship and headed to our next mission. Like it was on our first mission, we were at sea for about seven days before they told us what our mission was going to be—Saipan. Once we knew the objective we were thoroughly briefed on what to expect and what to do. We also continued with our physical exercise regimens, test firing our weapons, and then cleaning our weapons. We also sharpened our knives and bayonets. We were 3,700 miles from Pearl Harbor. Once we landed we were ready for action.

Saipan is an island that the Japanese had occupied since WWI. They had a large civilian population on the island and it was heavily fortified with bunkers, and machine gun nests. It was estimated that the Japanese had almost 30,000 troops stationed on Saipan and Lieutenant General Saito Yoshitsugu commanded them. The Marianas had been deemed the island as a more ideal stepping-off point for a Japan invasion than was the Philippines that General Douglas MacArthur wanted. The invasion involved 535 ships and three divisions: the 2nd Marine Division, 4th Marines Division, and the 27th Army Division, which was to be used as a reserve force. To lessen the Jap's ability to fight the Navy bombarded the island with heavy fire from the ships on both coastlines of the island. We had over 125,000 troops aboard the ships. The 2nd Marine Division was to invade the Red Beach and Green Beach, and our 4th Marine Division was to land on Yellow Beach south of Charon Kanoa.

The island terrain was ideal for the enemy defense: Mount Tapotchau had an elevation of 1,554 feet and had excellent observation with long fields of fire. There were also a lot of ridges, ravines, caves, cliffs, and jungle vegetation to make for a great defense for the Japanese. Their defensive plan was to kill the Marines as they landed on the beaches. The Japanese air defense had been destroyed, but some had been deployed to other battle zones. The Japanese had trained well for this and were extremely disciplined for battle.

D-Day for our landing was scheduled on my birthday. I took a lot of joking about getting killed on the same day I was born. But I wasn't concerned because I honestly didn't believe I was going to get killed. I felt my training had prepared me to survive. I was a squad leader by this time and I knew I had to lead my men.

The Marines were given reveille at 0400 in order to be ready for the attack. We were given a good breakfast while the troop transports were getting in position so the Marines could embark in the LVTs heading for the beaches.

We encountered heavy enemy fire as soon as we came in to the beach. It was different from our landing at Roi-Namur. Incoming fire was hitting a lot of the landing craft before they made it to shore.

The island was surrounded by coral formations and when we jumped out of the boats we landed on the coral—it cut us to pieces. The cuts would later get infected causing even more grief for us. It was really tough going for everyone there.

The Japs were really blasting away at us and we had to take defensive positions on the beach. The Japs had dug trenches and laid barbed wire to hinder our advance and cause more casualties for us, and we did suffer a lot of casualties on the first day. We were there for just a couple of hours when our battalion commander and our company first sergeant were hit with a direct shot from Japanese artillery. It was a big blow to us, but we had to continue our fighting. Several thousand Marines were ultimately killed in the invasion. The Japanese were committed to fight to the last man, and they were not willing to lie down and quit.

The next morning my gun teams moved farther inland, toward the island's hilly center. I could see Mount Tapochou standing fifteen hundred feet above the jungle below it. We had to set up a defense and I told my gunners to set up the guns in the holes that we had prepared.

The island had a lot of varmints and snakes, and we joked about what the hell were we taking this island for—let them have the damn thing. Conditions were really horrible for us, and we lived without necessities while we were there. The weather was very hot and humid, and we were running up hills and through the rough terrain. We had trained under similar conditions, so we were prepared for those conditions. The Japs had a lot of caves and positions they had fortified and it was slow going for twenty-five days. One day a sniper fired his rifle just as a scorpion stung me on my back. I thought I was shot—it burned real bad. A corpsman came over and pulled my shirt up and killed the scorpion. It hurt like hell. Nothing we had done in training prepared me for that.

The Japs would lay low during the daylight, hiding in their caves or bunkers. At night they would come out and make their charges in darkness because we could not hit them with artillery or airpower at night. We were warned of the Jap banzai charges that they would make in which large numbers of their soldiers would charge forward in overwhelming numbers that would create chaos and confusion. However, we had to have the entire field of fire covered, and we were fully prepared for those attacks.

We were being targeted with artillery fire after we had been completely set up in our position. We had our machine gun in place and had placed concertina wire in front, but our company commander, Captain Parks, directed us to pull up our position. We were angry with that, but we did what we were ordered to do. We then moved our position and we had no idea where we were headed. It was dark out and we just seemed to go on and on. Later on we noticed the Jap artillery was hitting about one hundred fifty yards from our position—it didn't make sense to us because they should have been moving closer and closer to our position. A little later I realized that when we had moved our position we were only one hundred fifty yards from our original location. It fooled the Japs—they thought we were in our previous location. Captain Parks was smarter than we realized. He was a tough Marine too—he came down with dysentery while we were there but he stayed with us the whole time. He was a real leader, and that was something the men really appreciated in combat.

We continued to move toward the east, but it was slow going as we slogged along with our equipment and guns. The further inland we went the more mortar fire we encountered. The Japs had set their mortars to hit all the main roads and clearings, or any approach the Marines might use. We did not take a lot of direct hits, but there was a lot of terror that came from being near a mortar blast or shell burst, especially when we didn't know where they were coming from. My gun teams had to leap-frog forward, one team a at time while the others fired toward the enemy to keep them low while we took cover in bunkers, rock ledges and anything that would protect us from the onslaught above. It was a horrifying experience, and I was glad we had trained so harshly with regard to discipline. We just never knew where the rounds were coming from, and that is a terrifying feeling to know such danger is a constant threat and not have any idea how to avoid it.

Our second day on the island was met with a lot of mayhem. Our battalion commander, Lieutenant Colonel Maynard C. Schultz, was killed by an artillery attack that came down on us very suddenly. Then our company first sergeant, Ralph Lilja, was hit by a Jap mortar shell and was killed instantly. First Sergeant Lilja was a real leader of

Marines and all my men pledged to make sure his death was not in vain.

The Japs were using guerrilla tactics and would sneak close in with very small units and attack the Marines before disappearing into the dense jungle. We had to be constantly on alert, but the heavy jungle cover made it extremely difficult and we were very vulnerable.

Japanese Lieutenant General Yoshitsugo Saito was the commander at Saipan and he was a formidable force to deal with. He used 105mm and 150mm artillery fire combined with light tank firepower to achieve a static defense. He constantly moved his troops around at night to confuse the Marines. The Japanese had a superior knowledge of their terrain and that gave them a big edge.

I moved my men through the thick jungle that had hanging vines and moss that was always in our way. When we could hear the birds high up in the trees and the monkeys that perched on the tree limbs we knew it was safe. But when the jungle sounds stopped we got real nervous and secured our defenses in anticipation of a fight looming. We had occasions when the Japs came bursting through the dark jungle night with their tanks while blasting their 37mm guns and 7.7mm machine guns at my Marines. We had to hit the deck to avoid being shot. Two of my best men died while trying to take out an enemy tank that had broken through. Sergeant Albert T. Burnowsi and Corporal Eugene T. Gladkowski approached the enemy tank and used hand grenades and a satchel charge to blow the tracks off the tank. The explosion stopped the tank where it sat. The loss of those two great Marines made my men and me become all the harder with the deaths. I was so upset that I promised to avenge their deaths and all the other men I lost in this combat, even if I had to die doing so. That was about the time I was given the nickname "Iron Mike", a nickname that has managed to stick with me to this day.

To defend against the bonzai charges I had my machine guns set up to cover all the areas around us. We had forward observers who would call in artillery strikes or even naval gunfire to stop the enemy attacks. But it was our mortar fire and rifle fire that mainly pushed them back when the Japs were close in around us. But the Japs sometimes broke through our perimeter, and when that happened it turned into hand-to-hand combat. We had trained hard for that very event so we knew what to do in that very dangerous way of fighting. It's one thing to kill an enemy at fifty yards with a rifle shot, but altogether a different matter when you stand in front of your foe face-top-face with the only thing between you and the enemy being a bayonet or KaBar knife.

There were snipers up in the trees and they would tie themselves to the tree in case they lost their footing so they wouldn't fall to the ground below. When we located them in the trees we would shoot them and they would then fall and dangle from the ropes. It was a weird sight to see.

I lost a lot of good friends and Marines on Saipan. One of them was our platoon commander, First Lieutenant Alexander Santilli. He was dubbed "The Saint" by his men because of his last name and also because he had studied for the priesthood at Fordham University. He was also famous for winning the Sugar Bowl when he blocked a punt into the end zone and caused a safety resulting in a 2-0 win. He was fatally shot by a Japanese sniper while on a patrol and he died where he fell to the ground. It was a real personal loss for me as well as for our platoon. The Saint always sought to protect the lives of his men by letting the more combat experienced NCO's run the platoon while he called for supporting fire and kept contact with the higher authorities.

The navy had decimated the Jap ships that were to resupply the military on Saipan and that determined the outcome. With no supplies the Japs knew it was over. They started to make some bonzai charges at us—they ran right at us with their rifles at fixed bayonets. We had a royal field day as they charged at us. Of course we lost more of our men, but they lost a lot more. They really were going to fight to the last man and they were not afraid to fight hand-to-hand. We had finally reached our primary goal at Phase Line 0-1, but we continued to face scattered remnants of Japanese units. The Japs were bone tired, bloodied, and practically out of food and water, and some even without ammunition. Despite that they continued to fight on—they sent their troops out to dash into our lines carrying explosive 'yellow powder' satchel charges that had enough power to knock the treads off our Sherman tanks.

My machine gunners became very skilled to the point of being natural born killers as they traversed their machine guns, mowing down the charging enemy as the attackers screamed "Bonzai" while running at us trying to break our perimeters with their suicide runs.

Our snipers begin to single out the Japanese officers making quick kills. The Japanese soldiers were at a loss without their leaders, as they relied on them for direction. That was a big difference in the Marines: if the company commander is killed then a platoon commander takes over, and if he gets killed a squad leader takes charge, and on and on down the line—we always have a person to take charge, and the men follow that man without question.

I was wounded by shrapnel while on Saipan and had to head back to the rear to be checked out by the doctor at the Army Field Hospital. He told me I would be sent back to the ship. I told him I didn't want to go back to the ship—I told him I wanted to go home to my family, which are my Marines. He thought I was kidding about home and he told me that home was thousands of miles away. But I explained that home was where my men were, and they were only two miles away. I finally had go UA (unauthorized absence) by sneaking out of the hospital. I found a tank retriever that was heading in the direction of my unit, so I hitched a ride with them and they drove me right to my company and I was finally back with my men—I was *home*.

My buddies and I continued to fight and forge our way ahead. In the next ten days my platoon battled our way to Hill 500, and then went on to Magicienne Bay where we continued to find fighting holes with fanatical Jap warriors resisting our advances.

There were a lot of Chamorro civilians on that island and they were being brainwashed and treated extremely cruelly by the Japanese who tried to convince them that the Americans were horrible and would rape the women and then slaughter them. The civilians were caught in the middle of the fighting, and unfortunately a lot of them were killed. But when we were able to take them prisoner we treated them well and they were surprised. We even had convinced some of them to make broadcasts to the other civilians to encourage them to give up and come to us.

But they still had a great fear of the Americans. The Japanese treated the civilians very poorly, and in the final days of our invasion I saw them take women and their children to the edge of a cliff where they made the mothers throw their kids over the edge and onto the coral far below. Then the women would jump, and if they didn't the Jap soldiers would shove them off. We used loudspeakers to try and prevent the suicides but they continued to jump to their deaths.

That was terrible to see and I hated the Japs even more after that. The waters around the coral reefs turned red from the blood—it was horrible to see. All of my men vowed to help the suicidal Jap soldiers accomplish their wish to die.

I had a corporal named Sandy Ball who came from West Virginia. He had somehow captured a motorcycle that had a sidecar attached to it. Unlike the sidecars on American bikes, this one was attached to the left side of the motorcycle because they drive on the opposite side of the road than we do. One day he said, "Hey Mervosh—let's go for a ride." I got in the sidecar and we took off on a narrow road and soon came upon some large trucks going real slow. He started to pull out to pass on the left side, but he couldn't see another truck coming. I was scared to death because I could clearly see the truck coming from my seat, so I yelled to the corporal, "*I'll* tell you when it's clear!" That was probably my last ride on the bike with him.

We were on Saipan for twenty-five days and finally we were given our first hot chow—it was chili. The flies there were so thick that we had to pry them off the food. That chili was great tasting, but later I got really sick from it. I had the "runs" for a long time. Lots of us had intestinal problems and we just had to deal with it. It took me over thirty years before I could eat chili again. They gave us an "APC" pill for everything because it kills every type of bug—that's what they told us anyway.

Water was a big problem on Saipan and we were on a strict water discipline—one canteen of water per day. It was really hot and humid there and we were dying for a drink of water. We put pebbles in our mouths and that helped a little. At times we even took the water from the condensing can on the machine gun—it was full of cosmoline, and when we drank it the taste was horrible, but it was wet, and that's all we cared about. Gunny Bringle used to tell us not to drink water from the streams. He was knowledgeable about a lot of things and we respected what he said. But one time as we were crossing a stream he took his cup out and tasted the water—he said it was okay and then we all drank water from the stream and filled our canteens. We didn't know it, but just up the stream were twenty dead Japs and we were drinking water that contained maggots.

We killed nine thousand Japanese on Saipan. In one Bonzai charge we killed over two hundred. I have no idea how many men I killed. The way we felt about killing was, "It's either him or me". I am beyond remorse—that is a common trait of Marines in those battles.

Tinian:

When we were done in Saipan we boarded ship and headed toward Tinian. Tinian was only a few miles from Saipan. We had been in almost constant battle with the Japanese since late December, and we were getting very battle savvy. Following a strong naval bombardment of the island we made our landing. It was considered one of the most efficient landings ever. For a long period before we landed the Navy bombarded the island with heavy shelling. Bombers then came in and dropped the first-ever napalm bombs on Tinian Town and completed destroyed the structures there. The napalm was also used to burn the sugar cane fields that also were hiding Japanese positions.

The weather in these islands was also very hot with high humidity. It took a lot out of us, and it was sometimes worse to deal with the weather than to deal with the enemy. But the fact was the weather was also hot and muggy for the Japs, so nobody had any edge in that regard. We just tried to drink as much water as we could to avoid getting heat exhaustion.

There were over nine thousand Japanese soldiers on the island and they had built up heavy defenses. They planned to destroy us when we landed on the beach. We fooled the Japs into thinking we were going to invade Tinian Town, when we actually would be invading a smaller beach, but a smoother landing spot. On 24 July we boarded Amtracs and headed for the beach. We landed on a small beach only sixty yards wide. The beach was so narrow we had to land in columns. Our Amtracs had to come in where the coral was, and we jumped out into water that was chest-deep. A machine gunner was trying to climb over the coral wall when he got shot in the chest. I grabbed him and tried to lift him up on the coral and at the same time plug the hole in his chest with my finger. It was a big struggle in the water and finally a doc came by and told me he was gone. The cuts we got from the coral would later become infected just the same as Saipan.

The Japs were totally fooled by our landing and we had virtually no significant resistance. We soon had a long stretch of beach secured and had moved inland about a mile or so.

Our enemy fought in a similar manner as they did on Saipan—they hid during the day and came out at night under the cover of darkness. We had to be constantly on the alert. Several days after our landing we were hit with a bonzai attack one night. The next day we had over eight hundred dead Japs lying on the ground in front of us. We lost a lot of Marines in that attack also. When the Japs attacked bonzai fashion it was better than when we had to go to the caves to get them out. They came running at us right out in the open, and the best way I can describe it is that we had a field day shooting them.

Tinian was also the first location that the U.S. used napalm bombs, and we dropped lots of bombs on the island to burn off the vegetation that was concealing the dug-in Japs. Napalm is a very effective tool and we used it a lot after that.

I've been asked before if we were afraid: I never consider fear as something we felt—we were together with Marines on our left and right, each one of us covering the next one. We were trained well for our job, and the fact is we had to kill or be killed. I am honestly more afraid of driving on I-5 than I was in combat.

The Japanese were desperate and eventually it came down to a lot of hand-to-and fighting. We used our KaBars a lot when defending ourselves in those attacks. That was when our physical training really showed up in our ability to beat our enemy opponents.

I had learned to chew tobacco when I was fourteen years old. I found that chewing tobacco kept me from being thirsty. One night at Tinian a Japanese jumped into my hole and he had his knife in his hand and was trying to stab me. I tried to get my knife out but it was stuck. In desperation I finally just kept spitting some chew juice into his eye and it blinded him for a moment. That split second was all I needed to draw my knife and kill the bastard. I guess I can always say that chewing tobacco saved my life.

The landing on Tinian is considered one of the best amphibious landings in Marine Corps history—it went very smooth by invasion standards and was perfect actions by the Marines involved. Tinian was extremely strategic, as our B-29's could take off from there and hit Japan. The Japanese lost over eight thousand men while the Marines only lost three hundred twenty-eight men KIA (killed in action) and had one thousand five hundred seventy-one WIA (wounded in action).

I got dengue fever while on Tinian. It is caused by mosquito bites and it causes every bone in your body to feel like it is broken. I ached all over and I was miserable, and frankly I wanted to just die. I went to sickbay and was given "APC's"—all-purpose capsules, and was told to go back and continue to take the capsules. I was on light duty for a week, but still ended up going into the battlefield to continue to fight. I was groggy from the fever and medication. We were given repellents to keep the mosquitoes away, but it eventually would wear off with our constant sweating and then the bugs would come back on the attack.

We finally secured the island and went back to our ships.

Maui:

We were supposed to go to Saipan for rest, but instead the ship headed for Maui for a much-needed R&R (rest and recreation). We needed to get replacement Marines to fill the empty billets that we had due to casualties. The wounded Marines were also able to get proper treatment to heal.

While in Maui I continued with my boxing matches when possible. I was training whenever I could, as I wanted to stay in shape, and I felt that boxing gave me a big edge in combat because it kept me very disciplined.

Once again we trained hard on Maui, going out to sea and conducting practices. Like I have said before, our training was harsh and miserable, and that made the actual combat actions seem easy. We were out at sea when they gave us the word we were going to Iwo Jima. We had no idea where that was. We were told that the island was only about six hundred miles from mainland Japan. Our B-29's were having a tough time taking off from Tinian because the fighters could not make the trip to escort them, so we lost a lot of B-29's. The fact that Iwo Jima was so close to Japan meant that the fighters could escort the B-29's and provide them the protection they needed from the Japanese defender Zeros. Iwo Jima had two airfields on it, and taking those airfields was our objective. The Japs had anticipated Iwo Jima would be a prime target for invasion and they had spent years fortifying the island into a fortress. They had dug tunnels throughout the island, and also built heavy bunkers for their artillery and machine gun positions. A five hundred foot volcanic mountain called Mount Suribachi stood on the southern tip of the island, and the Japs had built artillery positions inside the caves there.

Our convoy had to zigzag through the waters while en route to Iwo Jima to minimize exposure to Japanese submarines that slithered through the Pacific looking for American ships to sink. The troop ships only went about ten knot and the trip took over a month. The ships did not have commodes: instead, they had troughs and we had to sit on the edge of them. Water would slosh up and wash the wastes down the trough and into the ocean. The water would sometimes splash up onto our asses as well, and that was not a comfortable thing. We were using bunks that had so little space between the upper and lower bunks that if you turned on your side your shoulder would hit the bunk above. We didn't have pillows, so we used our jackets instead. There were so many men on the ship that after we went through the long mess hall lines we had to eat standing up because there was not enough room to sit down. When the seas were heavy the ships would roll with the swells, and a lot of guys would get seasick. They also would only turn on the fresh water for limited periods of time. When the fresh water was off the scuttlebutts (drinking fountains) were closed and we had to wait to get a drink of water. I always filled my canteens up when the fresh water was on, but some guys waited and couldn't fill their canteens full.

Iwo Jima:

We did not know it at the time, but we were preparing for what would ultimately become the fiercest battle ever to be fought by the Marine Corps. It would be known also as a perfect battle on a perfect battlefield. There were no structures on the island and no civilians there—only the enemy soldiers inhabited it. The island was devoid of brush, and it was just a very baron island. Worse for us, the Japs had been told by their commanders that they had to kill ten Marines before they could go to their graves.

The navy had bombarded the island for three straight days. They threw everything they had onto that place and it was hard to believe anybody could have survived. On top of that our fighter planes strafed the island everywhere they thought the enemy was hiding. I thought that there was not going to be anything left alive for us to get. What we didn't know was that the Japs were well protected in their tunnels and bunkers. We had grossly underestimated the enemy positions—we had thought there were about two hundred, but the fact is the total was more like eight hundred. The bombardment was able to take out some of the bunkers, but didn't have much impact on their soldiers—they were down five and six tiers below the surface unfazed by our bombings. The island was like a giant anthill with tunnels dug underneath. When the shelling was over our invasion started and the Japs were waiting for us.

The battle began on 19 February 1945. The first waves of Marines that came in had virtually no resistance. The Japs had planned it that way—they were going to wait for the beaches to be full of Marines before they opened up on them. Some Marines were coming ashore in Amtracs. My company boarded our Higgins boats from the ships and then landed on 'Blue Beach-2', and that was on the extreme right side of the attack. We jumped out of those boats and were immediately hit with a barrage of gunfire and artillery fire. There were bodies of dead Marines all over the beach and we had to step over them in search of cover. We were always crouching under artillery, mortar, and rocket fire, and even their anti-tank and anti-aircraft weapons were fired at us ground Marines. They threw everything they had at us, and when the shells hit the ground the impact raised plumes of dust and ash and sent shrapnel in all directions. When you consider the Normandy Invasion, twenty-four hours after they landed on the beach you could put a picnic basket out there with your grandmother or your wife, and then sit down to eat. But on Iwo you couldn't for the entire battle period—there just wasn't a safe place at any time during the battle.

My thoughts often fell back to the first twenty dollars I was paid in boot camp and how I had sent the money home to my mother. By now I was being paid forty-five dollars a month. I figured it out: we were battling twenty-four hours a day here, and our pay worked out to $1.54 per day. A buck fifty-four per day is not a lot of money to be paid to get shot at, blown up, and so on. But, we were Charlie Company, First Battalion, Twenty-fourth Marines, and we were here to win the battle. Our pay was never an issue to us.

The weather on Iwo Jima was different then Tinian or Saipan—on Tinian and Saipan the weather was hot and very humid, but here it was cool with rainy conditions. We went from temperatures over one hundred degrees to conditions in the sixties, and we were cold. We were shivering as the winds blew in off the cold Pacific Ocean. It hadn't rained on Iwo Jima for twenty-years, but it rained the first night we were on the island and it made us even more cold. The beaches were made up of course black volcanic sand, and there was a heavy mixture of ash. The ash made for poor footing and moving through it was extremely difficult. The Amtracs were getting bogged down in the sand and ash, and the equipment was starting to block the beaches when they became quagmired in the sand. The volcanic ash would get embedded in our skin. The ash made the ground soft and it no doubt was effective at lessening the impact of exploding shells, and it is hard to imagine the casualties we would have suffered had the ground been hard instead.

We were being hit with phosphorous mortar rounds and the phosphorous would fall down in chunks on top of us. We had to put our ponchos over ourselves to keep from getting direct hits by the chunks, and then immediately flip off any that landed on us. Our ponchos had holes burned in them due to the hot phosphorous. If the phosphorous made contact with our skin it would just keep burning through our flesh—it was horribly painful for those that were hit with it.

My company was part of the fourth or fifth wave to land. We had about two hundred forty men when we hit the beach. But by that time the Japs had opened up with their artillery fire from the hidden bunkers on Mount Suribachi. There was no place to hide on the beaches. The sand and ash did not allow us to dig foxholes. Dead and wounded Marines were lying all over the beach. We were being hit with machine gun fire, artillery, and sniper fire. We were pinned down on the beach with no place to go. We were in survival mode.

Charlie Company's objective was to secure airfield number two. We were on the extreme right flank of the landing. We had to change our objective, as there were heavy concentrations of Japs to our right and we had to attack their positions. We began to throw grenades at them. We threw more grenades than we shot our rifles. The battling was constant and very intense.

On 23 February the American flag was raised on Mount Suribachi. From our position on the beach we could see the flag, but we had no idea if it was American or Jap since it was too small to see clearly. I had a pair of binoculars in my pack so I took them out and stood up to take a closer look. I realized it was our flag, but at the same time the Japs zeroed in on me—anybody with binoculars was considered to be a leader and I became an immediate target. Bullets were coming at me like crazy. One round caught my cartridge belt and just about tore it off. I couldn't help but think that they poor shots. I ducked down and that is all I remember of the flag raising on Mount Suribachi. The photo taken by Joe Rosenthal of the second raising of the flag turned out to be one of the epic war photos of all time, but we were a little busy on the beach at the time. The truth is, the flag raising was no big deal for us—we were too busy killing Japs and dodging bullets to pay any attention.

We were using the artillery craters in the sand to try and stay out of the line of Jap firing. We had combat dogs that had also come ashore, and each dog had two handlers. One dog had one of its handlers killed and there was only one left. The dog and his handler had jumped into our crater to get out of the line of fire. Just then a heavy mortar attack was coming our way and the dog was scared to death. The dog kept nudging into my position. I was trying to push the dog away but the dog just looked at me and snarled and growled. I had to let the dog have my position in the hole.

We spent days at a time in the same foxholes, pinned down by heavy enemy fire. We had to piss in our helmets and then throw the urine over the edge of the holes. I don't remember taking a crap the entire time I was on the island, but I am sure I had to go at some point. It's strange how some things just don't stay in the mind—I think we were more concerned with the death and carnage all around us to remember about taking a crap. Since then I have asked hundreds of others that were on Iwo and they all said the same thing—taking a crap is something nobody seems to remember there.

The Jeeps and Amtracs that came ashore continued to get bogged down in the ash and sand. We were able to use those vehicles as cover from the constant shooting we were encountering. Japanese bullets constantly bounced off the metal sides.

We kept fighting whether we were wounded or not. The conditions were horrible and we relied on each other at all times. We were making maybe thirty or forty yards per day. The enemy was underground and well hidden from us. We had to eliminate their bunkers, and we used flamethrowers to blast the burning fuel into the bunkers to drive the enemy out. The Japs would scream as the fire blew in on them and their only escape was out the back hatch—we would be positioned there to kill them as they ran out. It was a horrible sight to see men on fire, but they were the enemy to us and killing them was our mission.

We didn't think too much about survival. We had a job to do. I didn't have fear because fear to me is complete loneliness. In other words, there's no hope, but I felt that there *was* hope because, man, oh man, I still have my Marines around me. It was, "Hey, let's go, *move out*!" That's my job to get my men to move out, and I was the first one to move out—I was leading my men, and that is what a leader is for. That is why they called me "Combat Crazy". But I told them I wasn't combat crazy—I was *combat oriented* and I told them to say that instead. I would also tell the man next to me, "If I die you are going to take charge." That is the way it goes because the fire team leader became squad leaders; squad leaders became platoon sergeants; platoon sergeants became company commanders—that is the way Marines handle facing casualties of their leaders. And that happened a lot on Iwo. We had complete decimation of our men. I always felt that if I lost an arm or a leg I'd be coming out ahead. I'm not kidding—I was ultimately one of thirty-one men in our company to walk off the island when it was all over, and our original strength at landing had been two hundred forty-one Marines.

Resupplying was no problem despite the havoc on the beaches—we simply used the ammo and food from the dead men lying on the sand. It might seem ghoulish, but that's what we had to do. Supplies couldn't be sent across the areas. We particularly liked the 'D' rations—those were the hard chocolate bars that came with the 'C' rations. The chocolate was so hard it could break your teeth if you bit down too hard. I used to let it just melt in my mouth. The chocolate bars were one of the few nice things we had on Iwo Jima, but it was no consolation for what we were enduring every minute we were there.

We couldn't sleep like normal, and all we could do was to take a short catnap. It was hard to sleep with all the loud noise from the explosions and gunfire. The enemy would come out at night and attack our positions and we had to be on the constant alert. We knew the only time we were going to be safe was when the island was fully secured.

We made very slow progress making our way to the airfields. We lost a lot of men. I became the company commander, as all the officers in my company had been wounded or killed. That was how the war was—the senior man remaining takes over. For me it was just another position of leadership and I was ready for the job. We were losing a lot of Marines and it was something we never got used to. We used flamethrowers a lot, and the flamethrowers had a range of about twenty-five yards, and that meant that the man with the flamethrower had to get very close to the enemy. It was a dangerous job, and all of us were trained on using them. I had one Marine by the name of Dominick Tutalo, and he was fearless—he would charge up to a bunker and blast the Japs with the flames. The Japs would run out of the bunkers on fire and we would shoot them. I told Dominic I was going to give him a reward when we got back—he simply replied, "Let's first get back!" When that time finally came there were fifteen or twenty privates that I had promoted to privates first class. Dominick was happier than a hog in crap to be a PFC,

The Japanese would take uniforms off dead Marines and then wear them in an effort to fool Marines. They would approach at night wearing those uniforms. We always had a password to use when approaching other Marines and the Japs didn't know the password. We would use a word like 'tree', but Marines would also forget the password so they had to come up with something that any American would know. If our password was 'tree' and they forgot we would yell out, "Give a name of a tree—any type of tree (like fir or some other tree type)." The Japs would often just say, "I'm a Maline." Their inability to say the letter 'r' would be a dead giveaway, and as soon as they said, "Maline", they were shot dead. We were learning on the fly for these types of enemy tactics.

We had made our way to a deep canyon that had the appearance of being created by a giant earthquake. I was low to the ground when I felt a heavy hit on my back—it felt like I was hit with a baseball bat. It was actually a piece of shrapnel that had hit my backpack and destroyed all my c-rations as well as the shrapnel hitting my binoculars. If I hadn't had that pack with the binoculars inside I wouldn't be here today. I had another close call when I dropped a white phosphorus grenade into a pillbox—Japs came flying out the backside and one of them raised his sword up so he could kill me. I quickly shot him in the face and then tried to shoot the other three. Unfortunately for me my rifle jammed. My automatic rifleman saw the Japs and it was his first time to see them, and all he did was start shouting, "Look—they're Japs!" I screamed at him to shoot the sons of bitches, and he then came to his senses and mowed them down. He was a replacement that was sent in and had little combat experience. A few hundred yards further up the hill he was killed by enemy fire. He had saved my life and I didn't even get to find out his name. I saved the dead Jap's sword and it is in my trophy case today.

I recall that on one occasion we had a slight lull in the fighting and some of my men lit up cigarettes that came in each K-ration package. They looked so relaxed smoking those cigarettes that I decided I would try one on our next break in the fighting—that break never came and I haven't smoked a cigarette to this day.

I had lost a lot of my ability to smell due to my boxing career—being hit in the nose will do that to you. But it helped me on Iwo Jima. The island has a sulfuric smell to it and a lot of men couldn't stand it. Also, the numbers of dead bodies on the ground created a real stink. A lot of guys would smell a decaying body and start throwing up, but it didn't bother me. In fact, when guys were complaining about the smell I would take in a deep breath to demonstrate a leader position by not letting it bother me. That type of action pushed my men to continue to use my nickname "Combat Crazy". I guess maybe I am lucky because of that, but it really didn't bother me at all.

One Marine, Sgt Oksandahal, had been at Midway during that battle. He had told me that the Japs had hit them with everything they had. I had read about that invasion and was familiar with the manner that the Marines were hit. He told me that Midway was no comparison to what was going on at Iwo Jima—Iwo was far worse! He didn't think he was going to make it and he started to dig a hole that he could get down in and get out of the line of fire. He dug in pretty deep and he was able to stand in his hole and still be able to fire out. I didn't follow his actions, as I just sat in the foxhole. A short time later a shell came down right on top of him and blew him up. There was nothing left of him, and what was left would have fit in a shovel, but I found his dog tags and saved them. I knew then that when it's your time to go you go—nothing you do is going to stop that. Another time we came under a mortar attack and a few of us ran and jumped into some large shell holes. Another round came into the foxhole and exploded and all the men were casualties except for me. I was knocked out and I have no idea for how long, but when I woke I had blood streaming down my face. I had been hit with shrapnel on my eyelid. I could not hear anything going on around me because the explosion had damaged my eardrums, but oddly enough I could hear angels singing. One of my men had a hole in the back of his head so I put a field bandage there and then carted him several hundred yards to where the corpsman was so the wounded man could be medivac'd. My future brother-in-law was also in the hole and he too had to be sent back to the ship due to his injuries. Luckily for me, about a week later my ears popped and I could hear again.

At one point I was in a hole with a lieutenant and we came under heavy sniper fire. We didn't know where the shots were coming from so I tried raising up out of the hole to see, but each time I was shot at and had to drop back into the hole. Finally, after several attempts resulting in almost getting killed, I told the lieutenant it was his turn. He raised his head up and almost immediately was shot in his head. The impact of the shot blew his brains onto me, and instinctively I tried to put his brains back into his head. It's odd what goes through a man's mind in such a moment. I quickly realized he was gone and just had to put the incident aside and deal with the sniper alone. I kept telling myself that war is *hell!*

There was a replacement captain that had arrived and was on his second day of battle as our new company commander. He had been an adjutant in his prior assignment, but now was in charge of our rifle company. We came under a very hard artillery attack and suddenly the captain was hit with shrapnel. He turned around, looked me square in the eye, and said, "I'm dead!" I looked at his eyes at that very moment and could tell the eyes were telling me, "You're in charge now." He dropped dead. That was when I became the new acting company commander.

We had reached an area known as the 'Boat Basin' and we had to throw grenades at the enemy. I threw so many grenades that my arm started to hurt. From there we went up to another area known as the "Quarry". It was there that I got wounded. I was hit in the stomach and my leg. The pain was intense. The corpsman looked at my wounds and gave me a shot of morphine—that really stopped the pain quick. He then and told me I had to be sent back to the ship. I looked out to the boats in the water and I could see some of the boats being blown up as they headed back to the ships. I decided there was no way I was going back, and besides, I was the acting company commander and I had to lead my men. I wasn't going to get on one of those boats and then get killed—if I were going to die it would be right there on Iwo Jima. The corpsman put a black 'M' on my forehead to indicate I was on morphine and tagged me to be medivac'd. The morphine had immediately taken the pain away so I wiped that 'M' off my forehead and went back to my men. The pain came back later on and some of my men told me to get another shot of morphine, but I wouldn't do it. I wanted to be aware and not chance being so drugged that I couldn't lead properly. I just had to endure the pain and carry on, but I am glad I didn't take that second shot of the painkiller.

The bodies of the dead Marines had to be buried to prevent the spread of disease. The graves were shallow—usually three or four feet deep at the most. We went through the dead Marine's pockets and destroyed any letters they had so that the Japs couldn't dig them up and use the information against us. The Americans would later be exhumed and the bodies returned to America for proper burial at home. We buried the Japanese soldiers in mass graves that were dug out by bulldozers

Toward the end of the battling the Japs that were left became desperate and began to come out of their underground positions. They would make bonzai charges at us. We liked it when they came up above the ground because that meant that we didn't have to go down after them.

The Japs staged their only organized night counter-attack of the entire battle against our lines on the nights of 8-9 March. From one thousand eight hundred to two thousand rockets, mortars, grenades, rifles and machine gun rounds fell along our lines followed by a systematic infiltration of the Japanese soldiers. Waves of Japanese hammered our lines, and some even broke through to the command posts. Many enemy soldiers carried land mines strapped to their chests and came running at us in attempts to blow them up in suicidal charges. Other Japs seeing their charge that was a failure killed themselves with their grenades. Hand-to-hand combat took place up and down our lines as the Japs pushed forward. Those of us that were lying in our foxholes killed the majority of the enemy—we blasted everything that moved as they charged our positions. The next morning there were seven hundred eighty-four dead enemy soldiers that were counted.

The end of the battle was in sight. At 1500 on 9 March the tenth patrol had reached the coast without encountering any opposition. However, the next day the Division front had heavy opposition in the wild terrain with its earthquake appearance as they advanced toward the ocean, except for the 25th Marines who were still meeting a pocket of heavy resistance where the enemy chose to make their last stand. On the nights of 15-16 March a party of over sixty Japs tried to break out of the pocket, and failing to do so, they slunk back into their caves and bunkers. The Marines finally were able to clear all the caves and bunkers out by 1000 on 16 March.

On 16 March our commanding general declared Iwo Jima secure, but we continued to get resistance from the enemy for another ten days on the far side of the island. The Fourth Marine Division Cemetery was dedicated that day, and naval support units sailed away. The 23rd had returned to their ships by 17 March, the 25th on 18 March, while the 24th Marines did so on the 19 March. We sailed away on 20 March. The division had a combat efficiency rating of just thirty-five percent.

The battle lasted thirty-six days and not one of them was an easy day. It was a bitter fight to the very end. Finally Iwo Jima was secure and we had won the battle. Out of two hundred forty men in my company that landed on that God-forsaken island we only had thirty-one left in the end—and half of us were the "walking wounded". We had lost over two hundred Marines on Iwo Jima. I was the highest ranked man at the end and was the acting company commander. We had a photo taken of all of our men that had made it to the end.

When we finally left the island and went back to the ships we had to climb up the netting along the side of the ship. After we got to the top of the netting the sailors were helping Marines get over the railing. I was wounded and in a lot of pain, and a sailor got me by the arms and I yelled, "Get away from me Swabby, I made it this far, I will do it on my own, by dammit, we're *Marines!*" Years later the expression "By dammit, we're Marines" would become the title of a book by Gail Chatfield.

Once aboard ship we were given a hot shower with regular water instead of the seawater we had previously used. They gave us our first hot meal in over thirty-six days. We had been totally wrung out during the battles, and it was very nice to be able to finally relax and not worry about being shot at.

Iwo Jima played a significant role in the final days of World War II. It became the way station of upwards of two thousand two hundred B-29 bombers and their crews numbering about twenty-five thousand, and the island would serve to save the lives of pilots and crews that would continue their bombing of Japan proper.

Countless acts of bravery and heroism under fire, with courage and determination and with a keen sense of duty under fire, went unrewarded because they were "all in a day's work," or went unwitnessed by any officers or Marines who lived to tell about it. Many of those Marines of valorous acts lie buried beneath the beach and volcanic ash.

Iwo Jima was recorded as the most demanding, toughest, and bloodiest battle in our illustrious chapters of Marine Corps history and heritage. The 'battle of all battles' was a perfect battle on a perfect battlefield. It was strictly fighting man against fighting man. In true words it was "kill or be killed". It was one-of-a-kind in the history of the Marine Corps, our country, and possibly the world. God bless the Marines who accomplished this mission.

I received my first Navy Accommodation Medal and a Purple Heart Medal. I had been put in for the Bronze Star but for some reason I never received it. Every Marine on Iwo Jima deserved a medal and most received none. Part of the problem was that most of the officers and witnesses had died in the combat, and there was nobody left to submit the required forms. Admiral Nimitz said of the Marines on Iwo Jima, "Uncommon valor was a common virtue."

Marines often took souvenirs from the dead Japanese. Many of the souvenirs were traded to sailors on the ships, and in exchange we received cans of peaches, or maybe even some whiskey. Guns would be carried home, but they had to be cleared with the censor officer first.

One Marine that I recall vividly was PFC Wallace Taylor. He was a machine gunner and had been in all four campaigns with me. I called him "Miracle Man" because he never got a scratch. It had to be a miracle . . .

I have been asked what battle was my favorite: it's sort of like being asked which was your favorite illness. But I would say that the Marshalls would be a favorite out of the battles because it was the shortest.

General Smith came to visit us in Maui. While in formation the general walked down the rows of men and was handing out Purple Heart Medals to those that had been wounded. He asked each man where he got wounded: their answered varied, "Saipan", "Roi-Namur", "Iwo Jima", etc. He came to one man and asked the same question: "Where did you get wounded Marine?" "Right in the ass sir!" replied the Marine. The general was a little flustered by the answer and reminded the Marine that is not what he wanted to know.

Marines had some good times back in Hawaii. On liberty we would go into town and the most popular places were the cathouses—there were long lines outside with the sailors and Marines waiting to go in. The lower floor of the buildings usually had a bar, and the second floor was the cathouse. The beer was fifteen to twenty-five cents, but the girls were two bucks. If anyone got venereal disease (VD) they would be court-martialed. We had "VD only" commodes in our heads that were specifically for the men who had VD. They were the cleanest of the commodes so I used those commodes. Word got out that "Iron Mike has VD" after Marines saw me using those commodes—it's funny how rumors start.

Some people consider me a 'survivor of Iwo Jima', but that is not the case: any Jap that came off that island alive is a survivor—I am a *conqueror* of Iwo Jima!

The End of the 4th Division:

We headed back to Maui to prepare for the assault on mainland Japan. While there I went to sickbay twice a day to have my wounds treated. It took over two months for the wounds to heal and I was placed on light duty. I was still in charge of training though, so it wasn't like I really had light duty. We had gotten new officers to replace the dead and wounded ones from battle, and our company was provided replacement Marines to bring us back up to strength. I was the Platoon Sergeant and held a staff sergeant rank. The training was intense, as we knew that landing on the mainland of Japan was going to be the real battle of all battles. Like all training it seemed like the training was harder than the actual battles we would be engaged in. But before we were deployed for the next phase of our battling the United States dropped the two atomic bombs on Japan, and with the Russians having also declared war on Japan just days earlier and were advancing through China, the Japanese finally surrendered. Those two bombs saved countless thousands of American lives because the invasion of Japan would have been a real dogfight and the Japs were not going to surrender until the very last one was dead. The war was over.

The 4th Marine Division went back to Camp Pendleton. We sailed on the USS Sgt Bay, a small aircraft carrier that took us to San Diego. We then moved north to Camp Pendleton and it was there that we had a ceremony and they cased our Fourth Marine Division Colors. It was a sad day for all of us. I am proud to say that I was one of the last enlisted men to have served with the 4th Marine Division. The Fourth Division had the most battles in that time frame, and those battles were among the harshest battles ever faced by United States Marines.

In Memoriam:

Sergeant Major 'Iron Mike' Mervosh wrote the following memorial to his fallen brothers. It reflects his unbending respect for his fellow Fourth Marine Division comrades who paid the ultimate price in battles that the division participated in. There is no doubt about his strong bond with those men and what they accomplished in their victories.

There were many Marines in the Fourth Marine Division who made the supreme contribution to victory. Like so many of their brothers in other divisions, and like those who fell before them on the shores of Tripoli and the Argonne Forest—they now guard the streets of Heaven. On Roi-Namur, the Marshall Islands, Saipan, Tinian, and Iwo Jima, they keep their ceaseless vigil. Of all the monuments to war, none will last as long to us of the Fourth Marine Division as the memory of the wooden slabs that glisten so brilliantly over their graves.

Many were killed on that first day of battle and on the very beaches where they are buried. Other Marines fought doggedly for weeks only to fall in their last skirmish, which preceded the raising of our flag in victory.

There were thousands of graves altogether. The dead were Catholics, Protestants, Jews and others. They were all Marines between eighteen and forty years of age. There were privates and then there were lieutenant colonels. They will not be forgotten . . .

The ceremony will long be remembered. Colors flew at half-mast. The firing squad stood at attention. Reverently the Marines paid tribute to their fallen comrades as a general rose and went to the altar.

"They are heroes all," the general said. "They died so we could live. They have written a glorious page in our country's history."

A slight breeze lifted the tiny flags on the graves for a moment and then let them down gently. A Catholic priest went forward to say Mass. He committed the dead to God's care. When he finished a Protestant chaplain took his place and recited the burial service for the dead. The Jewish Chaplain went forward, giving part of his talk in Hebrew and part in English.

Many Marines wept silently for their buddies who were among the fallen. Because we had come so close to death ourselves we shared more than the others the grief of its finality.

The Marine's rifles sounded three volleys over the rows of volcanic ash mounds. When they finished firing a bugler blew *Taps*. The generals rose to leave—it was a sign for us to follow. Some of us lingered briefly among the graves to whisper a last prayer, or to pay one final tribute to those who, out of the thousands of Marines in the Pacific, had to stay.

The face of every Marine who had come this day reflected the realization that there was an un-payable debt: the suffering of these Marines had led to our victory. Freedom was our password, death they had paid for holding high the torch of liberty. May we all meet in the great "Marine Barracks in the sky!"

Chapter 6

POST WAR ASSIGNMENTS

When the war was over the military began a massive wind-down. Men were being sent home, but the military had to do so in an orderly manner. They came up with a point system to determine who went first. For example, for each campaign we would get five points. We received five points for each commendation; one point for going overseas; one point for how long we were in the Marine Corps, etc. The cut was ninety points, at least until they had to lower it to increase the attrition. Most Marines had not enlisted to be career Marines, but rather had joined to fight the enemy that had invaded us, so when they had the opportunity to return to civilian life they were more than happy to go home.

In combat we had not been allowed to seal our letters being sent home, as the mail had to be censored by company officers. The officers had been schooled in censorship. We couldn't say where we were, or where we were headed, and we couldn't even mention things like palm trees and such—if we did it was blacked out so it couldn't be read. We weren't even allowed to mention Maui. It seems odd to think about it today, but that's how it was back in those days. So once the war was over we were no longer restricted. We were getting back to the freedoms we had taken for granted before the war started.

The chow we ate while aboard ships was fair, but not fancy. We had a lot of Vienna sausages, dried eggs, and sometimes Spam. The dried eggs were always bland and they were always greenish in color—hardly appetizing—at least not like I thought when I first ate them in boot camp. We didn't get really 'fresh' food until we got back to the States. My first meal upon my return was a double order of ham and eggs—it was eight eggs total. Immediately after I gobbled it all down I had to run outside where I puked my guts out. I guess I wasn't ready for real food yet.

We got a thirty-day leave and I met my future wife Margaret while I was home. My Marine buddy, John Hasara, had been discharged as a PFC after WWII and he had married my sister. I met his sister Margaret in 1945 and we ultimately got married in 1948—we wanted to make sure we were right for each other. We must have made the right choice because we were married sixty-three years until she passed. Margaret lived about ten miles outside of Pittsburgh and I had to meet her family. I thought they were rich because they bought a house for $4,700. My dad had paid half that much for our home in Pittsburgh.

I found out that my mother had saved all the money I had sent home to her, and when I got home she showed me the $300 cash. She gave it back to me. I went out and bought her a new refrigerator and an oven. My dad was upset because he liked the old icebox. My dad was very used to getting by with what they had; so getting new things didn't set well with him.

A couple of buddies and I went to the horse races and we ran into some horse owners that gave us some tips. We made the bets and ended up earning $184 apiece. That was a lot of money in those days.

While I was on leave I received orders to report to Camp Lejeune, North Carolina with the Second Marine Division. The Second Marine Division had occupied Nagasaki twenty-five days after the atom bomb was dropped. They were reassigned to Camp Lejeune and they became part of the Fleet Marine Force, Atlantic. The division participated in a lot of amphibious actions in the Caribbean waters. There were significant changes made to the makeup of the divisions, and that made the infantry battalions different than the former infantry regiments in brigades. The idea was to make the Marines more operationally efficient. They also improved the weapons for the battalions allowing that their weapons would be easier to transport thus allowing Marines to get them to a destination more quickly.

We did a lot of Caribbean cruises aboard the naval ships. The temperatures in the Caribbean were very hot and humid, and it was a lot like the islands we had fought on in the South Pacific. We did a lot of training for amphibious landings and assaults—that is mostly what Marines do in peacetime, as we always need to be ready at a moment's notice.

Ship life is a lot different from life on land. We always had to stand in line at the mess hall, and while standing in those lines I noticed a lot of guys tapping a spoon against a quarter. Quarters back then were made of silver and were fairly soft, and after tapping on the coin for a while the quarter would start to curl over. It took a lot of repetitions, but eventually the quarter would be formed into a ring. I made a ring and it was very nice looking. It took a long time to get it shaped to my finger too.

We made a lot of training cruises to the Caribbean. Those trips lasted from as little as two weeks to a long as two months. On the cruises we practiced a lot of beach landings and other military maneuvers. We got occasional liberty while in the Caribbean, but we mostly just stayed on the ships. Once, when we got back to the states, we were given a seventy-two hour liberty. Margaret was living in Pittsburgh, Pennsylvania at the time so I called her and asked her to meet me halfway. We went to a hotel and got a room for $6, and for six bucks we got a really nice room. Lawrence Welk was a polka player at the hotel and we went down to listen to his music and dance. We got a bottle of wine, and after pouring a glass for each of us I said, "Happy twelfth." She corrected me and said, "Happy fifth—that's how long we have actually been together!"

The 2nd Marine Division would often make Mediterranean cruises that involved several destroyers, a BLT, and we had about one thousand two hundred Marines plus our aircraft. We would be gone for six months at a time. My ship was the USS Latimer, a Haskell class attack transport ship. I liked those Med cruises because we went to some very interesting places—a lot of it was very historic too. By that time I had become a master sergeant and I was provided billeting in the chief's quarters where we were above the water line. That was a lot better than being below the water line like the lower ranked Marines. Rank did come with some privileges.

We had some really great liberty while on the Med cruises. Our ship stopped at great ports like Naples, the Riviera, Tripoli, and other good ports. When we were anchored off the Riviera the girls would come down to the beach and change into their bikini bathing suits. We would stand on the side of the ship and watch them, but they were always very careful when changing clothes and we never saw a damn thing! We stopped at Naples once, and I learned it was the most bombed city in WWII. When we went ashore we found Lucky Luciano's restaurant. Lucky Luciano was a notorious and ruthless American gangster who was convicted of racketeering in the U.S. He could have gotten life in prison, but he agreed to help the U.S. with information, so he was deported back to Italy. In Italy he opened a restaurant and it also had a cathouse on the upper floor. Luciano loved Marines and he came over and sat at our table to talk to us. He asked if we wanted to go upstairs and have a 'girlfriend'—I was married and had to say no, but some of my buddies took him up on his offer. He seemed like a really nice guy, but he was a hard-core murderer when he ran the New York Mafia.

We also made a stop at Sicily, and we all loved that place. There were olives growing on the trees and purple flowers all over the area. It had a really nice smell to it. We were not allowed to carry our rifles when we went ashore in Sicily, but we had all the rest of our gear on including our helmets and vests. The Mafia rules the area and has the local police and politicians in their pockets. The Mafia even have their own army of soldiers that walk around the area with rifles slung on their shoulders and bandoleers of ammo slung across their chests. Their job was to protect the various Mafia families and their turfs. When the Mafia soldiers came along the rode near us they smiled and were very friendly towards the Marines.

While on liberty in Rome we had a chance to see Pope Pius XII—it was a totally different experience from meeting Lucky Luciano. There were ten or eleven of us, and the Pope liked U.S. Marines. We gave him a "Hip, hip, hooray!" He liked that a lot. We were offered a tour of the catacombs. A priest led us into the dark caverns—it was pitch black and we were told we had to hold on to the shoulder of the person in front of us or we would get lost in the darkness. There were skeletons on our left and right as we walked along. When we were done the priest asked me for a cigarette. I didn't smoke, but I always carried a pack with me, so I gave him the pack of Lucky Strikes. He really loved that and he couldn't thank me enough. Back then we could buy a pack for ten cents and a carton was only eighty cents. American cigarettes were hard to come by in Europe, and our cigarettes were the most preferred type of smokes.

Once while on liberty in Tripoli we went ashore and bought some souvenirs. One of my corporals was a really good Marine, but when he got drunk he was a real terror. I had to pull his liberty card more than once. One day there was an announcement over the ship's loudspeaker for that corporal to report to the captain's office ASAP! I wondered what the hell the captain was requesting the corporal for so I went up to investigate. The captain looked at the corporal and said, "Corporal, last night you tried to bring a camel aboard this ship! I am confining you to five days of 'piss and punk' (bread and water)." I found out that he had gotten really drunk the night before and had bought a camel, and then he tried to bring it on the ship. The officer-of-the-day would not let him bring the camel aboard so the corporal left out on the dock. On another occasion the corporal put a nichol in a jukebox and selected the Marine's Hymn. The Marine's Hymn was all jazzed up and the corporal didn't like it, so he pushed the jukebox over. We had to get him back to the ship in a hurry to avoid trouble on shore.

While in Camp Lejeune I received a telegram that said, "It's a girl." My wife had a baby. I wanted to give my daughter a Serbian name and I suggested "Olga", but we settled on "Rosemary". It would be six more months before I would get my first look at Rosemary. Separation from our families was a major drawback of being a Marine.

In 1950 we were doing some land assault training exercises and we were using WWII ammunition left over from the war. I was in "C" Company and we had "A" Company on one side of us, and "B" Company on the other side. "A" Company called for artillery support fire. A "short round" hit the command post. One of our men, Charles Czerwiez—we called him "Pollock", had a small sliver of shrapnel hit him and enter his heart. He died instantly.

Pollock's wife and infant child had just come to see him at the base just before the incident. I was asked to take his widow and baby home on what was called "basket leave"—that was leave that was not on the books and could be as long as necessary. His widow lived in Pennsylvania, so I took advantage of the proximity to my home to call my wife and have her once again meet me halfway.

On my trip to Pennsylvania the widow told me she needed to breastfeed her baby but was very shy about doing so. I told her not to worry—that was what all the mothers did when their babies were hungry.

We finally reached her home and I dropped her off, and then headed to meet Margaret. When we finally met up it was the first time I got to see my baby girl Rosemary—she was six months old by that time. What a sight for me to see! She was beautiful and so tiny. It was a thrill for me to cradle her in my arms. None of the training, fighting, nor wars had prepared me for that moment. It made me realize how much I missed because I was a Marine away from my family. When it was time to go I hated to leave my baby daughter and Margaret, but I had to go. It was a very hard thing to leave home at that moment.

My brother Milan joined the Marines and he too went to boot camp at MCRD Parris Island. Following his boot camp he also went through his infantry training at Camp Lejeune and he had become a PFC by that time. He was assigned to "E" Company, 2nd Battalion, 6th Marines and he and I were housed just one building apart on the base. I thought it was pretty neat that we were so close together at that time. When I first I met up with him he wanted to have me take him to the Staff NCO Club. I told him I couldn't do that, but I would go with him to the enlisted club, also known as the 'Slop Chute'. I was proud that my brother had become a Marine and was taking after his big brother! Later Milan was transferred to the 1st Marine Division and was sent to Korea after the war started over there. He served in "I" Company, 3rd Battalion, 7th Marine Regiment, 1st Marine Division.

On my many cruises I took with the Fourth Marine Division I crossed the International Date Line ten times and went across the equator twice. We were on the ocean for over fifty thousand miles. Our mission while on the Mediterranean cruises was to show an American presence in the area and to enforce the peace. The Mediterranean can be a volatile area. The Marines first went there when they made a landing at Tripoli—the first American foreign invasion in U.S. history. It was a very historic area to be in.

I was on a Med-cruise when I received word that my brother Milan had been killed in Korea. It was a horrible feeling to know my brother had been killed. I had to take a flight from Naples to New York City and the flight took twenty-four hours. The flight was a very bumpy flight and the seats were all was bucket seats. When the military plane took off we had to go to the rear of the plane and lay down to shift the weight to the rear so we could get enough lift for takeoff. I had to pick up my brother's remains in New York City and then escort them to Pittsburgh. It was a very hard job for me to do. My family was not told how Milan had died, and for any family there needs to be closure, and with no information about what had happened there was none. We sent letters and made phone calls, but no information was ever received other than that he was "killed in action". It would be many years later that I received a letter from one of my brother's friends who wrote us and told us how Milan died in action—it was really tough to read that, but at last we finally knew what had happened.

I returned to Camp Lejeune and by that time the Marines were getting heavily involved with the Korean conflict and there were a few of us that were held back to train the replacements that were staging up to go to Korea. I was one of those Marines that were held back, probably due to my combat experience in the Pacific during WWII. I wanted to get to the action, but I was playing a vital role at Camp Lejeune.

Chapter 7

THE WAR IN KOREA

The Korean War began on 25 June 1950, when eight divisions of the North Korean People's Army crossed the 38th Parallel and invaded the Republic of South Korea equipped with mobile artillery that also included tanks from the USSR, as well as Russian aircraft. On 27 June 1950 the United Nations Security Council, proclaimed the North Korean attack a breach of world peace, and requested that member nations assist the Republic of South Korea. The United States was caught off-guard by the action because there was many who believed that because we had the atom bomb that nobody would ever mess with the U.S. Our military strength had been reduced to absolute minimal levels. Suddenly the U.S. was scrambling to build up sufficient troop strengths in order to send adequate help.

The Marine Corps' existence was under question following WWII, as some considered the Marines to be redundant to the Army, and few doubted that an amphibious military force capable of amphibious landings would ever be needed again. But it was the Marines that were able to rapidly pull together a force that could be quickly sent to South Korea to help stop the assault from the communists. The Marine Corps was pulling Marines from as many billets as they could, and then drew upon the reserves—many of which had served in combat during WWII, but a few had not even gone through boot camp.

The need for experienced fighting Marines was extreme and most combat experienced Marines were pulled from their duties to fill the initial Marine Corps' requirements of the war. They took drill instructors, cooks, admin men, and machine gunners—anyone they could. But they also left some of us back to train the Marines being called up from the reserves, and I was one of those men that did not get orders to go initially, as they felt I was needed more in a training capacity.

I really didn't know much about Korea at first. I knew from reading Marine Corps history that the Marine Corps had made several expeditionary missions in Korea during the 19th Century, and that Korea was in the Asia. I read about what was occurring in the daily newspapers and by listening to radio news reports.

For me, my involvement with Korea began with the death of my younger brother Milan in 1951. He had been stationed in Korea and was killed in action there. At the time we were not given a clear understanding of exactly what happened—we were just notified he was KIA (killed in action). I was asked by my mother to escort his body home for the funeral. It was a tragic occasion for the Mervosh family and everyone took his death very hard. As a combat Marine I was used to seeing death, but when it was my own brother it seemed much more different—it was *personal.* My mother wanted me to escort his body home so I had to go to New York City to pick up his remains, and then escort him to Pittsburgh. It would be my first and only military escort in my career.

In the fall of 1951, one month after burying my brother, I received orders to Korea. My parents really didn't like the idea of another son going to war in Korea, but nothing was going to keep me from going into another battle if I had the chance. It's a hard thing for parents to see their sons go off to war knowing that the outcome could be very bad news.

The Marine Corps had switched to the 'herring bone' utility uniform by the time the Korean War started. I liked that uniform because it had the buttons covered by the jacket so when we crawled on the ground the buttons didn't drag or break. The material was very tough and resisted tears. Of course we didn't worry about our appearance in the battlefield, and we wore the same uniform all the time. There was a Marine Corps emblem on the left breast pocket and the letters "USMC". A man once asked me what "USMC" stood for? I answered, "**Y**ou **s**aw **m**e **c**oming!"

I arrived in Korea in mid-October and was assigned to 'G' Company, 3rd Battalion, 5th Marines, 1st Marine Division. During October 1949, 3rd Battalion, 5th Marines had been reactivated on Guam and then in August 1950 the battalion deployed to fight the Communist force invading the Republic of South Korea.

The phonetic word for 'G' in those days was "George", unlike "Golf" today. We had a saying in our company: "They shall not pass by George!" 'G' Company was a rifle company and I was the company gunny as an E-6 gunnery sergeant. The company gunnies basically ran the company on a day-to-day basis. The 3rd Battalion had a nickname of "Darkhorse" and was derived from the radio call sign of its commander in Korea, Col. Robert Taplett, who was known as "Darkhorse Six". Colonel Taplett received the Navy Cross for his actions in Korea when the 3rd Battalion had battled at the Chosin Reservoir. We were a very proud outfit.

Korea was a very different type of war than WWII—it was a lot more similar to what WWI was like. In Korea we had trenches like they did in WWI, and between the enemy trenches and our trenches was an area we called "No Man's Land", and that was an area open to both side's line of fire and was extremely dangerous territory.

Aside from the danger of being in a war zone, our living conditions were pretty stark. For example, our field restroom facilities were very basic. A warrant officer by the name of Stinky Davis invented what we termed the 'four-holer'—it was a four-hole crapper with all four holes side-by-side. We dubbed him "Stinky", but he didn't care what we called him. Those four-holers were colder than ice when we sat on them, and we just prayed that no incoming rounds landed while we were on them. Can you imagine being blown up while sitting in the four-holer?

One day Colonel Taplett, our battalion commanding officer, came up to me and requested to know what the hell was going on with the company. The colonel was frustrated that he was not getting information he thought he should be getting from his officers. I just looked at him and said, "Well, get out in the company formation and you can find out." It was in our formations that we passed out our information and instructions, and I felt that was the best place for the colonel to get informed. The colonel took position and listened while I gave the report required of me as the Company Gunny.

The weapon I was issued was a .45 1911 pistol, but I also carried an M-1 rifle. The pistol was only for really close combat situations. I was a rifleman as far as I was concerned, and that required a rifle. I also could take over the machine gun if the gunner got hit. I knew all the weapons we had and I helped all our men whenever help was needed.

Korea topography had hills everywhere, and while on patrols we climbed hill after hill in what seemed like an impossible task to get to our objective. It was a lot different than what we faced on Iwo Jima where we almost had no hills, except for Mount Suribachi. Our demarcation point was the Imjin River, the seventh largest river in Korea.

Winter conditions in Korea were bitterly cold. The temperature was often below zero, but we never tracked it—we just knew it was damned cold. The winds blew hard and it made the temperature feel even colder to us. We were finally issued parkas, but initially we just had regulation-issue field jackets. The Marine Corps also provided heavy flannel shirts to wear, and those helped a lot. Our shoes in the beginning were boon dockers and we wore tan leggings above the boon dockers. The Chinese quickly learned to steer away from fighting with the Marines with the tan leggings—they knew we were fierce fighters and they avoided us and instead they preferred to fight the Army. We were eventually issued boots to replace the boon dockers and yellow leggings. In those days the boots were what were known as 'rough out' boots in that the outside surface was the rough porous part of the leather and the inside was the smooth side.

The North Koreans and Chinese seemed much better adapted to the cold conditions then we were. It was so freezing cold that I ended up with a case of frostbite on my toes. My toenails no longer grow because of the frostbite. It doesn't bother me now, but it was sure different in Korea. Everything was frozen. We had to keep the engines running on our trucks and Jeeps or they would freeze up. Our weapons were not immune from the freezing weather either—they would sometimes just get so cold that our M-1's wouldn't function. A cup of coffee would only stay warm for a minute or so and then would start to freeze solid.

Shaving was something we did when we could, but a lot of men avoided shaving and grew mustaches. I grew one, but when my nose would run it would freeze on the mustache. When I would try to drink coffee the mustache would get in the coffee, so I finally just shaved it off. One of my young Marines tried to grow a mustache, but he was not yet physically ready to grow one and I told him that he could put a finger between the hairs because his mustache was so thin. I told him that he needed to shave everyday until he had enough facial hair to make a mustache.

Korean rats were a big problem for us as well. They were all over the place and we had to be careful not to catch diseases from them. The rats carried a variety of mites and the mites could bite us. We were told that following the bite we would catch a fever and then twenty-four hours later we would die. I always thought how ironic it was that we were in a shooting war with an enemy but could die from a tiny bug bite. We had to get gamma globulin shots, and those shots hurt almost as bad as being shot, and worse, we could hardly sit for several days because our butts were so sore. A lot of guys joked that they should have gotten a Purple Heart for getting shot with gamma globulin in a war zone.

On Iwo Jima we had fought constantly for a full thirty-six days, but in Korea we had a lot of lulls between the fighting. We didn't have time to think about things on Iwo, whereas in Korea the lulls allowed men to have time to think, and we had to constantly motivate them to keep on going. Being cold-to-the-bone didn't help either. The Japanese had fought fanatically, but with the North Koreans and Chinese they just came at us in larger numbers—they were easier to mow down that way. When the Koreans and Chinese would attack they used bugles and whistles to signal their charges and other orders, and it was an eerie sound to hear. They really had a low regard for the lives of their men, as they had no problem sending waves of men that were bound to die in the charges, but more men were following behind them. For them it was just a numbers game.

We were assigned to "OP Reno" (Outpost Reno), a part of an area known for its Nevada names of 'Vegas', 'Reno', and 'Carson'. Reno was in the center of the other two and was the most vulnerable. The outposts were very important because we could observe what the Chinese and Koreans were up to, but also because it kept them from seeing what was going on behind us at our main line of resistance (MLR). Our outpost had the worst defensive position of the three outposts. At one point the Chinese were clobbering us really heavy, and when they over-ran our position we took huge casualties. The first sergeant told me to go out and write down the names of the wounded and dead Marines that lay in the field of fire. I was supposed to note who was KIA and how they got shot or wounded. It was really dangerous and the enemy was shooting the whole time. I just ran out into the field of fire and started gathering information. But there were a lot of wounded Marines so I just started picking them up and carrying them back. When I came back the first sergeant said he was putting me in for the Silver Star for what I did. The way I saw it I was just following orders. The Silver Star recommendation was downgraded to a Bronze Star with combat "V", and I also was awarded a Navy Accommodation Medal, which would be my second Navy Accommodation medal—my first had been awarded on Iwo Jima.

Author note: SgtMaj Iron Mike submitted a 'secret' document titled "The Defense of Outpost RENO" that he helped write as a review of the outpost defense. It was classified as secret at the time, but no longer carries that burden. Iron Mike felt that this was vital to help understand what his unit was doing in Korea in the outpost positions. It is entered below in the exact manner that it was prepared in the rear positions of combat in which it was typed with carbon copies on a manual typewriter. The report contains typographical and structure errors, but were not corrected to best replicate his report:

The Defense of Outpost Reno

"Forward of the MLR (Main Line of Resistance) occupied and defended by the 3rd Battalion, 5th Marines, three Combat Outposts are maintained on certain prominent terrain features. These outposts, commonly referred to as CARSON, RENO, and VEGAS, serve to maintain a line of contact with the enemy well forward of the MLR and are so located to deny the enemy as much as possible, unrestricted observation of MLR positions which he would otherwise enjoy. Although the enemy does hold higher ground forward of the outposts positions, certain portions of the MLR are not visible to him because of the intervening terrain features upon which the outposts are located. Freedom of movement of personnel and material is therefore possible to some enemy observation. MLR positions would be extremely vulnerable to all manner of fires were the presently held outposts not in friendly

hands and MLR dispositions could be readily observed by enemy at a relatively close range. Generally, under the present situations, movement on the MLR behind the outpost positions, about 800 to 1,000 meters can be traversed in relative safety from observed fire. Traffic to and from Outpost VEGAS can be accomplished during daylight hours because of a route most of which is in defilade, connecting that outpost with the MLR. Routes to Outposts RENO and CARSON are in defilade for some 800 meters forward of the MLR beyond which they are visible to the enemy. Supply, therefore, is conducted during the hours of darkness. Because of frequent patrolling in the area between the outposts and the MLR and because of observation into that are by both the outposts and the MLR positions; little to no enemy activity is encountered. Contact with the enemy has normally been made forward of the outpost positions. In the left of the battalion sector no friendly outposts are maintained. Dominating terrain to the front of the MLR is completely occupied by the enemy. Outposting, therefore on the low ground to the immediate front is neither feasible nor possible. It is notable that in this particular area, enemy artillery, mortar, and sniper fire is particularly heavy and constant. Movement on the MLR is extremely limited during the daylight hours and no movement forward of the MLR is possible at all during those hours.

"CARSON, RENO, and VEGAS are held by a number of troops consistent with the terrain, existing installations, and the availability of personnel that can be employed forward of the MLR without weakening the defenses.

"CARSON is garrisoned with a reinforced squad totaling 1 officer and about 36 men; RENO approximately the same; and VEGAS supports two reinforced squads at night and one during the day in addition to an officer who is present at all times. Organic defense of the outposts is based upon the utilization of numerous automatic weapons. From four to six LMG's (light machine guns) are kept on each position supplemented by a number of BAR's (Browning Automatic Rifles) and TSMG's (Thompson Sub-Machine Guns). Numerous hand grenades and napalm bombs (satchels) are also stocked for the close-in fighting that normally characterized the defense of an outpost. The outposts are organized for all around defense with the exception of RENO. Trenches

completely encircle CARSON and VEGAS so that a tight perimeter can be maintained and attacks against the outpost met from any direction. Such a defense is not possible however in the case of RENO, which is organized into a strong reverse slope defensive position. The forward slope of this outpost has been untenable by enemy artillery and mortar fire, which can be concentrated on any installations in that area. Construction on this position has been directed toward the placing of all installations below ground, with the exception of the trenchworks from which to fight. The effects of the continual H&I fires trenchworks received and the initial heavy preparatory fires usually employed by the enemy before an attack can in this way be minimized.

"From the MLR, eight direct fire .50 caliber MG's (machine guns) can be brought to bear on probable enemy approaches to the outposts, supplemented by the indirect fire .50 caliber MG's and by the fires of MLR heavy MG's. Artillery and mortar concentrations can be fired to completely encircle the outposts, covering particularly the areas inaccessible to supporting MG fires. Tank and recoilless rifle positions exist on the MLR, which can be employed so fire in defense of the outposts. Three searchlights can be brought into plan, illuminating a portion of the forward slope of RENO and terrain features to the front from which enemy fires can be delivered and reinforcements dispatched. Based on the utilization of the above weapons, a Battalion Outpost Fire Plan was developed to better coordinate their employment.

"Of the three outposts, RENO is considered to be the most critical because of its location some 1,350 meters from the MLR and well to the fore of the other two outposts. It, in a sense, dominates both CARSON and VEGAS, having observation to the rear over both of these outposts and also on all approaches from the MLR. CARSON and VEGAS are so organized defensively that both can support RENO by fire in the event of attack.

"Considering how the defense of Outpost RENO itself and the conditions described in the foregoing paragraphs, the following concept for defense was evolved. The organic weapons on RENO were organized as indicated on the RENO Organization of Defense Overlay. Thirty caliber MG's firing from CARSON and VEGAS were sighted to bring fire on portions of the forward slope and left and right flank of RENO (See MG Fire Overlay). Artillery, 4.2", and 81mm mortars were coordinated to provide close-in fire in the form of concentrations and search and traverse missions blocking all probable immediate approaches to RENO. These fires were to be used only in the event of an actual physical assault of the outpost position by enemy troops and then only on localities in which the presence of enemy troops were definitely established. Concentrations were also registered on probable enemy routes of approach and assembly areas located farther out from RENO. These fires were to be used only in the event of an actual physical assault of the outpost position by enemy troops and then only on localities in which the presence of enemy troops were definitely established. Concentrations were also registered on probable enemy routes of approach and assembly areas located farther out from RENO itself in contemplation of breaking up an enemy attack during the formative stages. The very location of RENO, and the frequent inability of friendly forces to detect the presence of large enemy elements until relatively close, made imperative registration of such close-in 'boxing' fires. Tanks and recoilless rifles in the various company sectors on the MLR were to be called on for direct fire on targets of opportunity by the company commanders concerned. In addition to support from weapons behind the MLR, on the MLR, and on the other two outposts, a mobile reinforced platoon was located on the high ground to the rear of RENO for ready support and reinforcement purposes. Study of enemy tactics employed in previous assaults on friendly outpost positions across the EU SAK front had indicated that at the time of attack the CCF recurrently blocked friendly routes between the MLR and outposts positions by use of troops, mortar, and artillery fire. To obviate this enemy capability and to economize on the length of time required to reinforce RENO from the MLR, the aforementioned platoon was dispatched each evening to set up in position behind RENO and was not returned to the MLR until just before daylight. It was contemplated that this force would support RENO by firing on enemy troops appearing between RENO and the platoon position; by maneuver to engage the enemy elsewhere in the vicinity; or by actual reinforcement of the outpost if in danger of being overrun. As a final defensive measure, FV could be fired around and on the outpost penetration itself without endangering friendly personnel once they had taken cover in the underground installations. As a further factor in the defense of RENO and providing the enemy attack were concentrated in that locality, it was planned to dispatch a reinforced platoon from another company to initiate a diversionary action on a known and nearby enemy position, to seize and occupy it for the purpose of denying enemy reinforcement from reaching RENO and to cut off the attacking enemy forces. Two provisional rifle platoons were organized from the Battalion H&S Company to occupy and maintain the integrity of the MLR when vacated by the maneuvering elements sanctioned, it was anticipated that RENO could be successfully defended against a large enemy force.

"The concept of outpost defense described in the preceding paragraphs was proven sound when on the night of 26 October 1952, the enemy launched a coordinated attack with the evident mission of capturing outpost RENO. From later developments, the enemy's plan of attack appears to have been: (1) To move through the trenchlines from Hill 150 leading to RENO; (2) To deploy from this trenchline on to the forward slope, right flank, and reverse slope of RENO; and (3) To send a portion of the attacking forces along the trenchline leading to the vicinity of the platoon position behind RENO with the mission of occupying that terrain and setting up a defense to prevent friendly reinforcement of the outpost.

"At approximately 1830, several rounds of artillery mortar, and rocket fire hit the outpost. This fire collapsed the three right flank bunkers, which had observation of Hill 1809, Hill 153, and the valley on the right of the outpost. Thereafter, there was only normal light enemy artillery and mortar fire received. There was no indication of the heavy barrage, which normally precedes an enemy attack.

"At 0036, friendly troops were deployed as follows: On RENO, two men guarding the end of the supply and evacuation trench leading into the outpost. Two men were on guard in the trenchworks of RENO. Four machine guns were manned and covered the crest and flanks of RENO. The supporting and reinforcing platoon from the MLR was deployed in the perimeter defense, with one squad on the right of the supply and evacuation trench to RENO, which ran through the position and the two squads to the left of the trench.

"At 0040, both forces heard bugles and whistles and what sounded like the slapping rifle stocks. Following this, an attack was launched against RENO; the enemy forces engaged the right flank of the platoon behind RENO. On RENO, the enemy moved over the crest of the hill, moved in from the right flank (location of previously damaged bunkers), and moved up the supply and evacuation trench toward the position. The initial enemy attack was characterized by the extensive use of grenades. Friendly machine guns went into action and were employed effectively against the enemy moving over the crest. The initial attack damaged two of the outpost machine guns and killed or wounded all machine gunners. The remaining two machine guns were then manned by riflemen and remained in action. The remaining two machine guns were employed with one covering the crest and right flank of the outpost and the other covering the reverse slope particularly the trench line leading to RENO. Fire was delivered by this latter gun on large groups of enemy between the outpost and the platoon position. This fire coupled with the fire of the mobile platoon itself succeeded in breaking up the enemy attack in that area by inflicting many casualties on the enemy.

"When the initial information that RENO was being attacked by a large enemy force was received, the 81mm and 4.2" mortars, artillery, and .50 caliber MG's appropriate prearranged fires were called down. Because of the close proximity of the enemy, supporting fires were brought in closer to the outpost position than normal safety precautions would have otherwise permitted. Maximum rate of fire was maintained for approximately five minutes; after which time the rate of fire was considered slackened.

"The initial approach of the enemy up to the right squad position of the platoon was met by effective small arms fire, particularly that of a BMG 1919A6 (Browning Machine Gun 1919A6) which was fired at point-blank range. However, by weight of numbers alone the enemy overran the right squad area. The platoon commander therefore moved one squad from the left of the perimeter to reinforce the engaged squad. As this squad was midway between positions, it was hit by enemy mortar and artillery fire. This fire fell also on the enemy troops, inflicting enemy casualties. As the enemy recognized the new threat and employed hand grenades, they were promptly taken under small arms fire by friendly forces. After a brief but intense firefight, the enemy was driven off and did not reengage the platoon position again although there was sporadic fire delivered at the position throughout the remainder of the night. The platoon's actions subsequent to this attack were to continue firing in support of RENO and to evacuate friendly casualties.

"On RENO, the action was progressing simultaneously with that described for the platoon positions. The initial attack consisted of two waves: the first using only hand grenades; the second using small arms. This attack was broken simultaneously with the cessation of the engagement on the platoon position. The enemy evidently withdrew to reorganize because friendlies could hear him talking and evacuating his casualties. Supporting fires were brought down in the vicinity of the reported enemy activity and shifted to cover probable enemy close-in assembly areas and approach routes. Friendlies used this time to move casualties under cover and to resupply fighting effectives with grenades and ammunition. The wounded loaded carbine and BAR magazines. A second attack on RENO at approximately 0105 generally followed the same pattern as the first. The enemy attacked from the forward slope, right flank, and reverse slope. During this attack, the enemy again employed grenades primarily. Several enemy troops were observed carrying planks, evidently to be used for reconstruction after capture of the outpost. This attack was repulsed by the combined small arms fire of the outpost personnel and the platoon position supplemented by MG fire from outposts CARSON and VEGAS. Friendly artillery, mortar fire and .50 caliber MG fire from the MLR fired in support as described during the first attack.

"Shortly after a third attack which began at approximately 0355, it became apparent that the enemy had penetrated the outpost defense. All friendly troops were moved into the underground installations and VT fired on the position itself. A searchlight was illuminated to cover RENO and machine guns were fired directly into the outpost. After about ten minutes of this heavy concentrated fire the third attack was broken up, the enemy withdrew, and no further action followed. Friendlies reorganized the outpost and began evacuation of casualties. Reinforcements and stretcher-bearing parties were dispatched from the MLR to both the platoon positions and RENO. All supporting fires were lifted from RENO and placed on probable withdrawal routes and assembly areas which were interdicted until first light in the morning. Several tanks in position on the MLR at that time commenced firing on targets of opportunity. During this interdiction phase, fire plans were prepared and later effected to smoke enemy terrain features in the vicinity of RENO in order to cover the removal of casualties to the MLR.

"The successful defense of Outpost RENO as described in the preceding paragraphs may be attributed to a number of factors. Small arms fire was used extensively and individual Marines were aggressive in their actions. All supporting fires had been planned and registered. Sectors of fire had been assigned to Outposts VEGAS and CARSON. A reinforcing and counterattack plan had been made employing several maneuvering elements. In anticipation of difficulty in moving rapidly to reinforce RENO or to counterattack, the policy of placing a platoon in a standby position directly behind RENO had been adopted. On RENO, the defense had been organized to provide all around security; partially completed and under construction was the extensive tunneling project. It was possible as soon as it was evident that the outpost was being attacked, therefore, to place all desired elements of the defense into effect. Although not needed or employed in this particular instance, a reinforced platoon from another company to create the diversionary attack previously described, was placed on standby as was a provisional Battalion H&S platoon.

"In any concept for the defense of an outpost, considerations must be given to the enemy's capability of employing overwhelming forces. It cannot be assumed that an outpost can ward off such enemy forces without timely assistance from other friendly elements. Carefully laid supporting fire plans; extensive use of small arms and ready maneuvering elements to engage the enemy by fire forward of the MLR and in support of the defense of an outpost, may very well be balance by which an outpost will be lost or retained."

By the time we had gotten involved in the outpost part of the Korean War the so-called peace talks were underway, but we were still under constant attack by the Chinese and Koreans. The Chinese had a real disregard for human life. They would shoot their artillery rounds onto their own troops. Their lack of regard for human life might have to do with their extremely large population they could draw upon for more troops. They did not make Bonzai charges like the Japanese did in WWII. They were not afraid to waste their men with their waves of attacks, as sooner or later they would be able to break through and get to their objectives.

Our tactics were very much like we had in WWII in the Pacific. We had intermediate and primary objectives. There were a lot of hills to take, but we could never go past the 38th Parallel. We weren't really held back like we would be later in Vietnam when we would get 'rules of engagement' that limited our fighting abilities. In Korea we killed the enemy whenever we had the chance. The Chinese came at us in waves, and I have never seen so many Chinese at one time as when they were massed in attack. It was pretty overwhelming for us, but we hung in there. The Chinese had buglers who blew different signals for attacks and withdrawals, and their men would yell and scream as they charged. It was an eerie set of sounds, not to mention their artillery and mortars blasting away. At night they would shoot flares into the sky and we could see them charging us. They were everywhere as far as we could see.

Resupplying our troops was much easier than in WWII when we relied on taking supplies of the dead Marines lying on the beach. Here we had H-34 helicopters that would fly in and drop off whatever we needed. The helicopters also took our dead and wounded Marines out, and that saved a lot of lives by getting wounded Marines back to the temporary field hospitals where they could get immediate treatment for their wounds. In WWII those same Marines probably would have died from their wounds out in the combat zones.

Replacements were brought to us in drafts of unit sizes of a company or two at a time. In the early part of the war these replacements were primarily reservists who had been called up, but as the war continued on we were getting inexperienced Marines just out of boot camp and infantry training. The inexperienced reservists during those times did not have to go through boot camp, and that was an issue we had to contend with—we had to teach them on the go. However, a lot of the reservists were combat-experienced from WWII and had remained with the Marines in the reserves.

As cold as the winter was in Korea, the summer was just the opposite—it was very warm and humid. Korea has four full seasons just like the eastern part of the US, and spring was the best. The weather was nice in spring and it would get really green out with occasional wild flowers.

We had some humorous moments in Korea: we had a company gunny that had a large mustache that he would put wax on to keep it formed perfectly. He was extremely proud of his mustache. One day while he slept soundly one of our men went up and clipped off one side so he only had half of it on his face. When the woke up he was really angry so he called the company into formation and demanded, "Who did this?" He never got an answer. Later our commanding officer Colonel Walt ordered that mustaches would no longer be allowed.

Another interesting story was about a Marine that had his testicles and legs removed when he received massive wounds there. In the hospital a nurse asked him where he was wounded. Without hesitating he told her it was in Korea. She then said, "No, I meant where on your body did you get wounded?" Feeling a little embarrassed by the location of the wound he simply looked at the nurse and reported, "I got hit in a place you could never get hit."

Sometimes we had to deal with conscientious objectors (CO) who would declare they were opposed to killing. A Marine draftee replacement came to our unit and declared he was a CO and did not want to kill anyone. My point man was young black Marine nicknamed Cobra. I told Cobra to take this young man to the point with him, but to not let him take a rifle or any weapon with him since he did not want to kill anyone. The next time I saw that young CO he fell out with his rifle! I guess he thought he was going to avoid action if he claimed he was a conscientious objector.

One day I noticed a little girl wandering about wearing only sandals and a dress. It was very cold outside and I could tell she was chilled to the bone and she was crying. She was a very cute little girl too. I heated up some C-rats for her and also gave her some candy. I had an extra pair of socks so I cut them with my Ka-bar and made some wrap-on mittens for her little hands. I wanted to adopt her because I felt so sorry for her—she must have been an orphan. However, there was no way we could take a child with us so we had to part and go our separate ways. I never saw her again and I have always wondered what became of her. That's a part of war that never leaves you.

Before we could leave Korea when our term was up we had to go to Inchon where we were required to take a physical and were also dusted with powders. They gave us malaria pills and during all this we stayed in tents. One of the last tests was to have a stool sample taken. We couldn't have worms in our stool or we would be held back and not allowed to go home till we were cured. We were sent to the head with a cup to crap in. Some of the men knew that I had passed the test before and knew they themselves wouldn't pass, so they asked if they could scoop some of my crap out of my cup. They scooped it out with their knives and then put it in their cups to be turned in to the docs. They all passed the worm test and were allowed to go home.

We had stored our sea bags when we had first arrived at Inchon, and when we were leaving we had to pick them up again. I grabbed a sea bag with my name on it, but was almost immediately another Marine asked what I thought I was doing. He told me it was *his* sea bag. I showed him the name and said, "See, it's got Mike Mervosh on it." He said that was his name! How odd to be thousands of miles from home and having another Marine with my name too. It was even odder that he was also of Serbian decent and had also come from the Pennsylvania area and was just nineteen miles from my home in Pittsburgh.

By 1952 good news came: there were peace talks and the war might be ending soon. We had lost more Marines after the Chosin Reservoir. One thing that I constantly think about is that there are over 8,000 men still missing from Korea. Later after the Vietnam War there were 2,500 missing and it was a big deal, but nobody said anything about the MIA (missing in action) from Korea. It *is* a 'forgotten war'.

I was in Korea for one year and a day. It was a long year and the last day was the longest day.

My return home allowed me to see my daughter Rosemary once again. It had been over a year since we last saw each other. When I walked in she started to cry—not out of happiness, but because she didn't know me and I apparently scared her. That was sort of a sad day for me because I realized how much my absence actually affected my family. But Rosemary quickly realized I was her daddy, and things went uphill from that point. It was good to be home with my family once more.

Chapter 8

THE COLD WAR

After WWII America and the Soviet Union began a tense period that was termed, *The Cold War*. It was a time when each country was experimenting with atomic weapons, each trying to gain superiority over the other. The Soviets were communist and the complete opposite of what America stood for. Tensions ran high at all times, and at any given moment America had to be on guard to react to any advance by the Soviets. While this tension was taking place between the two nations America was going through a very significant economic upturn. Employment was high and everyone was in high spirits. It was ironic in a way, because the good times were in contrast to the tension that was ever-present. The strategy of the military changed from before the wars, and it was necessary to think more global in concept, always with an eye to what the Soviet Union was up to.

After Korea I was given orders to report to Recruiter School at Parris Island, South Carolina. There was a lot I had to learn about recruiting, and one of the most difficult was all the paperwork involved. I had a big problem too: I couldn't type and had to use the 'hunt-and-peck' system. We also had to learn selling techniques, since recruiting is basically selling. The school was very demanding and a lot of time was spent on our appearances and the wearing of our uniforms—all of that would make a big impact on our potential recruits. We had a lot of inspections on top of the grueling class instructions, so we had to keep our uniforms in top condition.

I finally made it through the course and was assigned to go to Covington, Kentucky, a city just across from Cincinnati in Ohio. That part of the country got very cold and it rained a lot, but having grown up in Pittsburgh I was accustomed to cold weather.

Recruiting was a three-year tour of duty. We weren't at war at the time, and it was one of the duties that the Marine Corps needed, so I did what I was charged with. I would have rather been leading a company of grunts into a battle. On reflection however, it was one of the more important jobs that I did for the Marines, because it was the recruit that ultimately determined what the Marine Corps became, so what I was doing was going to have a major impact on the future of the Marines.

Our recruiting station had a pickup truck with a canvas cover on the bed. We would put recruits in the bed whenever we had to take them somewhere. On Saturdays and Sundays we had to wash and wax the truck to make it look sharp. We got our gas at a post office and it was free to us, but the government had to pay eight cents per gallon for the gas.

I talked with lots of teachers and parents, and my efforts paid off with what we called "send-ins"—that is, candidates that were referred by the teachers or parents. The send-ins made a huge difference in meeting our numbers. Having parents in favor of their son joining the Marines was a good thing—when they were opposed to it we had a much more difficult time, and we lost a lot of potential recruits after their parents finally got to them and talked them out of joining the Marines. Selling the parents on the Marines Corps was part of the job.

Recruiters had to always be seen in our best light and that required tedious time spent on grooming our uniforms each night before going to duty. I used to spend at least one hour each night spit-shining my shoes, pressing my uniform, and polishing all of my brass. We had to look our absolute best because our image had to reflect that the Marines were a cut above the others and we wear our uniforms with pride. Image meant a lot in this line of work.

One of the other things we did in recruiting was our participation at funerals. We often had to arrange the rifle squads and funeral details for the families of the deceased. It was always a sad event, but we had to help when we were asked. In many cases the recruiting office was the only military post that was available for families to come to for assistance.

The Marines are a well-respected branch of the military, especially with all the great press we had during World War II and Korea. The Marine Corps stood out even more so than when I was first desiring to enlist. The fact that we were no longer at war made a difference too—recruiting in wartime can be difficult, and that was a lesson we would later experience when the Vietnam War erupted a decade later.

My two tours of combat duty was a big help in my recruiting results. Young men look up to combat veterans. A lot of movies had come out about the Marines in WWII, and the young men were impressed by the way Marines were portrayed in the movies. We would go to high schools and put on presentations to the young men in the audience. The schools gave us the time to do this, and they were a big help. We spent a lot of time talking to teachers and coaches, as they were often able to steer the candidates to us. Our advertising slogan, "Marines build men", also helped our cause, because most young men had a strong desire to become a man, and the Marines were known as a good route to accomplish that. Having such a reputation was very important in conveying that we were different from the other services—it made a big difference.

The recruiters were held to high standards in terms of meeting quotas every month, and our jobs, and ultimately our careers rested on meeting those numbers. In the Marine Corps a quota was not a number that was just floated out there: it was a number that *had* to be met. The quotas were based on the area populations. I always met my quota. I took the job seriously. We sometimes had to spend twelve to fourteen hours per day traveling to towns that were often sixty to seventy miles away just to meet a recruit candidate. We met a lot of farm boys that had seen our signs that we had posted in the local small post office buildings. Often the town population was just two hundred or so, and many of those lived outside of the little rural town on nearby farms.

I was good at recruiting, as I had the experiences to talk to the young men about, and that seemed to motivate them to want to become Marines. I never took parolees, mental cases, or the men in the lowest category known as the "fours"—those men were substandard in physical strength, weight issues, or mental abilities. I spent a lot of time working with the kids—that was important when trying to meet our recruiting numbers every month. In fact, I was able to sandbag a lot and kept recruits in the wings. One time my commanding officer said he needed eight more recruits. I told him that there was no way, but I actually had the men already—I looked pretty good when I hit the numbers he needed.

We had some unusual recruits candidates that came in the door: one was a former Marine Corps master sergeant who had gotten out of the Marines after World War II. He wanted to come back into the Marines but due to length of the time he had been out of the Corps the best we could offer him was to come back as a PFC, but wouldn't have to go through boot camp again. However, there was another problem—he was married, and we couldn't take in married recruits. I felt bad telling him he couldn't come back to the Marines. He left our office dejected. About two months later the man came back to me and handed me some papers—it was his divorce papers! He wanted so badly to be a Marine again that he divorced his wife. We signed him up and he once again was a Marine. I met him later on and asked him if he was still a single man—he laughed and said he wasn't. As soon as he came back into the Marines he went back and remarried his wife. That's what I call real *dedication*!

I received orders to attend Drill Instructor School at Parris Island, South Carolina, and that ended my first tour of duty as a recruiter and was the start of my second tour of duty as a drill instructor. By that time I was a senior SNCO so my duties at Parris Island were to be a Battalion Sergeant Major, and I would not be pushing recruits through like my first tour. The McEwen incident was long past, but the pressure was on to keep the drill instructors from violating the SOP (Standard Operating Procedures) that had been established to better control the actions of DIs and protect the recruits from excessive force or ridicule.

Following my second tour at Parris Island my next role in the Marine Corps was going to the 3rd Marine Division in Okinawa in late 1958, a fifteen-month tour. I liked the fact that the 3rd Marine Division was basically an infantry division, so I was back with what I loved best about the Marines. When the division moved to Okinawa in 1953 they actually arrived by making an amphibious landing. My assignment was to be the 3rd Battalion Sergeant Major. We were part of the 9th Marines, so we were known as "3/9", and the best part for me was that it was a grunt battalion. The U.S. was not at war at the time, but we had to constantly train our Marines to remain in a readiness state. Early in my Marine career I learned how important training was when Marines hit the battlefields, so I was a strong proponent for constant training. We often made training landings, and my prior experiences with landings with the 4th Marine Division came in real handy for training my men. Sometimes we would go to the Philippines and do training in the jungles there. Jungle warfare is unlike battlefield warfare—the enemy is much better concealed and they are more likely to set up hard-to-detect ambushes. Enemy snipers were known to tie themselves to trees high above the ground and then shoot at the men below who often do not know where the shots are coming from.

I used to visit all of our command's areas at least once per month, and sometimes more often when I would go with our commanding general. We wanted to make sure that each command was in the proper state of readiness and were doing what we wanted them to do. I would take notes and then submit reports so that all the data was fed back to my command.

One time we made a landing and the colonel thought it was a really great landing. I wrote a report and ripped the landing to shreds due to the errors I noticed. I called things like I saw them, and I was not content to let our Marines get sloppy—when that happens the whole discipline erodes. We had to be razor sharp.

Our Commanding General, Louis Metzger, asked me to give a speech for him at Bataan—he was not able to make it and he felt I could handle it for him. There was a large audience in attendance, and there was a group of Philipinos that had been with Marines on the Death March. They had a speech prepared for me to give, but I ended up giving my own speech. It was very rousing and well received by the audience. This was one of the high points of my tour with 3/9.

By the late 1950's the Soviets put the first satellite into outer space and that shocked America—we had been one-upped by our enemy. We began to scramble to get our edge back, but at that moment the Soviets were ahead. When President John F. Kennedy was elected president in 1960 he made the space program become one of America's major challenges. He set a goal of landing on the moon, and that seemed almost impossible when he set the goal. America was charging forward in a dramatic fashion, and the pace of change was incredible at the time.

In 1961 I received my second set of orders to Recruiting Duty, and this time I was assigned to Birmingham, Alabama. The 1960's were a turbulent time in America, and America was going through a major transition regarding race relations, human rights, and other politically charged matters. The Civil Rights Movement created a large social change through marches and rallies.

As a sergeant major I had to oversee the recruiters in my district. If one of my recruiters was not hitting his numbers I would go out with him to see what he was doing wrong. My job was to make corrections when needed so that the recruiter hit his quotas. I only had two recruiters that I had to let go, and one of them was the number one student in his Recruiter School class. We had female recruiters back then, but they were mostly kept in the recruiting offices and did clerical work. It is different today, but it was the sixties then and the world was different—"women's lib" had not yet begun, and the Marines were still heavily entrenched in the paradigm of: "it's a man's world".

Toward the end of my second tour the people in America were starting to actively protest the Vietnam War, which was starting to heat up in a major way. That was especially true with the youth that we were appealing to. It was hard to get young men to enlist in the Marines when the Vietnam War was constantly being touted so negatively by the news on TV and in the newspapers. Recruiters were no longer welcomed on many college and high school campuses. In a way we were treated like *we* were the enemy.

The potential recruits we were seeking were the "Baby Boomers", the largest group of people our nation has ever produced. These young men and women were raised much differently than my generation. When I was young we had the Great Depression going on and everyone in the family had to help make things work out. We took odd jobs and worked two or three jobs at a time and then we gave the money we earned to our families to help make ends meet. But these young Baby Boomers had been raised in a totally different environment. They were brought up in strong economic times and had television and transistor radios, and they were easily swayed by the shows they watched on television, as well as the music they listened to. They were a generation of kids that didn't trust adults and they certainly didn't trust anyone over thirty years of age. On top of that, in November of 1963 President John F. Kennedy was assassinated in Dallas, Texas, and the accused assassin was a veteran Marine. There was such suspicion surrounding the details of the assassination that it fueled a suspicion that there was a major government cover-up going on. Conspiracy theories were rampant. Those were hard things to deal with when trying to convince a young man or woman that the Marines were the right choice.

The Civil Rights Movement was also in full swing in America at the same time the rest of the turmoil was taking place. Dr. Martin Luther King was rallying the black population to stand up for their rights, and marches and protests were common during that period. Birmingham, Alabama was almost the heart of the movement and we had a lot of turmoil to deal with.

But turmoil was what the Marine Corps was designed to deal with, and those issues were more like flea bites—it wasn't like the bullets that flew over my head in Saipan or Iwo Jima! We always met our quotas.

Chapter 9

DRILL INSTRUCTOR DUTY

"Then came the DI which stands for 'Devil's Instrument' who undoubtedly taught Satan tricks that he never dreamed of. He devised devious methods of agony and torment."

Every Marine remembers his drill instructors. The experience of boot camp is just too dramatic for any Marine to forget what their DIs put them through. The drill instructors are the ones that break down the raw recruit's civilian ways, and in a way it is like peeling a banana—removing the outer cover and then starting all over again molding the recruit into a Marine. The job of drill instructor is a difficult job, and many men do not desire to deal with the long hours and stress that a DI goes through in the training processes. The Marine Corps only wants their best men to take the task, as those men will forge the future of the Marine Corps.

I was given orders to report to Drill Instructor School at Parris Island, South Carolina. I hadn't been back to Parris Island since I was a recruit, and the place hadn't changed much since then. It brought back a lot of boot camp memories when I arrived.

At DI School we had daily inspections. In many ways it was just like being back in boot camp again, only we were now NCOs with a lot of experience in the Marines Corps. We had to stay in the DI School's barracks at night, and our families were not allowed to be with us. Families were not authorized to come until after we had finished DI School and were assigned to the Recruit Training Regiment. One particular DI School instructor was a real hard-ass on us and he really did treat us like we were a bunch of recruits. We didn't like being treated like boots, and his lack of strong leadership was apparent. Later in my career after I reached the rank of sergeant major this Marine reported in to my unit. I ultimately had to let him go, as he lacked the necessary leadership skills for the job his rank required of him.

DI School had classes on military history, and I was happy that I was part of some of the most epic battles the Marines have ever been involved in. My experiences in two wars gave me a huge edge in understanding our history. We also had hours and hours of learning drill—not just learning how to drill, but also how to properly teach each and every movement involved in close-order drill. We had to memorize each movement and subsequently execute our teaching of those movements in order to pass the course.

When we finally graduated from DI School we were assigned to our training battalions. Each platoon had a senior drill instructor and one junior drill instructor. The junior DI was either a corporal or a PFC. We wore a duty belt that was a WWII cartridge belt with a .45 pistol holster attached—we were considered "under arms" when we wore those duty belts, and we could wear our covers at all times, even indoors.

I was like most other DIs in that I emulated my own drill instructors and their styles. My DI's were whom I first saw as a Marine, and their image, and everything they did was engrained in me. It quickly made me realize that I too would make that same impression on the recruits in my charge—I had to make a lasting good impression.

Once I had my assignment to my battalion I was able to bring my family in to live in the military housing at Battery Park. Maggie was scared to death because at times we had water moccasins slither into our house from the nearby swamps. She was afraid to walk through the house in the dark, or even in the light for that matter. The weather at Parris Island was very hot and miserable most of the year, and the humidity could be put in a box and mailed overseas. At times there were hurricanes that blew offshore and in those scary times we had to stay indoor.

There were huge bugs that crawled everywhere, and spiders that hung down from the trees in the yards. It rained a lot in the hot summer days, and the rains could become real cloudbursts—very torrential and would come down extremely hard and fast resulting in the flat and low-lying areas being flooded for short periods. In the winter it got bitter cold and the winds would cut right through our clothing. Parris Island was famous for its sand fleas and they were the bane of recruits. They really came out in the heat of summer and their bites were a constant irritation and distraction for recruits to deal with.

Recruits were taught to discipline themselves and not swat the fleas or scratch the bites—it was very difficult to ignore the bugs though.

We used to pick up the recruits right out of the Receiving Barracks just after they received their 'bucket issue' (initial issue of needed supplies and clothing), and it was our job to get them processed through the medical examinations and other testing required of new recruits before their official training began. That first week or so with new recruits was some of the most trying times for DIs, as the new recruits were mostly in shock over their new life, and were very fatigued from lack of sleep and all the added stress we put on them. We rode them every minute just to keep them off guard. They had to learn to deal with the stress we put out, as it was nothing compared to the stress of combat they might encounter in their future.

Training was not broken down into phases like modern Marine training does—instead the training was pretty much just straight through training until the very end. During the middle of training there was a three-week period at the rifle range, and one of those weeks involved the recruits having mess or maintenance duty. Mess duty involved the recruits getting up around 0300 in the morning and marching to the mess hall where they then assisted the cooks with the preparation of the meals for the day and the cleaning and set up of the mess area. After we dropped the recruits off at the mess hall the chief cook took over their supervision for the rest of the day. The mess duty was a long day for the recruits and they mostly stood on their feet all day long. The mess cook kept them until after the evening meal and they couldn't leave until the mess hall had been thoroughly cleaned, and by that time it was often after 2100. The recruits didn't get much sleep during mess week, and mess duty would be something that all Marines below the rank of corporal would have to face throughout their careers until they reach NCO ranks. Some recruits were put on maintenance duty and were assigned to various details. One of the details was to make targets for the rifle range. Others were assigned to various organizations throughout MCRD wherever working parties were needed. Even though the mess and maintenance work details were long and often hard work, it was a little reprieve from the DIs, and the recruits were okay with that.

In my first DI tour the drill instructors were not under a tight regimented training schedule like they have today. We were free to train the recruits as we saw fit to do so. We did not have a lot of officer supervision and some of the drill instructors took advantage of their power and authority over the recruits. I believed in being stern and leading by example. I figured that what I had already learned in combat was that a leader sets the example, so a drill instructor must do the same thing in training. But I was also very firm and would not allow slack to occur. One time I had a recruit fall out and he had forgot to bring his rifle. On top of that he was standing in formation with his hands in his pockets. I walked up to him and asked him why he had his "army gloves" on. Once he realized what his army gloves were he pulled his hands out of his pockets—I was pretty stern in my diatribe to him and I am sure he and those around him would never ever consider putting their hands in their pockets. I also told him to fill his pockets with sand and then sew them up to prevent it from happening again. Years later I was attending a Marine reunion event and a master sergeant came up to me and he said he was a recruit of mine. I told the master sergeant I had a lot of recruits in my time and then I added, "You weren't the guy with his hands in his army gloves were you?" He laughed and told me he was not, but said he was in that platoon and remembered that incident very clearly!

Thursday nights were always 'field day' nights—that is when the recruits had to completely scrub down the barracks. All the recruits were given specific cleaning detail assignments. Every part of the barracks would be scrubbed down with soap and water. The recruit racks had to be moved aside so the decks would be swept and then swabbed. When the first side of the barracks was complete the racks were moved to the opposite side and the second half was done. The heads and showers were also scrubbed down. Recruits usually kept one commode open for recruit use until the full field day was complete, and then they would secure the heads and clean the final commode. The brass piping rising from the commodes and sinks were polished with metal polish creating a bright shiny look to the brass and copper pipes. All the faucets were wiped clean. Some recruits were assigned to clean the DI's quarters and duty office—they were all called "House Mouse". When the entire field day was complete we would then inspect the barracks. Inspecting the barracks usually called for finding dirt that was missed—we could never be satisfied. A failed inspection resulted in sometimes starting over from scratch, or maybe a lot of incentive training for the recruits. Incentive training involved strenuous exercises such as 'duck walking', push-ups, and a combination of exercises designed to be harsh punishment for poor results. Duck walking was one of the most hated of the exercises because the recruit had to squat down and then march forward from the squat position—it really put a strain on the leg muscles and often resulted in recruits cramping up. It didn't take too many doses of duck walking to get recruits to get the job done right the first time in future assignments.

Our voices were one of our best tools. We had learned to speak from our diaphragms and not the back of our throats, so when we bellowed out the sound was a deep roar. We would get right up to recruit's face and yell and scream at him—he would not forget that experience, and just the fear of a repeat was enough to cure a problem real quick. Some DIs would curse at their recruits, but I was raised as a Christian and I never found cursing to be a good way to communicate. Besides, I was the senior DI and to me that meant I was the leader, so I followed my "lead by example" style of command presence, but if needed, I could rip a good chorus of "in-your-face" diatribe.

We spent a lot of our time on close order drill, and recruits required a lot of extra time to get it down. Drill is important in Marine Corps training, as the discipline required and the instant response to commands is vital and can be related to the battlefield where orders and commands require instant obeying. For me, drill represented one of the best ways to instill discipline to recruits. Each movement requires precise moves, and the timing of those moves was critical to the overall outcome of the movement. If a recruit didn't pay attention to the command then he could make the entire platoon look bad—and if that was a battlefield situation a similar miscue could result in someone getting killed. We practiced those drill movements over and over until everyone had them down pat and could respond instantly. Drill also brought about pride, and when the platoon was clicking and popping in drill the espirit-de-corps was amazing. By the time a platoon was about to end training the recruits were at a point that when marching along everyone's feet were hitting the deck at exactly the same time resulting in a solid cadence of thump-thump-thump. It was like poetry in motion as they say.

Every Marine is a rifleman, and that is more than a saying—it is what the Marines are all about. Recruits had to learn to shoot the rifles at boot camp. We would march the recruits to the rifle range and for the first week of rifle range training they were taught how to aim the rifles, and how to get the correct "sight picture" when looking through their sights. A primary rifle instructor (PMI) was assigned to each platoon and he was in charge of rifle range training. After giving the classroom instructions about the sights and miscellaneous information about the targets and how the bullet trajectory works, the recruits would then have to practice squeezing the triggers—this was known as "snapping in". The recruits would be positioned in a large circle that had a barrel in the center of the circle, and the white barrel had tiny targets painted on the sides. The recruits would practice each of the shooting positions by dry firing at the targets. The whole idea of snapping in was to get the recruits used to the difficult firing positions, as well as practicing squeezing the trigger and not jerking it. By the end of that first week the recruits pretty much had the process down.

The second week at the range was the fun part for the recruits—they were then able to actually shoot with their rifles. The first four days of the week were practice runs so that the recruits could get their sight settings determined for each of the three distances involved. The first distance was a 200-yard range followed by 300 and 500-yard ranges. The recruits were firing the M-1 rifles back then, and the M-1 rifle used a 30-06 round that had a pretty good kick to it, not to mention the loud report. When the entire firing line was shooting the sound of all those rifles was very loud, and in some ways was similar to the sounds of combat. Everyone had to put cotton gauze in their ears to protect the eardrums from damage caused by the loud noise.

The most important day at the range was the "qual day"—that was the day the recruits were shooing to qualify with the rifle. We had taken a much more relaxed attitude with the recruits while at the rifle range because of the importance of qualifying, and qualifying as high as possible. The night before qual-day we would talk to the recruits in the barracks and explain the importance of qualifying. There were four possible rankings: the top ranking was 'expert' and required a score of 225 or higher. The second highest ranking was 'sharpshooter' and it took a score of 215-224. The lowest ranking was 'marksman' and that took a minimum score of 194-214. Any recruit that did not score at least 190 was a "non-qual", and it was a disgrace to not qualify. Back then we still kept the recruits that didn't qualify, but today it is a requirement to continue on in the Marines—a non-qual is now discharged if he doesn't qualify after some additional time and training. But we didn't take a non-qual lightly—when we marched back from the range the non-quals had to remove their utility jackets and covers and then tie the utility jackets around their waist. It was a dishonor to the platoon to have a non-qual, and he got no respect from the other recruits.

Being a combat veteran I knew how important firing the rifle was in combat. I always tried to instill that in my recruits. The rifle range was just a training field: the real test was in combat, and in combat there is no scoring—either you kill the enemy or the enemy kills you. That shot will count in combat—it's not about badges there: it's about survival.

In those days there were no flag conditions at Parris Island like there are today. Today, when the heat index (a rating of heat, humidity, and wind) reaches a certain point they raise a flag. The color the flag is determined by the heat index: the higher it gets the more severe the flag condition becomes. It starts with a green flag, then yellow, red, and finally a black flag—each color flag signifies what can and cannot be done with recruits in their training. The flags were brought out to protect the recruits from overheating that could result in heat exhaustion and heat stroke. But that would come long after my tour, and recruits and DIs had to just deal with the hot conditions present at Parris Island. For me it was like it was on Roi-Namur and Tinian, so I felt that the recruits needed to get used to conditions they might face in their future. We went out in all conditions and trained very hard.

My combat experiences in the South Pacific and Korea allowed me to relate to my recruits in a special way. I could make them understand how important it was for them to learn the basic skills we were teaching, and how those skills could later save their lives. My recruits respected that too. Recruits can tell when a DI is BS'ing them, and they knew I was not.

When my initial tour of DI duty was up I was given orders back to recruiting duty, and that gave me a rather extended experience in the process of recruit selection as well as the training of those recruits.

I received my second set of orders to Drill Instructor School at Parris Island. The infamous "McEwen Case" had just occurred in which a Marine DI marched his platoon into the swamps that surround Parris Island. The tide changes rapidly, and in the darkness of night the swift tides trapped some recruits who ended up drowning. It was a national scandal and there was a huge uproar over the events. It actually put the Marine Corps in jeopardy, as there were calls to disband the Marines as a direct result. It took the pleadings of MajGen Chesty Puller to save the Marine Corps. MajGen Puller spoke to congress and explained how the Marines have to have tough training in order to possess the types of skills and discipline that are needed for battles such as those that took place at Guadalcanal, Tarawa, Iwo Jima, Okinawa, the Chosin Reservoir, just to name a few.

Upon the formation of our new DI School class General Green met with us and he gave a welcome-aboard speech, only it was more like a real ass chewing than a welcome-aboard speech. He talked about what had happened in the McEwen incident, and it seemed like *we* were being blamed in a way. He made it clear that we were there to make things better. I didn't know what to think when he was done talking.

New drill was being introduced--it was a thirteen-man drill and it was very hard to learn. We had to know every movement for each man, and everyone had a different movement in the drill. Nobody liked it. We had been asked to give our anonymous opinions about the drill and to a man all of us said we didn't like it, that it was way too complex. They adopted it anyway. We spent many hours practicing the movements, and memorizing the various components of each movement. We had to present them to the instructors before we could graduate, and perfection was expected.

Things were a lot different the second time I was on the drill field. The Marine Corps adopted the campaign covers for the drill instructors to wear, as they wanted the DIs to stand out and have a distinct look. The campaign covers were the same type that Smokey the Bear wore, and we called them Smokey the Bear hats. A new Standard Operating Procedure (SOP) manual was created that gave specific rules for handling recruits and a training syllabus was established for uniform training of all recruits. More officers and senior NCOs were assigned to overseeing the training to ensure that the drill instructors were conducting training in accordance with the SOP. A lot of drill instructors were relieved of duties for violations of the SOP and it became clear that there was no room for doing things the old way. Recruits could not be abused in any way.

I was an E-7 first sergeant and I was billeted as a Company First Sergeant job. My job was to oversee the company's daily training operations and keep the DIs in line. We were under a lot of public scrutiny at the time. On 14 February 1958 I was promoted to Field Sergeant Major and became the 2nd Recruit Training Battalion Sergeant Major. At the time I had no idea I would eventually hold the rank of sergeant major for the next nineteen and one-half more years and rise to the position of the most senior man in all of the military branches.

I met with Major General Chesty Puller while at Parris Island. It was after he had been involved in the McEwen situation and had been called in to help settle things down. We shared a beer at the club. He told me, "Mike, before I leave I want you to have a smoke, drink a beer, take a chew, and then take a chance!" I took that as an order. General Puller and I shared a lot of views the same way—we had both faced the enemy eye-to-eye and knew what it took to lead men in dangerous situations.

One thing that occurred on my second tour was that there was a movie that came out called *The DI,* starring Jack Webb. It was a story about a Marine senior drill instructor and his dealings with a troubled recruit. Jack Webb had done his homework on learning what a Marine DI was like, and made sure his speech and mannerisms were consistent with the real DIs. He had a positive impact on what the public saw Marine training to be like, and it helped our situation. The movie even took place at Parris Island and many scenes included downtown Beaufort where many Marines spent their liberty hours or even had quarters at. The image he had projected was a blessing for the Marine Corps and the public ate up the strict discipline that he conveyed. Most of the Marines in the movie were real Marines, and he selected DIs to play some of the critical roles. Today that movie is considered a classic, but I've been told that young recruits today have no idea about the movie.

My drill instructor duties had occurred during peacetime, and most of the recruits coming in did not have the expectation of going into immediate battle like they did in WWII and Korea. That makes the job of a DI that much harder because the recruits have to be made to understand that at a drop of a hat they could be sent to a war zone somewhere in the world, and that concept is not an easy one for peace-time recruits to accept. As a result the DIs had to really stress the importance of the discipline they were demanding.

Today I always tell other DIs that I had two tours of duty as a DI but never graduated a platoon. They look at me incredulously and then I explain that in those days recruits did not "graduate" from boot camp—they "out posted" and left for infantry training for their next phase of learning the trade of being a Marine. I also received "flight pay": at the end of training out posting recruits would sometimes take up a collection from the recruits and put the proceeds into an envelope to present it to the drill instructor. I would call the platoon to the quarterdeck and lecture them that they were never to do that to any Marine, officer or otherwise, and then I would throw the envelope onto the deck, which caused the bills to fly . . . we called that "flight pay".

Being a drill instructor was a very rewarding job. We trained young men who came to us as boys, and in the end they turned into men and carried the title of *United States Marine*. The transition was incredible to observe, but the process was a little like watching paint dry—it took a while for that transition to fully develop.

Years after I got out of the Marine Corps SgtMaj Leland D. 'Crow' Crawford helped form the National Drill Instructor Association. SgtMaj Crawford was the ninth Sergeant Major of the Marine Corps and had been one of my men at one time. My pride in being a Marine DI made me become a Charter Life Member of that organization and I am Charter Life Member #0057. There are a lot of Marine associations for various Marine organizations, but there is something special about the Drill Instructor's Association because it is a group of unique men who have achieved one of the pinnacle positions in the Marine Corps—that of being a drill instructor. The National Drill Instructor Association has transformed into two separate groups: the West Coast DI Association and the East Coast DI Association. I am not real happy about that because we are all one group no matter where we served, but no matter, I am still Charter Life member number 0057 at both of the organizations and I participate at their annual reunions.

Chapter 10

THE VIETNAM WAR

Vietnam was one of the countries that were split into two countries following WWII. North Vietnam's leader was Ho Chi Minh and North Vietnam was a dedicated communist country. South Vietnam was a republic and was put under the care of the French who had previously held Vietnam as a colony prior to the Japanese taking over before the onset of WWII. Ho Chi Minh wanted to unite Vietnam into one country under communist rule and he developed a guerilla fighting force known as "Viet Cong" (VC). The VC would make guerilla commando attacks against the French, and the French quickly discovered that their position in Vietnam was not going to be the same as it was prior to WWII. Eventually the French pulled out of Vietnam and left the responsibility to maintain South Vietnam in the hands of NATO. Under the cover of NATO the United States took over where the French left off and were acting as advisors to the South Vietnamese Army in trying to develop their ability to defend themselves against the continuous attacks by the Viet Cong. In 1964 there were several incidents in the Gulf of Tonkin in which U.S. Naval forces engaged in a heavy sea battle with North Vietnamese forces. The result of this incident caused President Lyndon Johnson to get the 'Gulf of Tonkin Resolution' passed by Congress, and that opened the door for President Johnson to ramp up our troop strengths and engage in heavy involvement in what would become the Vietnam War.

President Johnson mandated that the U.S. services gear up for the new war, and the Marines began a large recruiting effort. Recruiting could not keep pace with the manpower needed, so the draft was used to increase the strength of the Marines. The young men being drafted came from the 'Baby Boomer' generation, the largest population bulge ever in America. These young men had been raised under peacetime conditions and the fifties and early sixties were considered 'soft' times. This generation of men did not have the harsh upbringings that the

WWII and Korea veterans had from their early lives in the Great Depression years. The Baby Boomers also had come to question authority, and they had been exposed to a radically different way of life. These kids were raised with television, transistor radios, and rock and roll music. There was heavy resistance to the war in Vietnam by Boomers, as most of those young people did not relate to putting themselves in harm's way in a country 8,000 miles from home. The idea of being pulled from their soft lives in America and being put into battle in a foreign land when the U.S. had not been attacked or threatened was a very hard pill for them to swallow.

I had two tours of duty in Vietnam, and my first tour started in 1967 and I was there during the Tet Offensive in January, 1968. The North Vietnamese decided to make a surprise attack on the U.S. forces in South Vietnam during the Tet holiday (Vietnamese New Year). The Tet was a holy period and a temporary cease-fire had occurred on both sides in honor of the Tet. But the North Vietnamese communists decided that making a sneak attack would catch the Americans off-guard and they planned to decimate our forces so badly that the South Vietnamese people would feel compelled to join the north's movement because they would be the victors. But they also had a secondary goal: the North Vietnamese knew that we had news correspondents that were feeding stories and news footage to the Americans in a manner that America was watching the war on prime-time news each night. They believed that once the American public saw the carnage they planned on creating with the American forces that the Americans would demand the withdrawal of the U.S. forces in Vietnam. I arrived in Vietnam just as the most heated part of the war was taking place.

When I checked in I was asked where I wanted to go—I told them I wanted to be in an infantry outfit. My initial assignment in Vietnam was as the sergeant major of 3rd Battalion, 7th Marines. It was an infantry battalion—exactly what I wanted! My role as a battalion sergeant major did not keep me from leading my men in battle. I was behind the scenes a lot more than in the prior two wars, but I still made all thirteen operations we were involved in. I was later assigned as the regimental sergeant major of 7th Marine Regiment and there I was more involved with helicopters.

Whenever I went into the field I was always armed with a rifle. On my first tour there we were using the M-14 rifle. That rifle was a very solid rifle and it worked in most all conditions. I always had an M-14 rifle with me plus my .45 1911 pistol. Eventually we preplaced the M-14s with the new M-16 rifle. The M-16 was much lighter than was the M-14, and it had a lot of plastic parts on it. The rifle shot a much smaller round, a 5.56mm NATO round instead of the M-14's 7.62mm NATO round which was a .308 caliber. At first I didn't think the smaller round would do the job on the enemy, but in the fairly close quarters we were engaging the enemy in the smaller round worked okay. However, the rifle itself did not function well, and at times the rifle would jam. A jammed rifle only occurs when you are firing it, and in combat that means it jams while engaging the enemy. A lot of men had that experience, and it cost them their lives. At first we were told the jamming was because the men were not cleaning the rifles properly. I am a weapons man, and I learned a long time ago how to properly clean my rifle, and my rifle jammed as well. I told the colonel that it wasn't the cleaning—there was a problem with the chamber's metal. Later on it was determined that there was a problem with the chambers and the parts were replaced with better materials, and that seemed to cure the problem. However, nobody really trusted the M-16 after the initial problems occurred, even after the fixes were made. That was not a good way to have our men go into battle action.

For me Vietnam was another opportunity to get back into action. I was born for action, and as a sergeant major I would be in charge of a large contingent of Marines. I was ready, and had two prior wars to get me ready for my mission. Our enemy was initially guerrilla fighters who are like 'unseen' enemies—they were hidden and then suddenly sprang up to fight and then disappeared quickly. Sometimes a young boy maybe twelve or thirteen years of age would be standing in the fields or by a water buffalo when we would approach. He would run into his hut, grab an AK-47 and take out three or four Marines, and then go back to the fields and look just like all the rest of the Vietnamese in the fields. That was a very difficult enemy to deal with because we couldn't tell who the enemy was—they wore the same clothing that the locals wore. Later on we were fighting the North Vietnamese regular army soldiers and at least we could tell that they were the enemy because they wore military uniforms. The Viet Cong used the Russian AK-47 rifle and it fired a 7.62mm round that packed a lot more punch than our smaller 5.56mm NATO rounds. Their rifles were actually better weapons because they could be dragged through mud, sand, and water and still would fire without fail.

In Vietnam we had base camps that we operated out of, but there were no front lines like in previous wars. With no front lines it made the battle much more difficult, as there was no special goal to achieve like we had in Korea and WWII—at least in those wars we knew when we were getting ahead.

The Viet Cong also had made a lot of land mines from our unexploded ordinance, and the mines and booby traps they laid were where most of our injuries stemmed from. One terrible type of booby trap was the pungi sticks—the VC would dig a hole and place sharpened bamboo sticks upright in the holes. They even went so far as to dip the pungi sticks in human excrement to increase the potential of infections once a Marine stepped on the ground cover that hid the hole and then plunged down on top of the sharp sticks. It was an agonizing wound and was very difficult to treat—the sticks went all the way through the soles of the boots and then through the Marine's foot. Beside the horrific injury to the Marine, the incident would then cause the patrol to have to stop to deal with the injured man, and that created the opportunity for an ambush. At the very least the injury would cause the patrol deviate from their planned patrol.

The trails were often set up with explosives that were triggered by a trip-wire that was triggered by a Marine tripping through the wire causing the bomb to explode. We had to be constantly on the alert, as we never knew what to expect. Land mines were placed under dirt on the trails and were triggered by stepping on them. A lot of men died or lost their limbs by such explosions. Another type of booby trap was a bomb that was triggered by a Marine picking up something that appeared attractive—something that aroused interest, but when picked up an explosion was triggered.

When a new man checked in to the regiment I would take him aside and tell him what to expect from the guerrilla war we were in. It didn't matter what their rank was either—all the new guys needed to know what they were in for. It also gave me a chance to find out what kind of men we were getting in.

I also found out that a lot of our Marines were not digging foxholes for cover, so I made it clear that all Marines were to dig foxholes when they settled in a position. I guess they just didn't want to take the time or spend the energy in the hot muggy climate, but having a foxhole to be in was a good way to increase a man's odds of survival under an attack.

One day I was given TAD (temporary addition duty) orders to go to Danang where I was asked to give a briefing to General Alexander Haig who was the Army's commanding general there. When I returned I was given a special certificate of appreciation for my presentation. It was a nice gesture, but for me I was just doing my job.

Just like WWII and Korea we had news correspondents with us, but during the Vietnam War the news correspondents would feed their stories to the U.S. to be shown either live, or on the same day on prime-time news. WWII and Korea were different though: during those wars the correspondents limited their coverage and did not cover really negative things. But in Vietnam it seemed like the newsmen were trying to put a slant to the war, and they did not hesitate to show villages burning, dead bodies on the side of the road, and just about every atrocity they could locate to film. The American public was getting a skewed idea of how things were going in Vietnam, and it was creating a major issue with Americans at home. Dan Rather gained his fame as a war correspondent in Vietnam, and he positioned himself so that the cameras were showing as much horrible war scenes as possible while he orated about what was happening. The media loved that war and they spent as much airtime as possible to flaunt their negative stories. Following the Tet Offensive it was Walter Cronkite who went in front of TVs largest TV audience and declared that there was no way to win the war—that virtually spelled the beginning of the end, because from that point the media started to rally the Vietnam protest and they fueled a large anti-war sentiment that resulted in furious demonstrations at many colleges and universities. The public hated this war and everything it stood for—that also included our military men serving their country during this time.

The war was what I would call a 'political war', as the politicians ran it instead of the military. We had rules of engagement that limited what we could do. Rules of engagement were actually rules of *disengagement*. In WWII and Korea we didn't have limitations and we could eliminate the enemy whenever and wherever we found them. There also was not a clear objective laid out that would determine if we won the war. There were no front lines in Vietnam—it was more like gang banging in the jungle. We were there to stop the communist aggression into the south. Ho Chi Minh knew that he could get to us in the long run by getting our very own people at home to turn against the war and demand our withdrawal. The Vietnamese have been fighting takeovers for a long time, and they had plenty of resolve to fight long past our resolve wore out.

The Secretary of Defense during the initial phases of this war was Robert McNamara, the former president of Ford Motor Company. McNamara was a brilliant man, but he knew absolutely nothing about the military or fighting wars. He first came in while John Kennedy was president and then later served under President Lyndon Johnson. He was one of the primary men responsible for the escalation of the war in Vietnam. In reality it was about buying arms and was weaved in with the military-industrial complex. Vietnam was a convenient venue. One of the things McNamara brought to the war was the "body count" as a means of determining our progress. He concluded with General Westmorland that our troops in the field should report all dead bodies and we would know if we were winning. Pressure became intense to come back with a high body count so the Army and Marines were pretty much forced to 'push' the numbers under their pressure. It proved to be a very faulty system and ultimately was dropped. It's just an example of the how the war was played out. If one were to believe the numbers it could be construed we killed *all* the North Vietnamese.

Vietnam brings back a lot of memories—some good, and some not so good. The same holds for Marine commanders I worked for. I was the Regimental Sergeant Major under Colonel Crossfield. He was ambitious, and to me he seemed to be working on getting his first star (brigadier general). We took a flight over the area in a helicopter, and for some odd reason he brought along the S-3 officer. Our M-60 gunner had a problem with the M-60 machine gun and he panicked while we were taking on fire from below. I dropped down to help him clear his gun, and at that very instant the S-3 major took a shot to his face and died instantly. Colonel Crossfield looked down at the dead major and with a scowl said to me, "Sergeant Major—that should have been you!" I will never forget him saying that. I rank him as one of the worse leaders I had while in the Marine Corps.

The sixties were turbulent times in America and aside from the resistance to the war in Vietnam; there were a lot of racial tensions. Back in the states Martin Luther King had been holding marches for racial equality, and the military shared in the strife that was occurring back home. There were some very radical black Marines in Vietnam, and they created a huge problem with regard to dealing with them. In some cases we had to really kick some ass just to get them to wake up. While there were a lot of very good black Marines, the small core of the bad ones became a living nightmare for us to deal with. They often threatened to "frag" those Marines (blow them up with a fragmentation grenade) that gave them any resistance. There were cases of men being killed that were due to the racial issues. These men called themselves 'Black Panthers' and their groups were much like the street gangs of today, and extremely militant, defiant, and aggressive. They thought nothing about refusing to go out on patrols, or just refusing orders in general. The whole situation created a tremendous morale problem for everyone.

Back in the U.S the Baby Boomers had adopted a new image for themselves—it was the Hippy movement. Hippies were about "free love" and peace was their theme. It was centered on the anti-war sentiment and disdain for the Vietnam War. Their symbol was the peace symbol—a circle with an upside down "Y" in the middle. They would signal "peace" by extending their hand with two fingers in a vee shape. It was a huge movement, and most of the colleges and universities adopted the Hippy movement as their theme. They created huge anti-war rallies on campuses. They despised the military and all the men that were in it—it was as though the military members were somehow responsible for the war. On top of this, many youths also became part of a drug culture and became users of marijuana, speed, cocaine, and a new hallucinogenic drug called "LSD". They resisted the military by burning their draft cards, and many just fled to Canada to avoid military service here.

I would often talk to my men about what was going on with the Hippy's back home protesting the war as well as the men in the service. I would tell them that the Hippies had no idea what they were doing—but the Marines do! When the Woodstock affair occurred it was a big anti-war protest. I participated with Woodstock—my rifle had a "wood stock" and that is how I participated!

I met General Westmoreland of the U.S. Army while I was in Vietnam. He was a good soldier with good military bearing. He asked what I did and then he praised the Marines that were fighting in Vietnam.

One of the things I always believed was that sports such as football, boxing, wrestling, lacrosse, and even bar fighting were prerequisites for combat success. Young men that participated in those contact sports and were in it to win made excellent combat fighters. But show me a kid who played sports like a wimp and I will guarantee that he will fight like a sissy, and will likely soon be killed in battle. It's all about mental toughness when it comes to combat. The Marines I fought with in WWII and Korea had a much tougher upbringing than the young men being brought in to fight in Vietnam.

I was out on a helicopter mission with Colonel 'Bulldog' Hall one time. He was a great regimental commanding officer and was a guy I would follow into hell if I had to. Our helicopter was unable to land in the normal landing zone due to the hostile enemy in the immediate area, so the pilot moved to another location nearby to set the chopper down. We were just about to land when we got hit with an RPG from a Viet Cong on the ground. The blast blew the colonel and me and out of the helicopter and we landed on the hard ground below. I was badly cut and bruised from the impact and it took a few seconds to shake off the stunned feeling I had. The colonel was hit in his leg by shrapnel and was much worse off than me. He looked at me and said, "We *won't* be POWs (prisoners of war)—you take the rifle and I'll use my .45 and we'll just kill anyone that tries to capture us. We didn't get captured and we managed to escape to safety. My greatest recollection of the two of us: we were uglier than a barrel full of assholes!

On another occasion, while out in a Jeep with Bulldog Hall, a fire team leader flagged us down after staggering up to us and asked if he could use our radio. I asked him why he needed the radio and he replied that he needed to call in artillery. I had to then follow up and ask why he needed artillery. He said, "There's a sniper over there and we need to take him out." I just looked at him and said, "You have a whole fire team and you can't take out one enemy sniper? You don't need artillery—Marine, take your team and go kill that guy!" It demonstrated to me how much our men have changed over time. Everyone seemed was looking for the easy button to push and had forgotten what good old hard work was about. Another example: I once noticed some Marines had not dug trenches around their tents, so I told a black Marine to dig trenches. He told me that he would get a working party together—I stopped him and said, "No, lets go down to supply and get a shovel. You dig and I'll watch."

Vietnam is a country that has monsoon rains part of the year. The rains are extreme and intense, and the torrents just seem to keep coming down and down. We were soaking wet during the monsoon rains, and even with our ponchos on the rain got inside our ponchos and we got drenched. When we got back to our hooches we wiped ourselves with a towel—that was our bath. Once the rain stopped coming down it would turn hot and muggy again. We didn't have to move to get soaking wet, as we sweated all the time.

Despite our baths from the wipe-downs after the rains, Marines still had a lot of body odor. I was thankful that my sense of smell didn't allow me to smell those odors, but others could. I always used a deodorant. The VC was already acclimated to the hot and muggy conditions, but it took me over a month before I finally get used to it. I don't recall if the others got acclimated, but it helped that I had spent so much time on the South Pacific islands in WWII. Every day we had to take salt tabs—large tablets of salt that we were told would help retain fluids and prevent muscle cramps.

Our cammies were pretty sturdy and seemed to last under the wet conditions. On my first tour in Vietnam I still wore my herringbone utilities. They finally issued jungle cammies to us and provided us with jungle boots—the leather boots just rotted away in the wet and soggy conditions. Today I see the new cammies worn by Marines, but they look like pajamas to me—sort of like "chocolate chip". They also roll their sleeves up today, but we never did—it was good protection from mosquito bites.

One time I walked out of the PX and saw a Marine walking by with his sleeves rolled up on his arms. I yelled out, "Hey Marine, get those sleeves rolled down!" The Marine turned toward me and I noticed he had two stars on his collar and he was our new commanding general.

I saluted him, and then the general turned to his aide and chewed him out for not telling him about the sleeves.

Vietnam was a country with heavy jungle growth that made fighting our fleeting enemy very difficult. To reduce the foliage and eliminate ground cover the Air Force was instructed to spray "Agent Orange" over the forested and jungle areas to cause the foliage to die. They also didn't hesitate to drop their loads on the jungles below while Marines on the ground. Even without having the chemical dropped on to of us we still had exposure to it as we navigated the countryside. It wasn't until we returned to the U.S. that we learned that the chemicals would have long-term affects on us and would cause a myriad of ailments on our men. To this day I sometimes get severe itching that requires putting a salve on my skin. I have to get the salve from the VA. Others aren't so lucky, as they have come down with cancer, kidney failure, and other similar maladies.

We had other dangers besides our own chemicals and the enemy—it was snakes! There were sixteen types of snakes in Vietnam, and some were extremely lethal. There was a snake that was so lethal it was called "Three Step"—if you got bit you could take three steps and then die. Mosquitoes were also a major problem—the large amounts of stagnant waters in the rice paddies were prime breeding grounds for those insects. Malaria was a disease that came from mosquito bites, and that ailment was a tough one to overcome.

The Viet Cong were very adept at creating IEDs (improvised explosive devises) that they would place in the ground where Marines walked. If the land mine was stepped on it would blow up, and with it a man would lose a leg, or maybe even be killed. They also dug holes in the ground and put pungi sticks (sharp bamboo sticks or metal) in the holes so that the sharp edges pointed upward. Then they would cover the pungi stick holes with a leaves and branches, but there would not be enough coverage to support the weight of a Marine—once he stepped on the thin cover his foot and leg would drop onto the pungi sticks and penetrate through the bottom of the boots. Often the pungi sticks were coated with human excrement so that the wounds would become infected. They were really nasty dangers that we always had to be concerned about. In addition, once a Marine fell prey to one of those dangerous traps the entire patrol was put in very high danger of being victims of an ambush or sniper attack. The wounded man would definitely slow down the patrol, which further endangered the group.

We were assigned to the southern part of Vietnam, and one of our primary missions was on Hill 55. Hill 55 was a large hill that had been originally full of land mines planted by the Viet Cong. Marine engineers had cleared the mines and we had to occupy the hill as a vantage point of the area below. I arrived just as the artillery unit was celebrating their one millionth round having been fired. They were really proud of that too. I asked how many enemies they had killed with one million rounds and they couldn't give me an answer. When I pressed them for what they had shot at it turned out that every request that came in for taking out a sniper in a tree or an ambush team in a bush caused a volley of rounds. I told them it was a waste of money because they should have just had men with rifles use a seven cent round from their rifles.

The NVA (North Vietnamese Army) had a better idea of military-wise fighting compared to the VC (Viet Cong) who were basically just guerilla fighters. The VC was more of a hit-and-run group than the NVA who would fight a more conventional military fight. Fighting a guerilla war was extremely tougher than fighting a war of conventional troops because the guerillas are insurgents who are able to blend in with the general population—they wore the same clothes. At least the NVA had uniforms and we knew they were the enemy.

One of the worst parts of the Vietnam War was how the American public perceived our military men. The press had done a good job of portraying Vietnam as a place where our military men killed babies, burned villages, and acted like a bunch of Vikings running amok. It was not an uncommon thing for civilians back in the States to yell out, "Baby killers!" to Marines passing by. They often would spit at Marines as they walked down the streets. That was in stark contrast to the way we were treated when we came back from WWII—we were honored and revered by the public back then. During the Vietnam War being in the military became a stigma for a lot of men, and many got out of the Marines when their tour of duty was over in Vietnam. We not only lost a lot of good men that were killed and wounded, but we lost a lot of good men that didn't care for the way they were treated by the public.

When Marines left Vietnam and returned home they did not come back as units like we did in WWII—instead each man was an individual returning. The result was that there were no parades or public displays of support. Nobody was there to greet the men as they returned other than their families. A lot of Marines became bitter over that slight, and the very fact that the war was so unpopular with Americans caused the Marines to withdraw. It affected me too, because I was also upset over how Americans treated us. Americans just didn't act patriotic and give the respect to our military men that they all deserved. These men laid their lives on the line for their country, and whether the public liked the war or didn't, these men deserve more respect for what they went through.

After the Vietnam War a new term was created: "PTSD", which stands for "Post Traumatic Stress Disorder". Many returning veterans were turning to drugs, alcohol, and violent behavior, and that was creating a severe situation for society to deal with. Psychologists said these veterans were suffering from their experiences in the war and needed special treatment. It turned into a prevalent ailment suddenly. I don't agree with it. We didn't have that problem in WWII or Korea—we called it "battle fatigue" and it went away with a little rest and relaxation. I think part of the problem is that the young people of the Vietnam era and even later on are being brought up too soft. Everything is provided for them and they want for nothing. In my day we had the Great Depression raging around us and we learned to do without things. We used to work hard and we had to overcome whatever came our way. It's gotten to a point where it seems like everyone that goes into combat claims to be negatively affected with PTSD.

My second tour of duty in Vietnam was different than my first. But the time I got back I was a senior sergeant major and General Wilson wanted me as the 3rd Division Sergeant Major. That meant I would not be in the field like I wanted, but when a general tells you what he wants you to do you listen and do it—in other words, a general's wish is his command!

When my second tour in Vietnam was done I had accomplished something very few men have ever done: I had participated in three major wars: World War II, Korea, and Vietnam (twice). I am extremely proud of those three conflicts and my contributions to each of them as a leader of Marines.

I've been asked how I would compare Vietnam with our current war in Afghanistan—well, put it this way: we have so much high-tech gear today and it's not being used. The Marines can't engage the enemy unless they are shot at first, and to me it's more like gangbanging than a real war. I say let the locals there do their own fighting and we should get the hell out of there. In fact, what the hell are we even doing there? We went to war there after the 911 terrorist attacks in 2001, and it's now 2015 and what do we have to show for fourteen years of battle?

Author note: Iron Mike Mervosh wrote the following article for the "Bush Beater", a unit newsletter in September 1965:

Why Vietnam?

Not long ago a mother wrote to President Johnson about the crisis in Vietnam. "I have a son who is now in Vietnam" the letter read. "My husband served in World War II. Our country was at war, but now, this time it's just something I don't understand. Why?" she asked.

Well, we can ask ourselves that question many times when it comes to the seemingly endlessness of conflict of Americans in combat. We could go on and ask why Lebanon in 1958? Why were we in Berlin during 1948 and 1949, and then again in 1961 and 1962? Why did we fight in Korea?

Ask a Marine in Vietnam and he'll tell you, "We're here to stop the Communists before they get to our country. Today it is here . . . tomorrow it could be home. I'd rather fight here."

You have read newspapers where a correspondent would seek out a nineteen-year old Marine and ask him why he was in Vietnam. When the Marine answered quite simply, "To fight Communists," the correspondent was horrified and proceeds to say so in about 1,200 words. Personally, we as Marines think "to fight Communists" is a good and concise answer. These relatively simple answers, and recent events, have caused a good proportion of the Fleet Marine Force (FMF) to be deployed overseas. Some of you will remember how we used to say during World War II, that there are two kinds of Marines:

those who were overseas, and those who were going overseas. In 1965 we still have only two kinds of Marines: those who are in the Fleet Marine Force, and those who are going to the Fleet Marine Force.

Having our FMF units all over the globe with the high state of readiness gives us the role of "first to fight." If the order is given—as it happened in Vietnam, the Marines were ashore within hours with the air and ground elements being employed together. The landing began at dawn the morning of March 8. One battalion landing team came across the beach. Another battalion came in by air from Okinawa. This was the first introduction of U.S. ground combat troops in South Vietnam.

The mission of the Marines was defensive in nature up to a few weeks ago until a major victory was won by our coordinated offensive against the Viet Cong. Marines learned long ago that one of the best countermeasures against guerrillas is to seize the initiative and maintain aggressive patrolling.

The Marines in Vietnam are fighting a military war and feel the war is being won. We in the Marine Corps are proud of our past performance, but past performance alone is no justification for our continuance. Our continuance can only be justified by what we are doing today and what we can do tomorrow and the day after that.

Chapter 11

SENIOR ENLISTED MAN IN THE ARMED SERVICES

When I first enlisted in the Marines the pay grades ran from pay grade 'seven', which was the lowest rank of private, all the way to the highest pay grade of 'one' which was a combination of either sergeant major, first sergeant, or master technical sergeant—the latter three higher ranks were dependant on the assignment. In 1947 the Marine Corps changed the pay grade numbering in a reverse order: private became an "E-1" (Enlisted-1) and the top pay grade was "E-7" (Enlisted-7), and the title of "First Sergeant" or "Sergeant Major" was dictated by the assignment—the normal E-7 grade was a master sergeant. Then in 1958 the Marine Corps changed the entire rank structuring to match the others services and had to increase the pay grades to nine grades. The top of the enlisted rank became specific ranks of 'sergeant major" or "master gunnery sergeant", and the first sergeant and master sergeant ranks became the pay grades E-8. The Marine Corps added the rank of lance corporal as the third pay grade, and that was the only rank in the Marines that I never held.

I was promoted to sergeant major in 1958. I held that rank for a period of nineteen and one half years, and when I finally retired in September of 1977 I was the most senior enlisted man in all of the armed forces. I could have become the Sergeant Major of the Marine Corps, but my wife was not in favor of me doing that—it would have meant being away a lot, and she felt it was time for me to buckle down to a little more normal life at home.

The job of a sergeant major is to be the senior enlisted man in units of battalion size and larger. While the majors, lieutenant colonels, and colonels are the officers in charge of those units, it is the sergeant major that basically runs the daily operations of the enlisted men in the outfit. In all of my capacities as sergeant major I always liked being in charge of grunt units the most. I always believed that the sergeant major's job was to be out working with the Marines and being visible. I was not the type of guy who stayed in the office out of sight. Leading men means to be out in front of them where they can see you there and know that you are part of their team. I was tough on my men—I knew that they needed to have discipline in order to be good in combat, and combat was what we were preparing to do at all times.

Despite my senior status I always tried to get billets that put me in charge of infantry units. I loved the infantry the most and being in charge of them was my idea of the best possible assignments. Of course, the more senior I became the more I was required to take larger command units.

I once met with General Metzger and I proposed to him that he might consider forming a battalion that had only enlisted men—with no officers at all. The battalion CO would be a sergeant major, the executive officer a first sergeant, and on and on down the line. He laughed and said it was a great idea and would probably work well, but was afraid that if he did that he wouldn't need any more officers. I guess he thought I was kidding.

Being a sergeant major carries a lot of weight with the billet. One time in the sixties I was stationed at Camp Pendleton and a navy corpsman was walking in my direction and he was wearing his blue navy uniform. It has been the tradition of navy corpsman attached to FMF units to wear Marine uniforms, so as the corpsman approached I called him aside and told him to either burn his blues or send them home and then get a full issue of Marine uniforms. He was upset with that order and he requested mast with the CO (a formal process of presenting a grievance with higher authority for resolution). We went to the colonel's office. I told the colonel that the corpsman did not want to obey an order. The colonel then asked the corpsman what I asked him to do.

The defiant corpsman said, "He told me to either burn my blues or send them home."

The colonel did not hesitate for a second and simply replied sternly, "Then do it!"

One thing that I realized over my extended tour of duty as a senior staff NCO was how the technology changed over the years and continues to this day. As an infantry man I only wish that we had the technology that our troops have today. In my day it was the Marine with his rifle and bayonet to get the job done; it was kill or be killed, to fight and win against all odds. During WWII the only real technology we had was radar, and that didn't pertain to us ground troops. The weaponry that developed over my years, and then even beyond my tour is absolutely incredible for our Marines.

If I were the Sergeant Major of the Marine Corps I would make a lot of changes, but the changes might be considered "unbearable". I would go back to the Old Corps ways, but I don't think modern Marines could tolerate the changes. For example, I once was summoned into an officer's office. As I approached his desk he asked me to remove my cover. "Why?" I asked him. "I am under arms."

He replied, "You're indoors."

"Sir, I have a pistol and duty belt on."

He just shrugged and said, "So?"

"Sir, I'm under arms and don't remove my cover."

"Well, in my office you do", the officer said.

"No sir, I don't."

It's that officer's lack of following our protocols that creates the erosion of Marine Corps traditions that makes me cringe. Another example is how recruits are no longer taught to start and end everything they say with, "Sir". Instead of "Sir, aye-aye Sir" it is now just, "Aye Sir." Traditions have been built over long periods of Marine history and should not be changed. I am proud to say that I upheld Marine Corps traditions during my entire thirty-five years, and I continue to do so to this day.

Another change I would make would be to go back to the old concept of barracks as the main form of housing Marine enlisted men. The modern facilities are more like apartments with Marines having their own rooms. That does not offer the kind of environment that builds teamwork and comradeship like we had in the old days. Having a field day on Thursday nights was a good method for maintaining discipline and keeping the young Marines constantly aware of cleanliness and maintaining their areas spic and a span. That is important for maintaining high morale and espirit-de-corps.

Chapter 12

ACTOR: HAWAII FIVE-O

Two years before Iron Mike Mervosh decided to retire he was asked to participate in the popular TV show Hawaii Five-O. Iron Mike was given a script and was asked to play a grizzled old Marine Master Sergeant—not a hard task for Iron Mike to play. He still has the full script in the tattered binder. Below is his recollection of his part as "Master Sergeant Langosta" exactly as he remembered it from the hand-typed script that he still has, although before the TV shoot took place changes were made in the names and some of the details that Iron Mike found to be factually inaccurate about the Marine Corps:

I got a phone call one day in 1974 and I was asked if I wanted to be in the TV show *Hawaii Five-O*. It was bit part and they said they would pay me. I was familiar with the show and I thought it might be interesting to take them up on their offer.

They gave me a script and my name in the script was MSgt Langosta but they took one look at me and decided I did not look Italian so they asked if I would mind using my real name in the show—I certainly didn't want that so they changed my name to SgtMaj Joseph Danvers. Then in the credits I decided I didn't want my real name used since the story line had sinister things and I felt that somebody might think I actually might know what really happened in real life so I had them use Joseph Monteleone. The story was supposed to be a true story in real life. It was about a murderous Marine named Raymond Parmel. He somehow managed to come across the bones of "Peking Man", prehistoric human fossilized bones from China that had disappeared after the Pearl Harbor attack in 1941. I was to be interviewed about Raymond Parmel and what I knew of him.

The story had a lot of technical inaccuracies and I had to suggest some changes to their dates and other matters needing correcting. They made the changes I proposed.

The shots of Parris Island were used as a backdrop in the movie, but the show was filmed in Hawaii. Jack Lord didn't like cigar smoke, and since I smoked a cigar in the scene he had another actor do his part. When they filmed my part the cameraman was right in my face—they told me not to worry, that this would only be seen in eighty countries! A makeup man wanted to put makeup on, but I wouldn't let him—can you imaging a Marine sergeant major wearing makeup?

Initially I received $400 each time they played the show on TV. Later it dropped to $375, then $350, and the amount kept dropping over time to where it is now $25. I just received a check from them for another $25 so I suppose the show is still playing somewhere in the world.

I guess I was selected to play the part of Master Sergeant Langosta because the part called for a senior Marine who had been around a long time—I fit that description. They aired the program very soon after we taped it. A lot of my Marines saw the show—I was a TV star to them. It was fun and I had fun making some corrections to their scripting because what they originally had was not correct. I still have the script—they gave me my own copy. It went something like this:

It described me as a "grizzled veteran". They opened the scene with me waving detective Danny into my office and to a chair after we shook hands. Then detective Danny sits down and is carrying a lightweight topcoat and an attaché case.

I looked at the detective and said, "Cops, huh? Lookin' for someone I know?

"Maybe." The detective replied with short answers as I remember.

The dialogue was short word answers and was almost comical. "Who?"

"Peking Man." Was the detective's answer—this time he used two words.

"What man?" My reply increased to the flow—two words!

"Peking." The interaction was hard not to smile to as I recall.

I had to puff on my cigar and then blow out a large cloud of smoke, and then I asked him, "What outfit was he in?"

His answer changed from one or two words and he rattled off, "Company 'B' of the 1st Battalion, 4th Marines. Sergeant Parmel's squad."

I had to look the detective in the eye and proclaim, "You came a long way for nothin', buddy. There wasn't anybody by that name in Ray Parmel's squad."

The detective then asked me something like, "What do you remember about that trip out of China in November of 1941?"

My reply came back to him with a certain amount of authoritive command presence—I am a natural for that: "'B' Company was stationed in Tungschow. About zero six that morning we got the orders to move south to Tientsin where a couple of transports were waitin'."

Danny the detective continued to ask me questions: "What else do you remember?

Since the timeframe of my recollections were a long time ago I had to pause as if I was recalling the memory: "The Japanese attacked the supply train around zero two in the mornin'. Lieutenant Groves came yellin' for Parmel to grab a truck if he could find one, and get the crates to those transports on the double."

Danny was reflecting on key things I was saying and he asked me, "What crates?"

I remember looking at him and casually saying, "The ones that were consigned to us for special shipment."

The detective got very excited at that point and in a very animated manner asked, "How many?"

I remained with a calm demeanor and simply said, "Three, I think."

"What happened then?" the detective continued.

"Then . . .? We did it." I recall that I had a long pause between "then" and "we did it" to add emphasis and position the detective to ask more inquiries.

The detective had to ask me, "Did what?"

Through the whole interview I remained calm and spoke matter-of-factly, and I simply said, "Got the crates on the transport and took 'em all the way to Honolulu."

The actor detective was portraying a lot of contained excitement, but his excitement was revealed in his tone when he asked me, "When was that? What was the date?"

I remember acting like I was thinking hard to recollect the answer and I finally said, "Let's see—that was two days before Pearl Harbor—December 5th."

Danny kept probing me and he prompted me, "Go on—what happened then . . . to the crates?"

At this point I had the look of someone that had fully recalled the incident and I confidently replied, "Once we dropped hook, Parmel and Crowe—Ed Crowe, was a member of the squad, buddy of Parmel's, told us to send the crates to Pearl Harbor and that's the last I saw of 'em. Two days later *it* hit the fan and most of us were shipped out." My reference to "it hit the fan" meant that Pearl Harbor was attacked.

His reply implied there might be more to the story, "That's all you can tell me?"

My answer was simple: "That's all I know." At that point the detective Danny got up and started to leave my office.

I blurted out, "Hey." His hand was already on the doorknob, but he turned around expectantly.

He looked at me and asked, "What?"

In a comedic twist I had to ask him about our original dialogue and I said, "Peking who?"

Danny went back to his one-word answers, "Mann."

I was still acting like I wondered who Peking Mann was, so I added, "There was a Sidney Mann in the second squad."

My scene was over when Danny looked back and as he was walking out the door he simply said, "Wrong man. Thanks anyway."

People that saw that show felt that I was more believable than the real actors. I guess it was because I was never really "acting" because I just acted like I normally do. But, as you can see, I never gave up my day-job to become an actor. A lot of people think of me as a TV star—but it was only a bit part, but it was a lot of fun doing it.

Chapter 13

RETIREMENT

Author's note: Retirement for a Marine like Iron Mike Mervosh is about the same as it would be for a Border Collie: the Border Collie is always going to seek a sheep to corral, and Sergeant Major Iron Mike is always looking for a battle to fight! After thirty-five years of hard and dedicated service to the Marine Corps and his country, Sergeant Major Iron Mike Mervosh finally called it a day. He held the position of sergeant major for nineteen and one-half years and was the most senior enlisted man in all of our armed services.

I could have made it twenty years as sergeant major had I taken one more assignment as the base sergeant major of Camp Pendleton but to me it was like a demotion after all of the higher leadership positions I had held so I settled down for a retirement instead. I volunteered to take the PFT (Physical Fitness Test) before I retired and I scored the same as a twenty-nine year old Marine. I was still fit, especially for my age. I always worked out and ran with my men. I also went to the rifle range and attempted to maintain my expert rifle ranking, but I was firing the M-16 and I only managed sharpshooter—I was disappointed, as my lower score was the result of the sitting position. I never felt the sitting position was a good one to teach because I never saw a Marine fire at the enemy while sitting down. On 1 September 1977 I retired, and at that time I was the most senior enlisted man in all the armed forces—that was quite an achievement!

My retirement ceremony took place at Pearl Harbor. I wanted it to be in a special place, and what better place then Pearl Harbor, the beginning place of WWII for the United States, and the event that motivated me to want to become a Marine. There were about seven to eight hundred people that attended my retirement. There were no speeches allowed at the parade, as they were concerned about our troops standing in formation in the hot sun. The parade was at the

Marine Barracks Pearl Harbor parade deck. The Marines were all wearing their dress blues, and it was a great parade. General Wilson was the reviewing officer—he later became the Commandant of the Marine Corps. General Wilson told me that I should have waited another six months so I would have had twenty years in grade. I always remembered how Ted Williams left baseball with a home run at his last at-bat, and that was the same way I wanted to go out.

After my separation I spent a month at my daughter's home, but after thirty-five years in the Marines I found myself still getting up at 0500. I still spit-shine my shoes for special events. I even kept my boots I wore in Vietnam even though they still have some of the Vietnam rice paddy mud on them. I go to Field Mess Nights three to four times a year and can still wear my Vietnam cammies.

I once told someone that my daughter attended seven schools, but she quickly corrected me: it was eleven! I often had received orders to go to another location before her school year term ended, but my wife always stayed back with her until the end of the school term so she had continuity in her schooling.

Margaret and I were married five or six times—we would often repeat our vows at different occasions. She was very happy about my retiring, and she often reminded me that it should have happened five years earlier. She wasn't fond of moving as frequently as Marine families have to do, but after the first two moves it became routine. The hardest move we ever had was when I was transferred from recruiting duty to back to the drill field. They only gave me travel days and no leave was offered. I had two days of travel time and four days of delay, so Margaret had to handle all the details of moving alone.

My daughter Rosemary eventually went to nursing school and became a nurse. When she graduated she had an all-white uniform that included white stockings and shoes, and also had the proper nurse caps they used to wear. She eventually joined the Army Reserve as a nurse, and held the rank of lieutenant—she always wanted to be in the military, and I suppose I helped form that idea. She never went on to active duty however, and she eventually resigned to go into the private sector. She always wore a bracelet she had received in nursing school—it had a red cross on it. She worked in the emergency room and also in ICU, but eventually the units became so busy that she decided to take a break and go back to school to study psychiatry.

One day I got a call from Sergeant Major Jones, Sergeant Major of Camp Pendleton. He said, "Mike, I need you to come to the Staff NCO Club." I got in my car and drove to the base, which is not far from my house. When I arrived at the Staff NCO Club I found that someone had taken the reserved space for the general and placed a sign on it: "Reserved for SgtMaj Iron Mike Mervosh". I parked in the space and walked inside the club—I was shocked to find over one thousand Marines inside! They were dedicating an entire room just for me—it was called the *Iron Mike Room*. The cost had been over $300,000. I ended up putting in a lot of my memorabilia in the beautiful cabinets they had installed, and we covered the walls with more of my things. That room was quite an honor to me and I sincerely appreciated it. Since the opening they have added even more changes, and it includes a special room that has cabinets on all the walls. I have filled all the cabinets with mementos, photos, and other items that I acquired during my thirty-five years in the Marine Corps—I ran out of room in my home to put all my things and I still have my den decked out with photos and mementos that cover every square inch of the shelf space.

Many years after I retired the Persian Gulf War erupted. I sent some letters and made some calls to Headquarters Marine Corps volunteering my services to return to active duty and serve the Marine Corps one more time. I knew I could be of help to the Marines, and I really felt my many years of combat experiences could be used to help save Marines' lives. At first I didn't getting any responses, but finally a colonel I had served with called me up to discuss my coming back. He complimented my service record, but added there was just one little problem: my date of birth! I told him they were discriminating against me due to my age, and then I went on to say I could teach the younger men a lot of things, and besides, there was a lot of sand over there and I knew a lot about holding sand bags. I tried to convince him I could save lives there. He laughed and told me he would see what he could do. I was a little encouraged by our talk, and I thought I had finally gotten through and made a valid point to the colonel. About a week later I received a large brown envelope from Headquarters Marine Corps. I was excited, and I really thought, "Hot damn, my orders finally came in!" I opened the envelope and in it was a letter dated 20 June 1991 and it said to the effect:

Thank you for your letter volunteering to return to active duty and once again serve your country in uniform. It is always a pleasure to hear from former Marines whose dedication to duty has remained undiminished over the years. Regrettably, since you have retired from the Marine Corps, we are unable to return you to active duty. Although you are certainly physically fit and motivated, we are sure you will agree that we must provide opportunities for younger Marines to experience challenges and rewards similar to those who enjoyed while serving in the defense of our beloved country. It is refreshing to hear from those will still possess the will and devotion to duty that have been the hallmark for over 215 years. Your sense of duty and patriotism is admirable, and knowing that we can count on your support is important to all Marines. I thank you again for offering to make such an important sacrifice.

My request was being *denied*—they felt that the younger senior SNCOs needed to get the experience. I was *really* disappointed. Maggie, however, was not, and she was glad I would remain home and retired. I still want to get over there and see what I can do to help—with or without their approval!

One of the modern things that are being offered to veterans of WWII and Korea is a free trip back to the battlegrounds where the veterans fought so bravely. The trips are sponsored by the non-profit *Greatest Generation* organization, and are primarily for veterans from the Greatest Generation while they still are able to go. I put in for a trip under them.

In 2011 I was offered the opportunity to visit Korea in a special Korea War group. It was a real experience landing in Korea and taking in the sights without being shot at. But it was apparent to me that the Koreans were not very fond of our U.S. Army men, but they *loved* the Marines. We arrived and the South Korean Marines treated us like kings. Their band was always waiting for us when we arrived and they would play great music for us. A lot of high dignitaries always met us and they made us feel very welcome. There were five of us on that trip, and all of us had been in the infantry. They held a special ceremony for us at the Punchbowl—that was where my brother had been killed. They had a monument there with the entire list of Marine's names on it, and my brother's name was right in the middle. A reporter there spoke good English and he interviewed me. I talked about my brother and what had occurred there, and also talked about our Korean War experiences. He ended up publishing the story in the paper there, but it was in written in the Korean language and I couldn't read it. Our trip lasted ten days and we traveled to a lot of the places where we had fought many years before. It was a lot nicer place when people weren't trying to kill us. When we returned I had to go through Customs and they asked me for my passport. I told the Customs officer that when I came before I didn't need a passport—now I need one? He laughed, but I still had to give him my passport.

The Greatest Generation also provided me with the honor of going back to Iwo Jima and the other islands that we fought on during WWII. Those islands brought back some special memories—some good, and some not so good. Iwo Jima looked totally different than I last saw it. The foliage had completely grown back and it was lush and green. I didn't notice the smell of sulfur that was there during battle, but then I actually didn't smell it years ago either since I don't smell certain things, but I didn't hear anyone talking about it this time. Some of the men were given a ride to the top of Mount Suribachi, but I decided I wanted to make the climb up the mountain. When we got to the top we were surprised to find a Japanese flag flying. It really pissed me off too—we lost a lot of men fighting for that island. The general we were with told us that since the island is a territory of Japan that they have the right to fly their flag there. We looked down at the black sands on the beaches where we had been pinned down for so long. Although it was silent at the time, I could still hear the horrific sounds of battle and the screams that accompany those booms and explosions. I could recall the faces of the many men that perished at my side on those beaches. The others that I took this trip with all felt the same way—it was nice to return, but the memories were hard to relive again. There had been a Japanese group that also was on top of Mount Suribachi, and they only spoke Japanese—we wondered what they were saying, and they paid no attention to us while we were there. It would be interesting to find out how the Japanese today feel about that battle.

I ran into an Army veteran who had received the Bronze Star. I asked him what he did to get it and he replied that he and all of his 8,000 men had received it on Iwo Jima. I asked what they did to earn it—he simply said, "We were there." It kind of blew me away that those occupying forces were honored with our nation's fourth highest medal of valor for just *being there*. Every Marine that landed on those beaches deserved to be honored, and not just because they were there. When medals of valor are handed out like that then the value of the medal drops significantly. In WWII there were sixteen million men that served and there were one million medals issued. Now there are one million men serving and the count is sixteen million medals—that should say it all.

During our trip to the South Pacific we stayed in four-star hotels and the one in Hawaii cost $490 per night, but the Greatest Generation group paid for all our expenses, so I never spent any of my own money on these trips. Ironically, after all the battles I have been in, and the wounds that I suffered in those fights, I ended up getting severely hurt while flying home from this trip. I was walking in the aisle of the jet when the plane suddenly lurched causing me to fall against some seats. The fall broke a couple of my ribs which then punctured my lung, and then upon our landing I medivac'd to a hospital. It was almost like I hadn't suffered enough during the war and was given a second chance to have more pain. In the hospital I came down with pneumonia and once again was on the verge of death. I recovered from the injuries and the pneumonia, and I couldn't help but think that perhaps *Hardcore Iron Mike* is more than just a name?

Maggie was stricken with ovarian cancer in 2001 and she suffered from that terrible disease for ten years. At one point the cancer went into remission, but unfortunately it returned. I had to do the housework and shopping since she was bedridden. I helped her with everything. I was with her at the hospital her last night but I left to come home to rest. I was woken by a phone call from the hospital telling me to come quickly, as Maggie was about to leave us. I rushed to the hospital, but by the time I arrived she had already passed away. Losing my wife of sixty-three years was the hardest thing I ever had to endure. Her cancer was an agonizing way for her to go. We had been shooting for at least seventy years of marriage before she passed. We buried her at the San Luis Rey Mission. My daughter and I will also be buried there. My wife's passing created a huge void in my life and I am very thankful that my daughter lives nearby, and I am able to see her often. I am frequently asked about being buried in one of the great cemeteries like Arlington National Cemetery, but I visited

Arlington one time and it was large and vast, and I felt that nobody would ever be able to find me. I like being close to home. The first several years of being alone were the hardest for me. I read a lot of books, but life was empty for me without Maggie. I still miss her and I think about her all the time. I think often about the great sixty-three years we had together.

About three years ago the Greatest Generation invited me to take a one hundred twenty mile rafting trip down the Colorado River. The trip lasted four days. We had daytime temperatures around 105 degrees, and there was no shortage of mosquitoes on the river. It was so hot out that we had to periodically jump into the cold Colorado River to get cool. When we would get out of the water the hot arid desert air would dry us off in a minute or so. We had eight people in each raft, and the rafts had plenty of whitewater rapids to traverse on the tour. We had one veteran who had no legs. The trips are designed to give these wounded Marines an opportunity to do some fun things that they would normally have no access to.

The Greatest Generation is working on a trip to Afghanistan for us. I would like to visit that part of the world. I wanted to go there after I retired but the Marines wouldn't accept my offer to come back. I suppose that once the Greatest Generation guys are all gone they will start honoring the Korea veterans, and eventually the Vietnam veterans. There are not many of us left. Their plan was to send us to Camp Leatherneck in Afghanistan sometime in the summer of 2014 or maybe later on. When I get there I want to go out on a patrol, and I intend to have a rifle and flack jacket issued. I will somehow find a way to do that even if they don't want me to—after all, they can't court martial me, can they? Anyway, since the area is a combat zone the dozen or so of us that go will probably have to sign a bunch of waivers. It's funny: they didn't ask us to sign a waiver at Iwo Jima!

One of the things I wanted to do when I retired was to further my education, so I enrolled at Palomar Community College. I was always the oldest guy in my classes, but that gave me a big edge—I had developed the maturity and discipline to buckle down and do the assignments while the other younger students partied. Dealing with civilians was a different experience for me, as civilians are not like Marines. It took a while to finally accept that they are not Marines, and I was not going to change them. But school was a fun experience for me and I was finally able to receive my Bachelor of Science degree and I graduated with High Honors. I had accomplished my education goals.

One of my proud achievements was that I had five men that at one time or other had worked under my command who all eventually went on to earn the highest enlisted position the Marine Corps offers—Sergeant Major of the Marine Corps. Not only did they achieve those statuses, but also they were some of the best at that position: SgtMaj Leland D. 'Crow' Crawford; SgtMaj Henry H. Black; SgtMaj Clinton A. Puckett; SgtMaj John R. Massaro; and SgtMaj Robert E. Cleary. I am sure that I had some degree of influencing them in their rise to the top.

My life's experiences seem to be a big attraction to others, and because of that I am often called upon to be a guest speaker at an event. In fact, I have had over one hundred and ten events that I have spoken at. I never plan my talks. I speak from the heart and I just seize the moment when I get to the podium. People seem mesmerized with what I say, but I think they are just awed by some of my experiences. I am not a politically correct person either. At my age and experience I say what I want and I don't care if it offends someone. I believe we have gotten to a point of ridiculous about being too sensitive.

I am not shy about saying that American values have eroded too far. My generation was brought up to believe in strong religious values with high moral standards. We did not flaunt our sexuality openly. Homosexuals existed then, but they kept it to themselves and it was not open like today. The Uniform Code of Military Justice prohibits homosexual activity and anyone caught engaging in those activities would be drummed out of the Marine Corps—literally! A formation would be formed up and the disgraced Marine would be stripped of all Marine emblems on his uniform and then walked off the base to the beat of a drummer. Somehow we have come to accept homosexuals and they are being allowed into the military. I see a major conflict ahead of us—homosexuals will not mix well in combat foxholes, and there will be conflicts. The military system is based on men living in close quarters and contact with their comrades, and there cannot be a mix of gay men with straight men in combat or even barracks lifestyles without negative side affects and conflicts. It is not about fairness—it is about common sense. The same common sense needs to be applied to putting women in combat. Combat is a very bad place to be for a man's man, let alone a woman—they have absolutely no place in combat situations. I have seen men literally blown to pieces and it was a horrible sight to behold—I cannot imagine seeing a woman in that same situation. It takes incredible amount of intestinal fortitude to handle the impact of seeing bodies mutilated by explosions, and then to continue on and fight the battle. The physical requirement of combat is extremely strenuous for able-bodied men, and women just do not have the physical ability to keep up. Ultimately the women will slow down the men and at that point the mission is compromised.

Tattoos used to be something that some Marines got while out on liberty and were generally limited to one or two tattoos that were usually the Marine Corps emblem on each arm. The young people have gone way too far today with the amount of tattoos they get. They don't realize that they are jeopardizing their Marine careers by the extent of tattoos they have etched onto their bodies, not to mention once they leave the Corps and go into private industry. Everything is done in excess today and the Marine Corps should make a strong stand against it.

The Marine Corps has been evolving a lot since I retired. Today they wear the cammies as their uniform-of-the-day, and they have lost the crispness and sharp look that used to be everyday stuff. They do wear their greens on Fridays, but they should be wearing them every day, and maybe have cammies on Friday, or when it is appropriate dress for the billet, and specifically when Marines are in combat, in the field, or on working parties. Even the Commandant wears cammies when he visits the bases, and to me that sends the wrong message.

Another change I am not happy about is that the Marine Corps no longer uses Marine cooks—they use civilians to run the mess halls. Junior enlisted Marines used to periodically be assigned to mess duty in the mess halls, and that helped develop a discipline that they no longer are receiving. They are even using civilians to guard the front gates of our Marine bases. I used to think our gate sentries added a special image of our heritage with their snappy dress and salutes to officers as they drove in. We don't get that with civilians as guards. We should continue to be self-sufficient and not have civilians doing jobs Marines can do, and have done for over two centuries.

I was raised by strict standards and we lived by the Ten Commandments. The world has changed, and now it's more like the "Ten Suggestions". In a lot of ways we have veered radically from our American values that used to be the way of life when I was a younger man. I am a very religious man, and I still attend church regularly. I still live by those standards I was raised by.

I have saved a memo dated 19 July 1971 that the Commandant of the Marine Corps, General Leonard F. Chapman wrote and it was addressed to all his general officers and commanding officers after he had received a letter from a distinguished friend. In the letter he quoted his friend who had been walking through an airport and was disturbed by the variety of military personnel with what he described as "very sloppy appearances". The men he observed had their jacket's button unbuttoned, ties loosened, etc. The man came to a Marine corporal who was just the opposite. When he pointed to the others and asked the Marine what the difference was the Marine responded, "*The Marines don't do that.*" General Chapman then went on to elaborate in his memo on what Marines "don't":

Marines don't: wear a scruffy uniform.

Marines don't: slouch around with their hands in their pockets.

Marines don't: fail to respond with a "Yes, Sir, or No, Sir" when speaking to a senior.

Marines don't: render a half-hearted or sloppy salute to the Stars and Stripes or to their seniors.

Marines don't: gang up on each other.

Marines don't: question lawful orders.

Marines don't: lie or cheat or break their word.

Marines don't: abandon a fellow Marine in time of need.

Marines don't: let down their fellow Marines by succumbing to drug temptation.

Marines don't: meet problems with, "it can't be done" or questions with the easy answer, "no."

Marines don't: the list is endless . . .

General Chapman finished by saying: Marines don't do that—but, why not? It's because the Marines are a breed apart. They are not the run-of-the-mill: they are but a few good men. They are proud members of an elite corps. They are as well trained as, if not better than, any military outfit anywhere. They have led the way, in war and peace, for 196 years. And they know that today they are ready—combat ready: to move out, anytime with the Navy, to go anywhere and take on anybody to fight and win.

Author's note: Despite SgtMaj Iron Mike Mervosh having been retired from the Marine Corps for thirty-seven years, longer than he was in the Marine Corps, he still has strong feelings he wanted to express so he took the time to hand-write the following dissertation:

"We Marines take pride in ourselves for battling with a lack of gear that is most needed. What puts this in my mind is the recent Secretary of Defense who came under fire for what he said: 'We go to war with we have.' Hell! That was very common in my days because that is what we did—we went to battle in what we had. That may be due to our principle of our 'band of brothers' concept, which tells us in part: 'nothing worthwhile comes easy, and if it were easy then we Marines wouldn't be needed.' But it applies to our Corps' values of: Honor; Courage; and Commitment that our Commandant, and all our commanders emphasize.

"I take this opportunity to pass on my Corps values that applied during my time in the Corps, which could be applied to our Marines today such as mental and physical toughness. Certainly our Marines have physical toughness, but they have to have the mental toughness as an equalizer to beat the enemy at his own game, and then possibly we won't have the post-traumatic stress disorders (PTSD) we have today.

"To add to those Corps values: self discipline; command presence; military bearing; total commitment to duty; dedication; force; endurance; good old basics and plain soldiering; hard work and team effort.

"Team effort was very essential in those bitter and bloody battles in the Pacific during WWII, Korea, Vietnam, Iraq, and today the war in Afghanistan.

"I want to quote a courageous combat Marine who was a giant in the Marine Corps; was an inspiring leader and a true professional; a patriot; a man who was a Marine's Marine in my lifetime, and a legend in all times; a man that was rarely politically correct but always militarily correct—Major General Chesty Puller: 'This individuality is a bunch of crap!' Therefore, our Marine Corps cannot afford to go to individualism, as it will tear down our fighting spirit, cohesion, unity, and will destroy the meaning of our espirit de corps. As far as I am concerned the only isms in our Marine Corps language should be: patriotism and professionalism, duty, honor, and country. I was overwhelmed with our patriotism that we had for a short time, but at the same time I was disappointed it took a wake-up call during 911. We can be proud by being flag-waving patriots. The wearing of the uniform we Marines proudly wear is a symbol of our patriotism.

"Patriotism at times is an abstract thing, and at times something that cannot be seen but is surely felt by all of us Marines who swear to defend the Constitution against foreign or domestic attacks. As far as Marines are concerned, anyone who desecrates our flag is a potential enemy, however, providing that person is in the process of burning that flag and the net results are most positive and providing that has our flag completely wrapped around himself while it is in the process of burning!

"Professionalism is not because our Marines have a certain job to do in their MOS (Military Occupational Specialty): I refer to those duties in a professional manner around the clock on a daily basis to accomplish the assigned mission. Being a Marine is not a job, but rather a way of life. Professionalism must be the heart and soul of Marines, especially our officers, Staff NCOs, and NCOs. They must be bold, prudent, and capable of dealing with and leading their Marines, especially in battle. Never will it be said that Marines lacked training and leadership by becoming a battle casualty.

"All our Marines are referred to as riflemen first and foremost, but to earn that prestigious title of 'rifleman' they must concentrate on 'one shot, one kill'—no exceptions. They must avoid being trigger happy: in other words, 'spray and pray' with a hundred shots and no kills wastes a lot of damn ammo, and that can't be useful during the course of battle.

"It's the duty of our Marines to strive to be the full-time Marines—the 24/7 type who are the leaders, warriors, and professional by being strong, tough, and decisive. They must maintain and participate in our proud traditions, or else we will become obsolete like a small worthless army or Navy police force. Believe me: that has happened before during my watch. I first heard of that argument during the Unification and National Security Act of 1947. I am sure that we may hear of it again in which we did as we almost lost our Marine

Corps entirely because of the recruits that drowned at Ribbon Creek in Parris Island, South Carolina.

"We certainly have our share of critics who claim the U.S. Army can perform any mission and assignment the Marine Corps can, and that there is no need for a second army with the title of *U.S. Marines.* Our Marines face the challenge of being different and better, and we also face the challenge of not becoming assigned as a second land army. Nor should we take the other service's route with their gender integration of recruit training that presently excludes the Marine Corps thanks to our Commandant. There is the experimentation of social programs, having liberal awards system. Most of us veterans feel that a definite reform is required to maintain the high standards and high plateaus of awards under our Corps—the Marines have always had the reputation as the most frugal and stringent of all the armed forces. If not, then the real combat awards won't mean a damned thing. The editor of the *Leatherneck Magazine* put it in perspective: There is medal and ribbon madness. Throughout our armed forces there is so much emphasis placed on counseling, anger management, and stress management, all of which was unheard of in any time in the Corps. Hell, we didn't need that crap to maintain our good old unity, cohesion, and to win all those important battles that have been our primary mission."

Author note: Iron Mike Mervosh is often asked to provide speeches as a guest speaker at numerous military and civilian events. Below is an example of a speech he gave to the Golden Gate Wing in a Prop Talk presentation:

"I liked the Marine posters. I liked: *The First to Fight, Kill or be killed.* I went to the Navy they said, 'Join the Navy and see the world.' I went to the Army and they said, 'Go to the Army and learn a trade.' I go to the Marine Corps and it was, "We offer you a rifle, pack, and a hard time. If you like to kill, join our outfit.'

"The first time I was wounded in combat a corpsman put a tag on me and marked a big old 'M' on my forehead. At that time I was leading my company as the company commander. The 'M' was for a morphine shot and I was told they were going to evacuate me. I wiped the 'M' off my forehead and ripped that tag off. I'll tell you that the morphine gave me a lot of adrenaline and I wasn't scared of anybody. I just wanted to kill more goddamned Japs. But when that wore off and I started thinking about what I did . . . I didn't want another morphine shot. I was hurting all over. I can see why some guys want another shot because it's 'no pain, no strain.' Thank goodness I didn't get that second shot, but then, I don't think they would have given it to me anyway.

"A bunch of us guys were enduring heavy concentrations of artillery shelling and mortar fire that forced me and six Marines into the nearest shell hole. I remember a guy named Cusimano who said he was getting out of that hole because there was too much stuff flying around. I told him, 'Where the hell are you going to go? You're going to get killed you dumb fool, they've got the place saturated!' As soon as I said that there was a loud 'boom!' A mortar shell went off right on top of the parapet. I don't know how long I was out—maybe minutes, hours, or what. I heard angels singing and I thought I was dead. I opened my eyes and the first thing I saw was blood all over me. I thought I was hit, but it was the other Marines' blood on me. I tried to stop the flow of blood on one of the Marines, but I soon realized that all five of those Marines were casualties. I had lost my hearing and it didn't come back for two weeks.

"Another time a sniper's bullet hit my cartridge belt—I remember feeling exhilarated that the SOB had missed me!

"I never took a prisoner on Iwo Jima. Japanese atrocities against civilians in China and Marines on Guadalcanal had hardened me against sparing any of the enemy soldiers I faced.

"On Iwo Jima we faced Japanese soldiers that had been given special instructions to kill any of invaders wearing red crosses on their helmets or carrying medical bags—the corpsmen, whose reputations of saving soldiers' lives preceded them into battle. We had twelve corpsmen in the company and only two of them walked off the island. That wasn't too bad, because some units didn't have any survivors. A lot of time we didn't want to burden the corpsmen with a lot of the wounds—they was too busy amputating legs, arms, and what have you. The corpsman couldn't be bothered with someone getting a bullet in his arm or leg—that's elementary crap to him. He had to get with the serious cases first.

"My company landed with two hundred forty-two men and only thirty-one were standing at the end. Our regiment had six hundred fifty-two killed and one thousand fifty-three wounded.

"When Marines were called to action during the Korean War I ended up serving with 'G' Company, 3rd Battalion, 5th Marine Regiment. My brother Milan had been killed in action in Korea before I got there. It was a sad time for me.

"Vietnam was another call to action for me. I had two tours in Vietnam with the 1st Marine Division. Between all these wars I served with five different Marine Corps Divisions, making countless operations and deployments around the world, in addition to attending Infantry Weapons School, Drill Instructor School, and Recruiter School for subsequent duty as a recruiter.

"Of the 232 years of the existence of our Marine Corps I have served only thirty-five years. During that time I embarked aboard ships many times, and made many amphibious landings, crossing lines of departure, lines of deployment, and participating in many 'D-Days'. As I crossed that last line of departure and joined the retirement ranks I can't help but feel the slogan, 'Once a Marine, always a Marine' is very much a reality.

"Retirement is inevitable though for a Marine. It has placed me in a unique position where I can sit back and enjoy the many successes of the Corps, and at the same time be disappointed at its many failures. And believe me: it's those disappointments that cause me to have a reoccurrence of heartburn. However, I do enjoy the many successes and past accomplishments of our Corps, and furthermore, I would like to commend all of our troops for a professional performance and 'well done' for the combat effectiveness during the surge for Operation Iraqi Freedom, and also Operation Enduring Freedom.

"You veterans have created the legacy, throughout the years, that our honor, valor, fidelity, devotion to duty, dedication, and reputation have remained unchallenged, is highly respected and has the highest order of being known throughout the world. And it's the duty of all of our troops today to be committed and continue and maintain that legacy.

"Previously I made a comment about being a career Marine, but I'd much rather be referred to as a combat Marine and a professional Marine. As a combat Marine and a professional, we did not join to be compensated with a fat paycheck. Nor to seek a second paycheck in some other type of employment that would deviate us from being a full time Marine, and at the same time enhance our monetary well being. We did not seek any personal gain at the expense of the Marine Corps, or to look for those perks and so-called 'goodings'. Nor to pass wars: we became instant and true patriots.

"We answered our nation's call. We joined because we wanted to serve our country and fight its battles. We're patriotic, loyal, and dedicated. There's no money in this world that can buy patriotism, loyalty, and dedication. And loyalty has to be a two-way street: it's something that must travel down as well as up the chain of command. And each link in the chain must be tempered with strength within its passing, all the way from the commanding general down to the platoon-to-company runner.

"You veterans have also created a legacy of having our elite fighting force, the nation's force of readiness, the true rapid deployment force: the first to fight, the first to kill or be killed, and win those battles that seemingly cannot be won against insurmountable odds.

"We prided ourselves in the lack of gear that was always most needed. Which puts me to mind that our former Secretary of Defense, Donald Rumsfeld, came under heavy fire by the media when he said, 'We go to war with what we've got.' Well, that was very common in our days because we went to all those battles with what we had. That's why we had the reputation that we could do so very much with so very little.

"Now this may be due to one of the principles of our 'Band of Brothers' concept', which tells us that nothing worthwhile comes easy, then anyone could do it and you veterans would not be needed. But it does come with those values that our troops are familiar with and all our commanders emphasize: honor, courage and commitment. But I would like to add a few of my own core values that applied to us during my time n the Corps that could very well apply to our troops today. Now these are not just mere words, but actions that are really required. In the likes of mental and physical toughness; self-discipline; devotion to duty; command presence; military bearing; enduring hardships; making personal sacrifices; total commitment to duty; dedication and determination; a heck of a lot of force; endurance; leadership by example; good old basics in regimentation, and plain old soldiering, hard work and team effort. And the list goes on. But these are just a few additional Corps values and those necessary ingredients in becoming a fulltime warrior, the 24/7 type: a leader and a professional.

"Hard work is something that comes naturally to us during a firefight. But it has to be practiced in that tough, good old Marine Corps training during the day, and especially at night, under all climatic and adverse conditions, and applied when contact is imminent. And we prided ourselves in training in misery, so we could do the rigors and hardships and miseries of battle, which means there's got to be *training*—more intense, realistic, and repetitive training to build up that needed confidence for the purpose of survival, having success on the battlefield by winning those important battles. Even though we pray for peace, we must always prepare for war.

"And I am sure that you old timers will agree with the fact that we've never seen or heard of a soldier or Marine that has drowned in his own sweat. I'm sure you've heard the old adage that 'the more we sweat in peace, the less we bleed in war'.

"Team effort was very essential towards our many victories in those bloody campaigns in the Pacific and the European Theaters during World War II.

"I would like to quote a courageous combat Marine, a giant of the Corps, an inspiring leader. He's a Marine who has never been politically correct, but always militarily correct. He's a true professional, a patriot, and a Marine's Marine during my time, and a legend of all time—Chesty Puller. He said, 'this individuality stuff is a bunch of garbage.' Of course, that was just pleasant terms—you should have heard the really good part of it! Yes, our soldiers and Marines have their so-called 'individual rights'. And that is, to a certain extent, while they are on leave or liberty. But once they're committed to duty status, and are out in the field training, and especially on the battlefield, then team rights supersede the individual's rights. Therefore, as leaders, warriors, and professionals, we cannot afford to be individualists or give a thought to individualism, as it will only tear down the fibers of our fighting spirit, our unity, cohesiveness and teamwork and destroy the meaning of our esprit d' corps. As far as I'm concerned the only 'isms' that need the most emphasis in our military language are: Americanism, patriotism, and professionalism. And those beautiful words that you veterans have lived by: patriotism, duty, honor and country.

"I am overwhelmed by the resurgence we had of our patriotism for a short while. But at the same time I was disappointed that it took a wake-up all due to 9-1-1 to bring it about, where it's something that should have been done right along. So we can all be proud and take the lead by being flag-waving patriots, and wearing that uniform that you once proudly wore, and earned the right to wear, that was a symbol of patriotism.

"Yes: patriotism . . . at times it's an abstract thing. At times it's something that cannot be seen. But I'm sure everyone in this room tonight who swore to defend the Constitution against all enemies, foreign and domestic, feels it. And as far as we're concerned, anyone who desecrates our American flag is a potential enemy. However, there may be one exception we can condone and that's provided the person who is in the process of burning that flag and has the flag completely wrapped around him or her while it's in the full process of burning. And one word that always remains in the pledge of allegiance to our flag is the 'almighty'. One nation, under *God*: no exception.

"Professionalism? Not because our troops have a certain job to do in their respective MOS's that they must have to perform at all times in a professional manner. Because being a Marine is not a job—it's a *way of life*. And if they still prefer to call it a job, then my type of Marine or soldier is the type that will run through a wall to get the job done. Professionalism must be at the heart and soul of our troops, and especially our officers, staff NCOs and our NCOs. They must be decisive, bold and prudent, and to be capable of dealing with, and leading our Marines and soldiers, especially in battle. And never will it be said that the Marine or soldier has become a battle casualty through any lack of discipline, leadership, or training that was due to him.

"All of our Marines are referred to as 'riflemen' first and foremost. But to earn that prestigious title as a rifleman he must always concentrate on one shot, one kill, and no exceptions. He must avoid being trigger happy—in other words, 'spray and pray', with one hundred shots and no kills, nor the probability of one and a waste of lot of damned ammo.

"Now to become a full time Marine, the warrior, the leader, the professional, they must strive for perfection and always persist in high standards by demanding more, by making the extra effort in performance of his duties to his own example and by making personal sacrifices. So it's the duty of all Marines and all soldiers—to become that full time warrior, leader, and the professional. Being strong, tough, and decisive in maintaining, participating, strengthening, and preserving our traditional values and the legacy we left behind.

"As those of you in this audience are pretty aware: our great generation of World War II veteran ranks are thinning out and fading at a rapid rate. Of all the battles that have been fought and won during World War II, and adding those illustrious chapters to our history and the heritage of our country, I would like to take one example of many, as never before, or never after, has there equaled the fighting on Iwo Jima. It was recorded as the most demanding, toughest, fiercest and bloodiest battles in the history of the Marine Corps. What many least know because you'll never read it in history books or view it on film clips, is that it was also a perfect battle on a perfect battlefield—a defender's dream. It was a battlefield that resembled the moon, with its bombed out craters, its earthquake appearance on the northern part of the island with its washboard terrain. Now what I meant by it being a perfect battle on a perfect battlefield was that there were no collateral damages assessed on civilian areas—there weren't any civilians or structures. There was not one single structure above the ground, or any semblance of any civilian, a harmless child, or a woman. It was strictly fighting man against fighting man—kill or be killed. It's the only one of its kind in the history of the Marine Corps, our country, and possibly in the history of the world.

"On Iwo Jima there were so many unselfish unrelenting acts of bravery, courage and heroism that occurred routinely as a cool and keen sense of duty, that it was taken for granted. It was unrecognized and most of it went unaccounted for. Yet it brought forward the inspiring message by Admiral Nimitz that will live on forever: 'Among those that fought on Iwo Jima, *uncommon valor was a common virtue.*'

"Now Admiral Nimitz could have meant that message towards the enemy, as they performed in a brave and courageous manner. However, we Marines have experienced many times their fanatical and suicidal ways, as every one of the enemy on that island was ordered by his commander that he would kill ten Marines before he made his defensive position his gravesite.

"While this 'battle of all battles' was raging on had to be the toughest and most demanding assignment of my lifetime. I'm one of the very few infantrymen who didn't miss a day of that battle, even though a good many of us were the walking wounded and continued on with the fighting. On D-plus-4 our Marines, with fierce hand-to-hand fighting, finally seized and secured our primary objective, Mount Suribachi.

"The flag raising at Mount Suribachi was not the culmination of the battle. The battle was just getting started, with many more deadly objectives to follow, and where most of the fiercest fighting and casualties occurred on both sides for an additional thirty-two days. Those came with the likes of Hill-382; Hill-362; The Amphitheater; Turkey Knob; The Meat-Grinder; The Quarry; Boat Basin; Cushman's Pocket; Katana Point; Charlie Garden Ridge; Airfields One and Two, just to name a few.

"There was no place to hide and take cover. No place to run, except toward the enemy, as they had been preparing for the longest time in those well entrenched, concealed underground fortifications which monitored eight hundred pill boxes, blockhouses, and gun emplacements. They were interlocked with miles of tunnels and caves that were several tiers below the surface of the island. The enemy did not fight on Iwo Jima—they fought *within* it.

"Every square yard of that island was covered with intense interlocking fire, supplemented with land mines, with heavy concentration and the well-coordinated enemy's artillery, mortar, and rocket fire. And even anti-tank and anti-aircraft fire that was solely used on us ground Marines. Of course, at that particular time there was no availability of any high-tech weaponry or probably we would have secured the island in four or five days as predicted. Guided missiles; unmanned flying drones like the Predator and the Reaper; robots that search out the enemy and explosives; night vision goggles—not even the availability of a flak jacket. Because all we had was the green utility jacket while being armed with that deadly rifle and bayonet, hand grenades, demolition charges, flamethrowers, and with sheer determination and guts.

"And run? Hell yes we did run, as well as possible in that ankle-deep volcanic ash, but we did it the good old Marine way by being ever aggressive and forging ahead to attack and assault, time and time again until ultimate victory. Which brought forth another inspiring message by then Secretary of the Navy, James Forrestal, that the ferocious fighting Marines and the flag-raising on Iwo Jima, 'guaranteed the Marine Corps for the next five-hundred years!' I am sure that at one time or another you have heard about the first and second flag raising where the smaller flag was replaced by the larger flag. And Joe Rosenthal, the photographer who took that classic and emotional photo with the split second timing said, 'Anyone could have taken the picture. I took it, but the Marines took the island.' And the last survivor of both flag-raisings details, Corporal Charles Lindberg, who participated in the first one, modestly said, 'first flag raising, second—it doesn't make any damned difference, because every damned Marine who fought on that island, raised the flag!'

"Now, get back to those guaranteed five hundred years. Thank God our Marine Corps and our country survived sixty-three of those years. No pun intended, but we have four hundred, thirty-seven years to go. Therefore we cannot afford to be complacent, and rest and live on our past sentiments, glories, laurels, and past accomplishments. What our Marine Corps must do, and I am more than certain they are more than capable of doing, is face that challenge and strive to be a heck of a lot different and a heck of a lot better than any military organization in the world. And to be committed to continue and maintain our legacy as the finest and proudest Marine Corps it can brand has been for the past two hundred thirty-two years of our Corps' existence.

"Lastly, let us pay tribute and honor and give a thought and a prayer to our silent and unseen comrades, as they have given up all of their tomorrows for our today's. As they all wanted to live to fight the enemy but were not afraid to die. They asked so very little, but they gave so very much in preserving, protecting, and defending our precious freedoms we all cherish, and for making this evening possible for us. In addition, I charge all our Marines across this great land of ours with this mission: ensure our motto, 'Semper Fidelis' continues to mean 'always faithful': to our God, our country, and our Corps.

"God bless you, and Semper Fidelis!"

In May of 2013 I went to the annual reunion of the East Coast DI Association at Parris Island, South Carolina. I was put up at the Beaufort Inn, a place normally reserved for colonels and generals—the depot sergeant major arranged for me to have a room there. It was a great event and hundreds of drill instructors came. I had been asked to be the Parade Reviewing Officer by the Depot Chief of Staff, Colonel Rick Grabowski, who himself was a former drill instructor. During Colonel Grabowski's speech to the new Marine graduates and their families he spoke for over thirty minutes. His speech was primarily about me, and my experience that started during the Pacific campaigns in World War II. It was a great experience standing there with the colonel as the newly graduated recruits marched by. We returned the unit's salutes as they passed by. When it was all over Colonel Grabowski turned to me and saluted me—I quickly snapped a salute back. Some of the DIs that witnessed that said they never saw an officer salute an enlisted man before, but I just told them that the colonel was trying to show me respect the best way he could think of. I stood there for quite a while shaking the hands of drill instructors and new Marines who wanted to meet an old Marine like me. I felt honored to be so respected by the Marines.

Over the years many Marines have asked me which of the three wars I was in was my favorite. It's hard to pick a favorite war since wars are hell, but I would not hesitate to say that World War II was the best one of all, and Korea was my second favorite. My reason is simple: we had no rules of engagement like we later had in Vietnam. In WWII and Korea we were there to win and we killed the enemy wherever and whenever we came upon them. Vietnam was a whole different story, as we were required to engage the enemy only when we were attacked. In Vietnam we fought a guerilla war in the jungle, and the Viet Cong looked just like the people living in the many villages we came upon.

In 1997 the Assistant Secretary of the Army Sarah Lister, someone I personally call a 'Lister bag' (a water bag), gave a speech to a Harvard University group, and in her speech she described the Marine Corps as "extremists" who were at risk of "total disconnection with society." "Wherever you have extremists," she said, "you've got some risks of total disconnection with society, and that's a little dangerous. I think the Army is much more connected to society than the Marines are," she said. "The Marine Corps is, you know (sic), they have all these checkerboard fancy uniforms and stuff. But the Army is sort of muddy boots on the ground." Her remarks offended all Marines, especially the Commandant of the Marine Corps, General Charles C. Krulak. Marines instantly despised her, and she made a half-assed attempt to apologize by saying that is not what she meant. It's hard to see how she could have meant anything else. Even the Army had problems with her statement. So Marines just think of Sarah Lister as a "Lister bag".

Chapter 14

ONE CIVILIAN'S VIEWPOINT

Author note: In preparation for writing this book I solicited Marines and people who know Iron Mike to write to me and provide any stories or anecdotes that could be put into a special chapter in the book. One person, Jim Cerenelli, wrote such an eloquent story that I decided to make it a separate chapter. Jim Cerenelli was a Marine from 1971-1975 and achieved the rank of sergeant. He currently is a life member of the Marine Corps League Tri-State Detachment 494. While in the Marines he served in Headquarters Battalion at Headquarters Marine Corps, and later in the Office of the Commanding General, Fleet Marine Force Pacific at Camp Smith, Hawaii. After getting out of the Marines he spent the next thirty years as a policeman and achieved the rank of captain. His last assignment was as Operations Supervisor. Following his police career retirement he became a high school educator/coordinator and teaches public safety and criminal justice. He also coordinates firefighting and EMS training. His talents include being a professional musician dealing with vocals, guitar and keyboards, and also is a songwriter. He was so impressed with Iron Mike that he took my offering to task and wrote the following story—his writings mirror some of the other stories in the book, and yet they validate all the other stories.

The morning of May 3, 2013 dawned in a cold, rain-soaked and windy bluster aboard the U.S. Marine Corps Recruit Depot, Parris Island, South Carolina. For the three hundred-plus new Marines of Platoons 2032, 2034, 2036 and 2038 of Golf Company, 2nd Recruit Training Battalion, however those weather conditions were barely noticeable, if at all.

This was graduation day, and their three-month whirlwind ordeal of the intensive mental and physical training crucible of hard work, pain and discipline known as Marine Corps boot camp was finally over. Today, these young men-turned Marines were embarking upon the next phase of their challenging journey; that of joining ranks with the most storied warrior brotherhood in the history of warfare. The events of this day would be indelibly burned into their minds and the proud sense of accomplishment they felt made it uniquely unlike any other day they would ever experience.

Eventually the rain subsided, though the damp chilling wind refused to remit. Nevertheless, like a thousand before it, the ceremony moved smartly along as all parades should. Following several entertaining selections by the excellent Parris Island Marine Band, a small group of stone faced, razor-sharp drill instructors moved into position on the rain-darkened asphalt. The DIs were soon joined by four large, tightly knit rectangular formations of impeccably dressed military figures, deftly advancing to their pre-designated places on the hallowed parade deck.

The band ended the preliminaries with a stirring rendition of the Star Spangled Banner, which was then succeeded by prayer and commentary, courtesy of the depot chaplain. The remaining narrative oratories concluded shortly thereafter. Then at last, to the delight of the anxious crowd, the final great procession of troops began to unfold.

Every young man on that parade deck knew exactly who among family, friend and sweetheart was present in the reviewing stands, straining to get a glimpse of their favorite Marine. Each was also aware that among the multitude of honored guests was a contingent of retired drill instructors, returning to the depot for their 26th annual reunion. Every graduate was cognizant of the deep distinction with which Marine Corps tradition: its membership, alumni, and America herself regarded a historical reputation for honor, glory, and esprit de corps.

They had undoubtedly been told that the honorary reviewing officer, in front of whom they were about to pass for one memorable last inspection, was an extraordinarily special and honored guest indeed. In the modern gladiator kingdom that *is* the United States Marine Corps, that official could arguably be considered the *most* honored guest of all.

For what these newest members of America's most elite fighting force may not have fully understood was that they were about to share their glorious day with true Marine Corps royalty in the person of legendary Sergeant Major Michael D. "Iron Mike" Mervosh.

Iron Mike's resume is nothing short of remarkable. As a combat veteran of World War II, Korea, and Vietnam, a conqueror of Pacific islands like Saipan and Iwo Jima, and one of the longest serving, most distinguished enlisted Leathernecks in the history of the Marine Corps, his escapades and longevity rise to the heights of Olympus.

For me, being afforded the opportunity to view the graduation ceremony from the VIP area of the reviewing stands as a guest of Iron Mike made the entire spectacle even more awesome to behold. The cold blowing wind did little to dampen the spirits of those in attendance as the parade got underway, and I gleaned particular pleasure at the sight of Iron Mike taking his place, front and center of the meticulously geometric platoons, and then hearing his still strong, authoritative drill instructor voice engage them to, "*Pass in review!*"

Fittingly then, with those three words, the longstanding and well earned dream of the Golf Company Marines became reality, as they marched proudly into their own glorious chapter of the Marine Corps' diary.

An asterisk here should point out that despite the wail of the wind, every person in attendance clearly heard Iron Mike's commanding words as they set that procession of khaki and green into motion. This seems to me the appropriate juncture to proffer the great respect and admiration I felt for this ninety-year old warhorse as he stood on that parade deck, as stoic and erect as the historic Parris Island statue bearing his famous nickname.

I thought about what cultivated levels of strength and self-control it would take never to waiver in that gusting chill, as platoon after platoon came under the scrutiny of his expertly trained eye. To his credit, Iron Mike maintained perfect military presence and bearing until every Marine of Golf Company had passed, and in doing so, easily paralleled the efforts of the staff NCO, a man perhaps a third his age, standing beside him.

My recognition of the sergeant major's forte paled in comparison to comments by the bevy of former and current drill instructors, many of whom were combat veterans themselves, as Mike's military career achievements and battle record were broadcast by the public address announcer. A tinge of awe could be detected in the voices of these Marine-makers as they bestowed their valued gifts of praise and sincere expressions of approval. My favorite laudation came when an old gunny turned to his Marine friend in the seat beside him and stated most seriously, "*Holy shit, I wonder if this guy can fly?*" The positive karma I felt proved itself to be a consistent presence throughout my return to Parris Island, the first after forty-two eventful years.

The reunion with Iron Mike, combined with visiting many locations associated with my own boot camp days (enhanced courtesy of my former senior drill instructor, now retired MSgt. Donald Flick), melded with a plethora of happenings over the next three days to create memories fresh and anew, memories which I must say, left me humbly grateful.

Nothing however, rose above the most dominant theme of that unforgettable excursion, which revolved around Iron Mike himself. I had served with him decades before and it was his invitation that had motivated me to make the pilgrimage back to the proverbial Mecca of Marines that is Parris Island. Doing so would prove to be a glowing point of light in my personal Marine Corps universe, and as I watched him on the parade deck, my mind returned both of us to a time when the sergeant major and I were much, much younger men, and to a lucid replay of how Iron Mike Mervosh and I came to cross paths in the first place.

When I joined the Marine Corps not long after New Year's Day in 1971, I felt like I already knew about Iron Mike. Well, not directly by name, but from the time I was a kid and saw my first set of dress blues, I *knew* that someday I'd be a Marine. For reasons I still don't completely understand, it turned out to be the tales and images of the Pacific island-hopping Marines of World War II that captured and cultivated my ever growing imagination the most. By way of some strangely kindred spirit, these camouflage helmeted, M-1 carrying Devil Dogs became the fighting role models and American heroes I most wanted to emulate.

Let me be clear: every Marine who served honorably prior to and since that worldwide conflict is my brother or sister. All are America's military elite, some obviously more so than others by virtue of their missions and sacrifice. But for the juvenile Jarhead wannabe that *I* was, the combat veterans of those epic Pacific battles against the Japanese, with names like Guadalcanal, Tarawa, Kwajalein, Saipan,

Tinian, Peleliu, and Iwo Jima represented something exceptional. It was true back then and remains so to this day. The chronicles of those campaigns continue to stir my soul like no other engagements, in any theater of war, fought by any combatants, at any time in history.

Given this preamble, it's easy to understand my ebullience when, while stationed in Hawaii in 1973, a young Marine corporal, newly assigned to the Office of the Commanding General, FMFPac (Fleet Marine Force Pacific) at Camp H. M. Smith, first met Fleet Marine Force Pacific Sergeant Major "Iron Mike" Mervosh.

Even back then, Iron Mike was already enshrined into the annals of Marine Corps folklore, replete with a combat record that went way beyond impressive as a veteran of three wars and several Pacific battles, including Roi-Namur, Saipan, Tinian and Iwo Jima. Those actions laid the precursory groundwork for his prodigious combat resume, which would eventually include the Korean and Vietnam theaters of war.

I can still recall the day I was introduced to this cigar chomping, sporting a high-and-tight haircut, and was a fireplug of a man. Iron Mike is a grinning, growling, human pit bull, who is aptly arrayed in a gentleman's demeanor. While spoken words would soon sustain the virtues of his worldly savvy and acute intellect, the "Iron" in Iron Mike was unmistakable and tangibly locked and loaded inside that well conditioned frame.

Despite his hard-earned mileage, he still looked every bit the Fourth Marine Division Middleweight Boxing Champ he was when he wasn't storming those enemy-held islands. Poured into that perfectly tailored summer service uniform, Iron Mike Mervosh was without a doubt the consummate poster child for the U. S. Marines

Thrusting out his right hand, he looked me square in the eye as he boomed, "Welcome aboard Marine, where are you from?" My slightly unassertive response elicited from him an, "Oh yeah . . . Youngstown, Ohio, I know right where that is," as he proceeded to indoctrinate me to the fact that my hometown sat a mere hour or so northwest of his own home in Pittsburgh, Pennsylvania.

Although that introductory conversation was short, I left his office pleasantly bolstered by the perception that a man with such a lofty Marine Corps pedigree and wearing so many ribbons (as in: Navy Commendation and those Purple Hearts) should come off as being so down-to-earth friendly with the new kid from Ohio. I came to realize later that the occasion had presented me with a single, cryptic snapshot of this fleet sergeant major that personally and passionately cared about his Marines, regardless of their rank.

As I got to know him better, I found Iron Mike to be a man of character, humor and personal integrity. Above all, he displayed those quintessential qualities associated with the most basic tenets of Marine Corps doctrine: courage, discipline, loyalty, honor, and dedication to duty.

Not to sound cliché, but with Iron Mike, what you saw really was what you got, and still do now. It was not unusual to see him around the gym or with other Marines, and aside from the character essences already mentioned, another telling example of his ironclad will and physical prowess was his stalwart warrior fitness ethic. Despite the wounds he received in combat, this sergeant major's workouts were always Marine Corps worthy.

For those seeking additional credence of his toughness and endurance, I would offer as evidence his record as Fourth Marine Division Middleweight Champion: Iron Mike fought a total of thirty-eight fights, of which he lost just four, count 'em—*four*. Even more significant is that all of those losses were to other Marines! He made it a point to remind me once that he "never lost to anybody from the Navy or Army." Note too that he won eighteen of those bouts by knockout. I will own up to my own occasional speculation about just how many *really* tough guys there must have been in the Pacific Fleet during World War II and respectively, where that would place Iron Mike in the pecking order of *greatest global war bad asses*. Pretty damned high, I'd say.

Before leaving the subject of workouts, I would surely be remiss if I failed to relate one lighter moment, which emanated from an encounter with Iron Mike outside of the Marine facility at Camp Smith. Not long after we met I was leaving the weight room and found him standing outdoors, cooling down after his own sweat session. We began to talk about a now-forgotten topic of conversation at the time. Looking down toward the pavement, I happened to notice that he wasn't wearing any shoes or socks, causing me to inadvertently zero my gaze onto his bare feet. I have no explanation as to why my subconscious mind was prompted to pursue this particular line of thought, but I suddenly found myself totally engrossed in the image of those leathery grunt appendages embedded in black volcanic ash. In a moment of what I can only describe as enlightened lunacy, I felt a soft, autonomic surge of air traverse my throat as the speech mechanism spontaneously engaged. Then, as if but a thought, I whispered, "Holy Jesus . . . those dogs were on freakin' Iwo Jima!"

He didn't hear me and in my defense, historians as well as the likes of John and Jane Q. Public visit the Marine Corps museum every day to view with bountiful reverence the weapons, uniforms and 782 gear our fighting men used on historical battlefields. So how much greater the treasure should we consider the flesh and blood of a man who actually lived such an experience? Yes, I do state this contention with tongue firmly in cheek, but agree or not, to me there is a scintilla of sound logic here (well, somewhat sound anyway). The redeeming quality is humor, because the truth is that even after all these years, I still smile when I think about it. Besides, there must be some validity in my madness, for when I finally did relate the story to Iron Mike many years later, he got a chuckle out of it too.

Regarding FMFPac, I would regularly contemplate my good fortune at having been selected for such coveted duty. Out of the multitude of Marines in the largest of Corps commands, destiny had favored *me* with the assignment of serving with not one, but *two* legendary Marines of the Second World War: Sergeant Major Iron Mike Mervosh on one flank and the late General Louis H. Wilson, a Medal of Honor recipient on the other. General Wilson received his MOH for gallantry in action on Guam and later closed out a brilliant four-star military career as the 26th Commandant of the Marine Corps. Truth was, even without those stars, we all respected him as a man and me as a youngster who grew up with such an affinity for Greatest Generation Marines, daily contact with the CG and Iron Mike equated to nothing less than situational manna from heaven.

My duties at Camp Smith enabled me to observe, and in varying degrees to participate in daily activities, protocols and functions supportive of the offices of the commanding general and the sergeant major. This included many peripheral and often mundane tasks conjunctive to military, diplomatic, and civilian guests of FMFPac. During the course of these duties it became pretty obvious that Iron Mike was both socially comfortable and proficiently interactive within these circles. Then as now, regardless of his opinion of those with whom he might be associating, his interpersonal skills were highly developed and his conversation always learned, respectful, and articulate. He could always be counted on to coolly hold his own with everyone and anyone present at any official proceeding or social event.

In the end, given his own inimitable style and vernacular, Sergeant Major's stated viewpoint on any topic, combined with his worldly experience and competence in the area of human relations, meant others in attendance could not help but mark his presence.

Projecting the world according to Iron Mike proved to be a strong and fundamental element of whom he was, but he knew the meaning of discretion, too. In other words: the man spoke his mind but was smart enough to know when he was better served by holding his fire.

In his position as Fleet Sergeant Major, Iron Mike had the responsibility of being the enlisted point man for the commanding general during their inspection visits to Marine installations. Mike's vast knowledge of, and his diverse experiences in the Corps, tempered by his blue collar background, provided him with an extremely high level of awareness and uniquely broad insight into the state of each unit or man's readiness. This gave him the ability to bring the authority and power of his office and that of the commanding general to bear for the benefit of all Pacific Marines and those matters affecting them.

As a result, the Marines of FMFPac were extraordinarily well served by Iron Mike's dedication to their personal well-being and operational effectiveness. The enormous value of his input was certainly not lost on General Wilson, who relied heavily on his sergeant major's rapport with the troops, as well as his intuition and POV regarding what was right or wrong within their world. The general knew that Iron Mike's enlisted status, background, and service qualifications gave him a higher level of clearance within the enlisted circles and a more empathetic line of communication with these Marines.

Not that we peons didn't like the general: quite the contrary, as I've said, General Wilson was an outstanding Marine and a marvelously splendid individual. It was simply that the protocols and privileges afforded general officers were not conducive to assuaging the average "Gyrene" (Marine) concerns that such high rank could not accurately relate to life at lower levels of the olive drab green food chain. Contrarily, they knew where Iron Mike came from and felt much more comfortable opening up around him. Despite his elevated stature within the Corps, he'd marched beaucoup miles in their boots and was one of them.

A typical day at Headquarters, FMFPac involved a variety of duty assignments. Consequently, at any given moment Sergeant Major would call upon members of the staff to assist him in one-way or another. Often, those assists involved serving as his driver and it was in that capacity that one of the more memorable, albeit atypical missions of my tour of duty came to pass; that glorious Hawaiian morning when he summoned me to his office for a briefing on the necessary logistical support for his latest adventure.

Recalling the conversation, it was something along the lines of: "Hey-uh Cerenelli", he says, "how about goin' down to the motor pool and get me a vehicle. You can pick me up out front in about twenty."

Now I'll stipulate that forty-some years may have rounded the once-sharp edges of that dialogue a bit, but trust me when I say the events themselves are crystal clear. My standard reply of, "Yes sir," was accompanied by my slightest degree of confused abeyance. Unfortunately the delay failed to elicit the required info that subsequently spawned my next inquiry of, "Where to, Sir?"

Now I, along with any other NCO in the staff who might be driving the sergeant major, knew we could count on him providing destination coordinates at some point of his choosing. But something in his facial expression intimated that this exploit might be just a tad different—and it was.

His matter-of-fact response to my question admittedly caught me off guard when he said, "Well, it looks like I'm gonna be on *Hawaii Five-O*."

"Really?" I replied with an unavoidable grin and a sophomoric, "*The* Hawaii Five-O?"

"That's affirmative," he went on, "Appears they're doing an episode about some military guy getting murdered and they want somebody to play a senior Marine Staff NCO".

My disciplined grin exploded into a full blown laugh as I thought; "Geez, talk about your typecasting!" So, with the latest intel now assimilated into the battle plan, and my energized, "Aye-aye, Sir," we crossed the line of departure and headed for Iron Mike's next great safari.

The Oahu-based television show was in its prime during that period and the prospect of being able to watch the filming of an episode, not to mention chauffeuring McGarrett's latest cameo guest star, just tickled me out. Double-timing down to the motor pool I checked out a ride and picked the sergeant major up as designated location. Passing by the sentry at the gate I remember thinking, "Hawaii Five-O…no shit. How cool is *this*!"

While en route to the set, Iron Mike seemed genuinely amused to be a participant in the filming. At the same time he displayed absolutely no sign of anxiety, even though he was about to jump into a situation that would be a pretty daunting proposition for most folks. Imagine: you are about to play a character, with lines, on camera, in one of the most popular, star-studded television series in show biz.

Oh yeah, by "popular" I mean: as in 'currently viewed by *millions* of people encompassing a pretty good chunk of the free world-type popular!' Most of us would be looking for everything from Rolaids to a Valium, to a sitting head call. Hell, I was antsy and I wasn't even in it!

But, then again, nobody else is Iron Mike Mervosh. No stage fright or pre-camera willies whatsoever. On the contrary, he was calm and deliberate to the extent that you would've sworn he was a veteran actor versus being a Marine veteran. Clarity suddenly dawned when I heard this voice in my head suggest I consider how a brief appearance on *Hawaii Five-O* might compare to landing on enemy held Roi-Namur or Iwo Jima?

In the end, this confident assurance of his Emmy Award-worthy acting potential would be definitively validated, for time would reveal that Iron Mike was not only right at home on the set, but believe it or not, that day he had an even better grip on the scene and delivery of his lines than did the actor with whom he was working. The title of that episode was *Bones of Contention*, and it remains in the good sergeant major's portfolio of out-freaking standing acting credits. The vivid recollection still brings on a laugh or head wag among those who hear me describe it. As for his small screen fame, the Five-O mission shines as but one twinkle in his eye. Just a day in the life of Iron Mike: TV star.

All good things, as they say, must come to an end and eventually, the day arrived that saw me trade my military service for another enlistment in an outfit with a slightly different mission. Iron Mike subsequently chose to secure his illustrious career about two years later. Though the Marines would ever be a proud, invaluably relevant and abiding presence in my life, once we moved on, Iron Mike and I didn't communicate for many years. He stayed active enough in his "retirement", so much so that I occasionally read about his speaking engagements and travels. It was nice to know he was alive and kicking and I harbored the ideation that someday, perhaps our paths would cross again.

For the next thirty years, I put my Marine Corps training and experience to proper and positive use in my new career as a law enforcement officer. When the passage of time brought the fruits of that calling to conclusion, I found myself affably retired at the rank of captain. Not unlike Iron Mike, retirement for me was short lived, and it wasn't long afterward that I became involved in yet one more challenge, this time as an educator to the next generation of public servants, now serving as high school juniors and seniors.

The curriculum consisted of law enforcement, firefighting and emergency medical courses with the daily format and protocols strongly geared to the paramilitary. Uniforms, inspections, command structure, academics, and heavy doses of discipline were the norm. It was not high school as I had ever known it, but right in the wheelhouse of any career police officer and especially one with USMC tattooed on his arm. It was during the run of this endeavor that fate decided the time had come for Iron Mike and I to reconnect.

It all began when I became acutely aware, and I might add, more than a little disturbed, by the realization that the majority of students had little or no concept of what men like Mike Mervosh had accomplished on *their* behalf, not to mention for the sake of the free world. None were cognizant of the reality that it took the bloody sacrifices of men like this Marine hero to afford today's technology-rich, history knowledge-poor young men and women the opportunity to sit in air conditioned classrooms and complain about the overwhelming volume of homework, via cellular phones and a hodgepodge of social media.

It was while reaping those benefits of freedom and privilege, which had literally been granted them, that the fourth estate-defined "Generation of Entitlement" was failing to recognize and appreciate the verity, that as of this juncture in their young lives, most had yet to render *any* sacrifice, satisfy *any* obligation, or facilitate *any* requirement for obtaining or maintaining the quality of their own state of being, or that of any other living soul.

The amassed lack of knowledge about World War II and its veterans was, to say the least, unsettling, and to say it more grandly, nothing short of *appalling*. The contemporary teenager's capacity to understand or morally quantify what men and women of the Greatest Generation had done to preserve their right to bitch and moan about the deficiencies and inadequacies of their limited existence had proven itself to be virtually nonexistent (minimal exception granted for watching *Saving Private Ryan*).

It is important for anyone reading my words to understand that they are not an indictment of today's youth, but rather a statement emphasizing the misguided priorities within our educational and social systems and to highlight the negative impact these omissions of ignorance are inflicting upon the moral, ethical and spiritual ideologies of our children.

Thus, the existence of this historical vacuum eventually inspired me to seek out the one person who in my estimation represented the greatest example of that period: Sergeant Major Iron Mike Mervosh. During the interim since we left the Marine Corps, I had randomly searched out his name on the Internet, taking note of whatever mention of him was documented online. He obviously continued to be very active and I watched with interest his comprehensive interview for C-Span, in which he talked about the Saipan and Iwo Jima campaigns. I also noted how fit he still looked for a man of his years.

The notion then came to me that Iron Mike should become the veteran with whom my students would identify in order to learn about and remember those patriots who came and went before them. Furthermore, I vowed that for as long as I was called to teach, these young men and women would not only know who Iron Mike Mervosh was, but that they would be taught to appreciate the meaning of his sacrifice, the worth of what he and others like him had attained by virtue of their courageous service.

Finally, I would require each member of every class to somehow, in some way, become personally interactive with Sergeant Major's persona on a daily basis. This was accomplished by utilizing standardized military protocols and patriotic practices within our training routine, such as the Pledge of Allegiance, participation in Veteran's Day events, and via the exchange of communication, written and otherwise, in expressing their personal perspectives to or appreciation for him.

It took awhile, but finally, through contacts with Leatherneck Magazine and another former Marine with whom I had the pleasure of serving at FMFPac, Lieutenant Colonel David Tomsky, I was able to secure a telephone number for Sergeant Major. I will admit to a smidgeon of apprehension as I dialed the phone: after all, forty years *is* a long time, but with each cycle of the ringtone that feeling was dispelled and soon replaced by a tincture of schmaltz.

When he answered, I immediately recognized his distinctive voice, still strong and clear. I told him who I was and where we had served together, surmising of course that his ability to individualize one Marine's identity from among the many thousands with whom he had served over such a vast span of time could test anyone's faculties, let alone those of a person with ninety-plus years of accrued memory to sort through.

But again, this was Iron Mike Mervosh, and God bless him, he was sharp as a tack and didn't miss a beat. His first question was direct and apropos; "How would I remember you?" Naturally, the prompt that made the most sense was to resurrect *Hawaii Five-O*, to which his animated response was, "Oh yeah, I remember that very well!"

Obviously, my next salvo had to be that I was the guy who drove him to the set from Camp Smith. Well, that nailed down the recognition factor and he shot back "OK, I've got you!" The confirmation tied up any potential lack of familiarity, even given the years, and from that point our conversation flowed freely. We talked about the roads we had travelled since Hawaii, our families, and whatever else came to mind. Eventually I told him of my intention to ensure that his story, and by vicarious association, the stories of untold numbers of World War II vets would always be a part of the educational criterion for my classes. I assured him that during my teaching tenure he would always have a special place in the hearts and minds of those young men and women who would comprise our current and future generations. To facilitate the process, my only request was a photograph that I could frame and post in the classroom, so that all who entered and particularly the students, would have an image to match up with the legacy.

He not only agreed to the photo, but his generosity in providing educational materials that became a veritable flood of memorabilia. Now books, literature, photographs, newspaper articles, magazines, and even a vial of black volcanic ash he brought back from his 2012 return to Iwo Jima, adorn the "Iron Mike Corner" of the Trumbull Career and Technical Center Public Safety classroom in Champion, Ohio. This is a place where neither Sergeant Major, nor any American veteran or their service will ever be taken for granted.

One interesting, and I might add effective, element we use for injecting the Iron Mike awareness factor into the daily thought process of our young people occurs at the close of every morning formation. Upon completion of their uniform inspection, both junior and senior cadets recite the Pledge of Allegiance, replete with the words "One nation, under God". Noteworthy is the fact that although no one is ever forced to articulate those last three syllables, the vast majority of students always do. Then an addendum of honor is attached to this staple of American patriotism as the focus turns to Sergeant Major. Every Cadet renders him a proper salute as they proclaim in unison: "God bless you Iron Mike, wherever you are!" This heartfelt tribute to the Marine these kids have come to know and respect as one of the greatest men of The Greatest Generation is something I look forward to every day, because with time the understanding in their voices and in their eyes becomes palpable. More importantly, the positive effect this circadian gesture continues to build in them has become part of their spiritual, moral and ethical DNA. In other words, *they're getting it,* they really are!

These future servants of the people have become so well indoctrinated into this ritual that for some, the desire for heartfelt expression transcends the limitations of the classroom. Take for example junior cadet and aspiring writer, Ms. Hope Weckerly: Hope was so moved by the story of Iron Mike that she wrote her own version of his biography, which was then published in the local newspaper. The result of her efforts meant that many area residents learned about Mike Mervosh. Hope herself went on to win worthy accolades for literary quality and excellence. Her work also succeeded in generating a higher degree of public interest in the Marine sergeant major that had inspired her. When he received a copy of her story, the ever-appreciative Iron Mike sent the young author his expressive written thank you along with an autograph. She, in turn, was so grateful and excited to receive the gift that she remarked in open class that, "she would never part with it" and, knowing her as I do, I am convinced she won't.

When Mike came to visit the Youngstown area in the summer of 2013, he toured our classroom, where the look of approval on his face pretty much said it all, as he perused our "Iron Mike Corner" for the first time. I only wish school had been in session so his kids could have met him in person—a detail to be resolved next time, for sure.

While Iron Mike was in town, the Marines of Tri-State Marine Corps League Detachment 494 held muster in his honor at Kenny K's, a local establishment where the food is road-house gourmet and a profound variety of spirituous liquids flow quite freely. It began routinely enough, but before anybody knew it, that evening morphed into a rerun of the Parris Island celebration of his life and times, with autographs, photographs and memorabilia abounding.

Once the festivities finally ended sometime around zero-dark thirty, Mike's Leatherneck rock-star self had provided the catalyst for old friends to acquaint with new, for Marine Corps League Detachment 494 to obtain a genuine, autographed Larry Smith work of literary art, and for Kenny K's staff to close the business day around an amply satiated cash register and a signed 8x10 glossy of their favorite Marine sergeant major. Oh yeah, lest I forget: for a company of happy, well-fed, and *ahem, well oiled* Marines, to return to their home ports of call and hit the sack dreaming of camaraderie and good times shared. Instances like this denote the positive energy Iron Mike just naturally infuses into such situations by virtue of his presence. Marines can't avoid the feeling that it would be an honor to share a foxhole with him. That's the way Marines are supposed to feel about their leaders and it reinforces the core belief that Iron Mike still holds this affinity for his troops. I appreciated it back in 1974 when he appeared at my wedding reception, and I still do today. He didn't have to come, but he did because he wanted to be there and because he *was* there, things were naturally better. That's just the way it was and still is.

My personal relationship with Iron Mike took on an added dimension during his recent visit when he, along with fellow 4th Division Marine Glenn Buzzard and Glenn's son Jeff, sat down for dinner with me, my wife Angie, and our two sons James and Christopher. I have to preface whatever else I'd say with the comment that Mike and Glenn together are a trip unto themselves. Another Greatest Generation veteran of the Roi-Namur through Iwo Jima campaigns, Glenn and Mike have been close friends since their World War II days. Glenn still lives in my hometown and their coming together over dinner that day proved to be a wonderful occasion. Just seeing these two longtime and loyal friends in each other's company made the day special. They had been through so much together and their tremendous mutual respect was clearly evident. The conversations were captivating, as we listened to animated accounts of fierce front line fighting and funny recounts of life in camp. Powerful first-person documentaries fed the imagination and left all of us who weren't around back then with greater insight into the era that was the last world war.

The spiritual essence which seemed to enfold all who were present that day was special, as if we were indeed all a family, long separated by time, distance and circumstance, reunited once more within the circle of true kinship. Marvelous too, was the feeling that intangibly played itself out as thought it was meant to be a lesson in the awareness of Divine Order. That lingering thought brings me full circle, back to Parris Island, back to the East Coast Drill Instructor Reunion and Iron Mike's enduring status as an icon of the Corps.

I must mention that after so many years, crossing the Depot causeway rekindled an absolute flood of emotion that continued as I drove past the old 1st Battalion barracks area, the parade deck and the Iwo Jima Memorial. Anyone doing likewise that day was conspicuously reminded of the sergeant major's presence symbolically by way of the "Iron Mike" statue and officially by means of the large marquis in front of the Depot Theater which proudly proclaimed in all caps: "WELCOME ABOARD SERGEANT MAJOR "IRON MIKE" MERVOSH".

Motoring out to the extreme end of the installation, past residential streets appropriately titled Tarawa, Guadalcanal and Peleliu, I made my way to the Traditions SNCO Club, located in a lovely setting along the banks of the Beaufort River. Inside, I found Iron Mike sharing a table with several friends, whom I would soon be exponentially blessed to call my own friends as well. For a time I couldn't get close enough to properly identify myself. I did manage to gain a sufficient degree of his attention to get in a, "Hello Sergeant Major," which he politely acknowledged, however, forty-plus years of my own physical mileage would prove to be an effective disguise and any attempt at a clarifying follow up was deftly precluded by yet another Marine.

Content to mark time pending the call of opportunity, I chose an empty seat at the bar, introduced my parched muzzle to its first cold draft brew and sat watching what I came to realize would be an ongoing pilgrimage of individuals desiring to share Mike's company. Eventually, I did manage to forge a shallow crossing in the stream of well-wishers, again made my presence known and this time managed to successfully secure a place at the table with Iron Mike and his companions.

Upon proper introduction, I came to know one of these beautiful people as the former *Parade Magazine* editor, accomplished author and adventurer Larry Smith and his very lovely wife, Dorothea. Joe Paulini, a Christian brother and highly gifted individual whose late uncle had served with Mike on Iwo Jima, and finally, Dominick Tutalo and his son, Danny. I could not have imagined what a pleasure it would be to spend the next few precious hours with these quality individuals.

Dominick was yet another Iwo Jima veteran (or as Mike prefers to define the battle's surviving participants: "Conquerors—we were *conquerors* . . . the Japs were the survivors!" It is with due respect that I digress for a moment to say that Dominick Tutalo impressed me as being one of the nicest, most decent, unassuming men you'd ever want to meet. However, listening to Iron Mike and later, Glenn Buzzard's vivid accounts of Dom's battlefield prowess with a flame thrower and demolition charges underscored the fascinating contrast of how drastically warfare can adapt the character traits of peace loving men to the facilitation of survival and victory in combat. Dom Tutalo's soft spoken and endearing humility was an admirable compliment to the tiger he was in battle.

The high regard in which Dom, Iron Mike and Glenn Buzzard still hold each other is very moving. These men share a deep and eternal bond, which can only be forged by mutually shared participation in such harrowing and horrid exploits as human combat to the death. To their credit, the sincerity, degree and longevity of their covenant are real, rare and admirable.

I didn't immediately grasp the life span of the phenomenon that evening, but time would soon confirm that Iron Mike seemed destined to be noticed, recognized, and socially advanced upon by a constant flow of his adoring fans for the next three days. The skirmish line of Marines continued to matriculate into his personal space, be it simply to listen to what he had to say, buy him a beer, chat a bit, or request an autograph. It continued for the remainder of our time at Parris Island.

The evening at Traditions concluded after adequate portions of interesting conversation and laughter. Our party had consumed our beverages of choice. Then answering the bugler's call to chow, this group of friends (now larger by one) proceeded past the distinctly spotlighted tribute to Iron Mike hanging on the wall leading into the SNCO Lounge. The large pictorial montage, aptly titled, *Sergeant Major Iron Mike Mervosh*, photographically chronicles his Marine Corps career. Exiting the club, our contingent then carpooled to the Dockside Restaurant in Port Royal for a fine seafood dinner.

Afterward, we returned to our accommodations in the VIP quarters (arrangements courtesy of Iron Mike—thank you, Sir) where ever more stimulating conversation, imbued with a nightcap and quality cigars, closed out the remainder of a splendid Parris Island social. I was billeted in the suite next to our gracious host, while the Smiths, Tutalos and Joe Paulini occupied quarters in the upper portion of the building.

At this point it should be said that quite often, that which occurs spontaneously in life could prove it the better of that which is scripted. This day was an excellent example, as it elicited for me a warm and personal cocktail of sentiment for both the people and the place. I didn't know I would meet my new companions when this excursion was planned, but I felt an immediate affinity and it again seemed as if I'd known them far longer. Not surprisingly, Iron Mike had once more provided the medium for the chemistry.

In the end, those seventy-two hours seemed to pass at light speed and on that last day, while perusing the sights and sounds as I drove my final lap around the Depot, I struggled to secure the substance within the barrage of melancholy and memory I'd found there. Among my many reflections were:

It was a vivid image of Iron Mike in his role of Honorary Parade Reviewing Officer. As was his custom, he fit that part to a tee. Decked out in quasi-formal attire and not without his favorite "Combat Veteran of 3 Wars" ball cap, he arrived by chauffeured military limousine to a warm, personal welcome by Parris Island's Chief-of-Staff and Depot Sergeant Major. (One note of precedent; the graduation ceremony later that day marked the first time in my life I'd ever seen a sergeant major saluted by a colonel).

There were many other veterans, as well as the large contingent of former drill instructors and family members of the recruit graduates who were in attendance at morning colors. At the parade deck and the graduation exercise I couldn't help imagining how well the magnificent spirit of American patriotism might be served if every American man, woman, and child were to attend a Marine Corps graduation ceremony during their lifetime. I pondered how the increased level of appreciation such an experience might generate for the enormous sacrifices of our veterans; especially if Iron Mike Mervosh were reprising the role he played that day.

The rock star treatment so righteously accorded Iron Mike, including during the DI Reunion picnic at Elliot's Beach, where he and author Larry Smith (*Iwo Jima, The Few and the Proud, Beyond Glory*) held a book signing.

The ongoing column of Marines who interacted with the sergeant major, purchasing books, engaging him in photo ops or requesting his autograph on everything from Larry's books to illustrations of the Iwo Jima flag raising, as well as T-shirts and DI Smokey- the-Bear campaign hats. They seemed to be genuinely inspired by Iron Mike's eagerness to preserve their remembrance of the moments they personally shared with him. I'm sure they did so for many reasons, not the least of which being the sake of posterity. But they all appeared to be keenly aware that in their presence was someone they, as Marines and Americans, wanted their children and grandchildren to recognize, applaud and contemplate. Some wanted these mementos, validated by Mike's own hand, to become heirlooms and affidavits, which they as parents and grandparents could employ as forward payment toward the legacy and virtue each item represented for future generations. It was a moving and respectful demonstration that I will always remember.

Through it all, Iron Mike proved to be as gracious and patient as you'd ever want him to be. These were his Marines and he loved being among them as he basked in their attention. While every Marine bought into the concept of esprit de corps, we all knew that on that day, the glory of that spirit had been made brighter and stronger by what Iron Mike brought to the table. If you knew and cared about him, you were proud and happy to see him enjoy it and to nod your head as endorsement of how richly he deserved every *"by damned"* second of it!

The culmination of both the Drill Instructor Reunion and the closing salute to Iron Mike, which came the final night in grand style at the formal dinner held in the Lyceum. I make no apologies for the redundancy of saying that throughout the event, his admirers continued to pass in review until inevitably, as it had for me some forty-two years ago, our last night on Parris Island came to an end. We returned to our quarters for a bit more conversation, one more toast and then all acquiesced to a good night's sleep. The next morning, heartfelt farewells and embraces consummated, a group of friends, separate courses charted, returned better served to their previous lives.

The last two people in each other's presence could only be Iron Mike and me. As we shook hands there was talk of future reunions and hometown visits. "Keep takin' that thirty-inch step," he said, as my assurances to do so were given. Then, with everything done that needed to be, I turned the polished brass handle and moved to the other side of the door.

I learned long ago that the only time we are guaranteed in this journey of life is the moment we find ourselves in. It's a philosophy to live by and it ensures that nothing or no one is ever taken for granted. It was not lost on me that every significant happening of this Parris Island safari was connected in some way to the remarkable Leatherneck standing in front of me. Looking back with a smile, I had to let him know; "Thank you Mike, you're a good man. God bless you, take care of yourself." Fittingly, my last words were Semper Fi, Marine," and "Semper Fi" he echoed. I said a little prayer as I closed the door behind me.

EPILOGUE

I felt proud and fortunate to be a United States Marine as my Parris Island homecoming concluded. Driving toward the main gate I set out to fulfill a little promise I'd made to myself. Passing the old barracks and parade deck for who knows, perhaps the last time ever, I turned left and traveled about a block or so. Parking and exiting the car, I walked down an empty street to the front of an official-looking red brick and glass building. A U.S. flag and the Marine Corps colors flanked the two large silver doors embossed with circular brass renditions of the Eagle, Globe and Anchor: This was the entrance to Recruit Receiving. It was Sunday morning, and not a soul was in sight. Standing alone in silence save for the wind, I felt a tightening sensation in my throat as I read the bold brass lettering above the doors: ***"Through these portals pass prospects for America's Finest fighting force—United States Marines".*** Tradition dictates that a man will pass through these doors but once. That tradition proved true for me and as I looked down the four long rows of yellow footprints, my mind's eye saw the bleak afternoon drizzle resolve itself into that dark and rainy night of March 25, 1971. Aligning my feet into the right front pair of prints, I executed a sharp facing movement toward the ever-waving American flag.

From deep inside arose the spirit of a kid filled with visions of island battles and dreams of dress blues, all the while proclaiming, "I *am* a United States Marine." Standing at attention now and rendering my best hand salute, that kid, and the Marine he became, fully understood that the very fabric of those visions, those dreams, and ultimately their reality that was woven from the character, courage and deeds of men like Sergeant Major Iron Mike Mervosh. It turned out to be the last thing I did on Parris Island, in the rain . . . *and I loved it!*

I have no qualm about stating that Iron Mike Mervosh *is* the United States Marine Corps, or the enlisted man's Chesty Puller, or a living paradigm of the Corps' doctrinal template. To say that he is as tough as they come and that he both understands and promotes the finest traditions and tenets of the Corps like few others, amounts to accurate and succinct verbiage in my book.

Still, for him and for the multitude of veterans whom he vicariously represents by virtue of his service and longevity, he *must* be defined, his exploits *demand* to be chronicled and his legacy *will* be remembered.

I never served with Iron Mike in battle, but I wish I had, for combat may well be the glowing forge of ultimate revelation when it comes to the analysis of a man's character. But even absent that component, I am confident in my belief that the Good Lord imparted me with an innate ability to discern certain qualities within those whose paths would cross my own. I also believe those virtuous qualities which The Creator places in Marines to be among the greatest and most valuable to the human species.

In that context, Iron Mike's position in Marine Corps history is sovereign. He *is* the archetype of an adept, well-trained and highly motivated combat operative, willing and able to physically close with, engage and destroy any enemy using skill, strength, strategy, courage and tactics. He *is* the ultimate patriot, willing to sacrifice life itself and one to whom the words "Semper Fidelis" represent a mantra of literal expression; the stated value of his existence.

Conversely, the civilian side of Mike Mervosh is a rare, intelligent and articulate man who has lived a long and celebrated life. A complex and private individual who often chooses to play his personal hand close to the vest. He is a man who clearly recognizes the importance and blessing of family and friends. One not ashamed to say how much he loves and looks forward to reuniting with his late wife, Margaret, or the degree to which he loves and values his daughter, Rosemary.

Mike's blue-collar philosophy of life is entrenched in his Christian faith, having been refined in the fires of deadly conflict, personal tragedy, and diverse life's experience. He stands as one for who honor, loyalty and integrity remain at the core of his being. He is a man whose passion in war emanates from his passion for peace and for life.

An excellent communicator with a memory sharper than a Marine KaBar, his ability to effectively yet uniquely express himself is an accepted staple of his personality. He speaks his mind when the situation requires and is far too comfortable with what he has to say about any subject to be offended when others disagree. His personal side can be prone to rather comedic outbursts of the brassy, unabashed sergeant major, as during one instance on Parris Island when he observed my privately cold hands stuffed inside my publicly visible pants pockets (a faux pas for a uniformed Marine). Accompanying the undeniable squint of a drill instructor came his inquiring indictment, "Hey, what's the matter, your hands cold?" The impromptu scolding drew an open laugh from me . . . immediately followed by the expeditious removal of my hands from my pockets.

During our times together I've never heard him utter gross profanity, only his trademark "By dammit" (Gail Chatfield's choice for her Mervosh-inspired book title *By Dammit, We're Marines*) or the socially acceptable four-letter description of the devil's eternal residence. He loves to use phrases like, "Keep on chargin'," or "Continue taking that thirty-inch step," and like Gail's fine book title, these and other idioms have come to be identified with vintage Iron Mike Mervosh.

He ranks in the top tier of blue-ribbon storytellers, with his vivid recollection of historic battles and specific events of his and other wartime adventures. His penchant for and accuracy of detail is nothing short of amazing. I could listen to him talk about his exploits ad nauseam, for he really is a remarkable treasure chest of encyclopedic yesteryear in human form. I've spoken of his proclivity as an ambassador for the Greatest Generation, but do be advised, he is not without a line of proverbial BS that has served him as well and for longer than his M1 Garand.

For those blessed with the intuitive understanding of social consequence, Iron Mike will ever maintain his flesh and blood presence in our midst, even as he continues his forward march into an even greater eternity. This warrior, ambassador and family man has overcome unimaginable adversity, while carving out his niche in the noble service of humankind and in doing so, has earned the right to become the image and resume's we, as Americans, love to love in our legendary figures.

It is only fitting then, that the concluding tribute of this perspective should reflect the most carefully considered thought. He is forthright, memorable, impassioned, and worthy of the legacy of both man and Marine. Having once written him a letter in which I characterized how warmly God might greet Iron Mike at his ultimate landing on the beaches of Heaven, I find myself inclined to reference that profoundly beautiful prospect as the staging point for these last few paragraphs.

The challenge lies in the reality that Iron Mike's life and times probably contain sufficient volume to fill a library with books. So much more of who he is exists in the vast archives of his extraordinary existence than can be justified by any one conglomeration of words. Therefore, I felt it appropriate that Mike's earthly epilogue should in no way depict an ending, but rather a symbolic, historically representative glimpse into the transcendent inauguration of one eternal Marine's crowning and perpetual glory.

Attaining proper mindset requires the reader to entertain an imaginative, ethereal vision of our Supreme Commandant who, while lavishing celestial praise and honor upon Iron Mike in recognition for his successful accomplishment of every earthly mission he was ever assigned, now prepares to decorate him with Heaven's ultimate commendation;

As He places the Heavenly Order of the Medal of Honor around Mike's neck, The Good Lord commands St. Peter to read these words of The Kingdom's Proclamation:

Whereas; In the course of a bloody and horrible earthly engagement of Good versus Evil known as the Battle of Iwo Jima,

Whereas; Michael D. Mervosh, platoon sergeant, United States Marine Corps, himself wounded during the battle, assumed command of Charlie Company, 24th Marines, 4th Marine Division,

Whereas; Michael D. Mervosh did so, due to every Marine officer and NCO his senior having been either killed or wounded in that epic battle,

Whereas; Michael D. Mervosh then proceeded to lead the men of Charlie Company through the remainder of this great conflict and on to victory, wherein the island of Iwo Jima was wrested from the Japanese Empire and declared secure,

Whereas; Michael D. Mervosh, no doubt worthy of the Medal of Honor for his heroic actions on Iwo Jima, was approached by his battalion Commander.

Whereas; Michael D. Mervosh was rendered a firm handshake by his battalion commander and in lieu of nomination to receive said Medal of Honor, was offered the words . . . "Suddenly, Almighty God stops Saint Peter before he can finish speaking."

The Good Lord turns and casts His loving eyes upon Iron Mike, as the enormous Gates of Pearl swing widely open. Our Heavenly Father's thunderous voice reverberates to the far corners of The Universe as He once again commends Mike for his magnificent life of service on Earth.

Then, in the presence of Saints, Souls and Angels, Almighty God Himself welcomes Iron Mike into his eternal glory with the words: ***"Well done Mervosh, well done indeed!"***

Chapter 15

STORIES ABOUT IRON MIKE

Iron Mike Mervosh has touched thousands of Marines in his lifetime, and many of them have written letters to him, or have written stories about him. This chapter is dedicated to sharing some of those stories and letters.

Sergeant Brett Dingerson, (USMC Veteran):

In October of 1971 I reported for duty at Camp H. M. Smith, Aeia, Hawaii with orders to replace a departing corporal on the four-man Marine Detachment assigned to CINCPAC (Commander in Charge Pacific) headquarters. CINCPAC himself was Admiral John S. McCain, Jr., a crusty veteran of submarine warfare in the Pacific.

We guarded his office from unauthorized personnel, escorted him on and off the base, carried classified information, and drove him around wherever he needed to go when his regular Navy driver "Boats" was off duty. Since Boats usually just worked during office hours it fell on the Marines to drive the Admiral to parties and social functions most evenings and on weekends. The junior Marine normally covered that duty so I got to interact with the admiral in a pretty relaxed atmosphere. He never knew my name, or the name of any Marine on the detachment, and for that matter, we were all "sergeants" to him. I wasn't about to correct him, as I was a corporal, so if he said that was my name then that's what I answered to.

The admiral loved his Marines and I don't remember any time he bitched at us for anything. Of course we were dedicated to being the best Marines possible due to the responsibility inherent with the post. But he would, and did, scare the shit out of any senior Marines he caught giving us a hard time: we were *his* Marines.

The commanding general of Fleet Marine Force Pacific, Lieutenant General Wilson, occupied the floor directly above Admiral McCain. General Wilson had been awarded the Medal of Honor for incredible bravery as a company commander on Guam. His sergeant major was a salty Marine named "Iron Mike" Mervosh, another legendary Marine who fought in the terrible battle of Iwo Jima and was awarded the Bronze Star for heroism. Iron Mike wasn't accustomed to a desk job so when he first arrived at his new post he liked to get away from his office and march around to inspect the Marine sentries, and the Marines on guard duty could expect a visit at any time. Once I happened to have the post at the Admiral's door and saw SgtMaj Iron Mike Mervosh coming down the passageway. The sergeant major came right up to me and started to examine my uniform and shoes. I instinctually snapped to attention even though this wasn't a formal inspection and I wasn't required to come to attention for an enlisted man. But this enlisted man was 'Iron Mike'.

My shoes were midnight-black spit-shined mirrors, my brass spotless, and my uniform was fresh from the dry cleaners that morning with creases still sharp enough to cut your fingers. Iron Mike's eyes slowly ascended up my body until he was looking me directly in the face—he wasn't smiling.

"Your mustache is too long, corporal. It covers up some of your lip. I want to see a better trim this time tomorrow, there's a lot of important people that come through here and you can't let your appearance slack one iota."

"Yes, Sergeant Major, I'll take care of it."

"Great, you look fine. How's everything going for you? Where are you from?" He was smiling now because he was a genuinely nice guy, a great marine, and like all Marine NCOs was concerned about everyone in his command. What happened next was totally unexpected and completely out of my control, but it was hilarious because he was about to meet Admiral McCain, and appearances can be deceiving.

The admiral's door opened and Sergeant Major Mervosh knew whose door it was, so he snapped to attention as Admiral McCain walked out into the hallway. We were only a few feet away and the admiral saw what he thought was somebody messing with one of *his* Marines, "Sergeant, are you giving one of my Marines a hard time?" he thundered, walking directly over to Iron Mike.

"No sir, just checking the sentries on duty sir."

"My Marines are the best Goddamn Marines in the whole Goddamn Marine Corps; they wouldn't be on my staff if they weren't."

"Yes sir, you have some fine Marines here and they are great representatives of the Corps."

I had to grit my teeth to keep from laughing; this was some cool shit to see the admiral come to my defense, even though I didn't really need it. Everyone who knew him idolized Mike Mervosh; I'd shave my 'stache' with a K-bar if he asked me to.

"All-right Sergeant, give my regards to General Wilson." With that comment McCain stuffed his cigar back into his mouth and walked away to attend to his original errand. Iron Mike looked at me as he turned to go and smiled when I silently mouthed the word, "Sorry".

"Don't worry about it," he whispered, "after Iwo Jima a little bitching doesn't bother me. Trim that mustache, got it?"

"As soon as I get off duty."

SSgt Gregg Stoner, Veteran Marine, author of this book:

I am a docent for the MCRD Command Museum and one of our display galleries features World War II. In that gallery we have two large displays of Iwo Jima showing the beach landings with Mount Suribachi in the background. Recruits are brought into the museum on their training day-56 and docents are assigned to take two squads each through museum and give twenty-minute talks in each gallery bringing the Marine history alive in the process. I thought it would be great to have SgtMaj Iron Mike Mervosh come the museum and station him by the Iwo Jima displays and then have him talk to the different squads as they came through. He was absolutely great with the recruits—his command presence was outstanding, and he completely mesmerized them with his stories of his thirty-six days on the island of Iwo Jima. The recruits couldn't believe their eyes that they were in front of a real-life hero of that epic battle.

When we were done with the recruit visits I gave the sergeant major a brief tour of the museum, as it had recently been changed since his last visit. One of our new galleries is called "Forward Deploy" and it features all Marine Corp activities since the Vietnam War. One of the first displays in that gallery is a U.S. flag that had flown in Iraq and was signed by the men of a company to commemorate the names of several Marines that had died in a battle there. Iron Mike saw that flag hanging on the wall with all the signatures and he went ballistic over the flag being "desecrated". He demanded to know who was in charge of the museum, as he wanted to have the flag immediately removed and burned. I was actually a little concerned about his health because he was so incensed and worked up. I walked him down to the Museum Director, Barbara McCurtis, and he immediately made a demand that the flag be removed from the wall and burned. She tried to calm him down by explaining that she could not destroy the flag, as it was a donation to the museum, but Iron Mike was having no part of her explanation. He demanded to know who had donated it, and when told it was another sergeant major he was inflamed even more. I had to walk him out to his car, and he was fuming the entire time. I was actually a little afraid he might have a stroke or maybe even a heart attack because he was so worked up. I checked with him after he got home just to make sure he was okay. I figured he would eventually get over it.

On a recent visit to his house to continue interviewing him about this book he brought the matter of that flag up again, asking me if it had been taken down yet. I had to tell him it was still on the wall, and he got worked up all over again. He told me that he would tear it off the wall if it were still up the next time he visited the museum and then would burn the flag himself. I have no doubt that Iron Mike would do that—his passion about the American flag is immense, and to be honest, I would not stop him if he followed through.

Iron Mike's feelings about the American flag are immeasurable. He told me of his ire about the Iwo Jima Monument at Camp Pendleton because it flies a fifty-star flag. He insists that the Iwo Jima Monument should always fly a forty-eight star flag to be correct. He didn't just complain about it either—on a recent visit to his home he proudly showed me a forty-eight star flag that had just been delivered to his house, and he could not wait to get to Camp Pendleton to switch it with the fifty-star flag on the monument. To me that is the epitome what being a true American is about.

SSgt Gregg Stoner, Veteran Marine, author of this book. More insights:

This book came about in an unusual way—Iron Mike and I ran into each other at a Tuns Tavern Tea event at the MCRD Command Museum a few years ago. We were standing in a short line to get some appetizers and he commented to me that he had seen my book

Ooorah about SgtMaj Bill "Ooorah" Paxton and he asked if maybe we could get together and do a book about his past. I told him I was interested and I gave him my card and then I asked him to call me to set up an interview. I wasn't sure if he was just doing "small talk" with me, as that often happens at these types of occasions. But to my surprise and pleasure he did call me a couple of weeks later and we agreed to meet at the Bay View Restaurant at MCRD San Diego—the book was on!

Over lunch at the Bay View Restaurant in San Diego we began our first interview. I took copious notes. This meeting gave me some insight as to how to approach this book. I realized how his participation in World War II was a key aspect of his story.

Our second interview was at the Iron Mike Room at the Camp Pendleton Staff NCO Club and while there I took a lot of photos of the really neat museum that was specifically built to house his prized memorabilia. We were to meet there for a third meeting, but somehow our wires got crossed on the dates and after I first went to the Iron Mike Room at Camp Pendleton's Staff NCO Club, I ended up going to his home in Oceanside a few miles to the east. He lives very close to Mission San Luis Rey and it was a pleasurable drive to his home. I arrived and immediately noticed an American flag flying proudly from the side of his house—I pictured Iron Mike putting the flag up each morning and then standing back to give it a proper salute. His yard was well manicured and it showed pride of ownership. I somehow wasn't surprised to find the interior of his home to be fit for an inspection—it was spotless and everything was in its proper place.

Iron Mike took me to his den—wow, what a den! It was more like a museum and it had shelving on all the major walls that didn't have a window, and every square inch was filled with his Marine Corps memorabilia. He had hundreds of photos on the walls and many were of him with some very important people—President Gerald Ford for one. He later took me to his garage and on the walls was a lot more of his posters, photos, and other Marine Corps memorabilia. His whole house is a treasure chest!

Iron Mike was always prepared for our interviews. He would often have pages and pages of hand written notes that he had written just for the interview. His notes told of the many stories that made up his fascinating history. He also had letters from many individuals that gave additional insight about him. It became obvious to me from the onset that he was most proud of his time with the Fourth Marine Division fighting the most epic battles of the final days of World War II with Japan. I am still in awe of his memory recall of those hard-fought battles. I never had to press him for details—he showered them each time he told a story. I often found myself caught up listening to the stories like a child listens to his grandfather telling stories—I had to remind myself to take notes and memorialize the stories for this book.

For me personally, this book has given me an invaluable insight into one of the Marine Corps' icons of the modern times. I was given an incredible opportunity to sit with this legend and get to know him very well. The way he describes the events that happened on Iwo Jima and other islands he was on made me feel like I was there with him. I could smell the sulfurous odor he described from Iwo Jima, and I could feel the thundered sound of artillery hitting the ground. I could picture the many Marines lying dead on the beach and those that were horrifically wounded by the explosions and screaming in pain. It was very powerful to sit with Iron Mike and relive his life's experiences. I am eternally grateful to him for sharing his life with me.

Gene Fioretti PLLC, Chemical Engineer, B.S., M.S.:

'Iron Mike' is one tough marine, even at his age. I met him at a WWII conference at the National Museum in New Orleans. He was a guest speaker at the opening ceremony, representing the Marine Corps. On stage each of the service branches had a vet, but none grabbed the audience like Iron Mike did. When he stood up, erect, chest out, and chin in, he spoke about big issues like duty, honor, and country. It was impressive. He voice was strong and convincing.

Later that afternoon, there was a beer & sausage tent out in the parking lot. I approached him and thanked him for the great talk and his long storied service to the Corps and country. While eating, he made a comment that he wished he had a good dark beer and some chew. I immediately went into action and found a convenience store nearby and delivered both. We've been friends ever since. I visited Iron Mike in San Diego and got to see his personal collection of memorabilia, which is quite impressive. He knew that I liked to collect WWII stuff and I was dumbfounded when he went into his closet and handed me a B-2 unit ration pack. The only catch was that he made me promise not to open it up. The beef slices and potatoes might not be edible after seventy years! Mike has also given me a small amount of sand from Iwo Jima. Both of these items as well as the autographed pictures are very special.

I write just for fun and a short story about Iron Mike is in my plans. Recently, I had planned go down to see him and attend the 68th anniversary of Iwo Jima ceremonies, but I tore my Achilles tendon, so the trip was cancelled. I try to routinely call him. Anyway, here is one that I think reflects the character of the man:

At the onset of Desert Storm, Mike talked and talked to his wife about volunteering to go active again. He epitomized the concept of 'once a Marine, always a Marine'. He must have pestered his wife until she relented and told him to go ahead and volunteer. I don't have a copy of that letter, but I am sending you the response letter from the Defense Department. If you could secure Mike's letter, I think it would be an interesting story. That's what I hoped to write about.

Mike is certainly opinionated, and he has every right to be. When you spend a major portion of your life in a career where people are trying to kill you, a few slings and arrows from civilians who think he may be a dated dinosaur are not going to bother him in the slightest. Case in point: on my last visit, Mike was proud of his one-of-a-kind Iwo Jima cap. It seems that the original inscription had read: Iwo Jima *Survivor*. To that Mike responded, "I'm no survivor, I'm a *conqueror!*" He sent the cap back to his benefactors and told them such. They in turn, redid it to Mike's specification.

During our phone conversations, he told me about the bronze head of Sadam Hussein that was brought back stateside by the 1st Marine Division. According to Mike it was displayed somewhere in the Marine's Hall of Honor Room in the Mike Mervosh Lounge at Camp Pendleton's Staff NCO Club. Mike didn't think much of Sadam or the idea of dishonoring the distinguished Marines honored there, him being one. He told the brass such, and according to Mike: "Get that thing the hell out of here!" They did.

I once asked him about his R&R experiences. He said after Iwo, he had five days in Hawaii. Marines are "men's men", and I would be interested in knowing some of the details of those five days. When you don't know if the next day will be your last, some of the normal civilian constraints must have be ignored. That would be an interesting story.

Mike's Korea experience might have been more painful than WWII. If I am not mistaken, his brother was killed in Korea.

Please give my regards to Mike. I miss him. You would really be in good standing if, when you visit, take him a six-pack of good dark beer and a pouch of Mail Pouch chewing tobacco.

Captain Ed Garr, USMC Retired:

'Iron Mike' was my Company Gunnery Sergeant as a Tech Sergeant (E-6) in 'C' Company 1st Battalion, 6th Marines from October 1950 to late December 1950 at Camp Lejeune North Carolina. I was a PFC (private first class) just out of boot camp, and was assigned to a machine gun platoon as an ammo carrier. I was not quite eighteen-years old.

I cringed every time Gunny Mervosh came into the squad bay and bellowed orders to fall out or stand by for a junk-on-the-bunk inspection, or to field day the squad bay. He really scared the crap out of me and I tried every way possible to avoid contact with him.

I was never allowed to go on liberty because the duty NCO always told me that the Company Gunny would not allow me to have a liberty card until I got squared away! One time, while on the rifle range at Camp Lejeune, some other Marines and myself went out the back gate at Sneads Ferry. I still didn't have a liberty card or even a military ID card. I believe I used someone else's. We went to a bootleggers place and bought some moonshine and got drunk as hell (I was only seventeen at the time). The gunny found out and chewed my ass out big time about getting drunk and leaving without an ID or liberty card. He said as long as I was in his company I would never get a card.

Many of us got orders in December 1950 to go to Korea and we were granted leave prior to departure. We still had no ID or liberty cards, but we were issued approved leave papers.

When I returned from leave we drew cold weather gear and were told that Iron Mike was not going with us. I was a little surprised and felt somewhat dejected that he was not going to war with us kid PFC's.

The years flew by and I often read or heard some scuttlebutt about Mike Mervosh. I thought he was one hell of a Marine. I later became the Company Gunnery Sergeant of 'H' Company, 2nd Battalion, 4th

Marine Regiment in Hawaii/Vietnam from 1963-1966. I employed the same tactics with the troops as he did. I restricted some troops to extra duty, no liberty, and at times used knuckle drill by squad leaders and platoon sergeants the same way Iron Mike did or would do.

I got commissioned in 1966 after sixteen years of enlisted duty and became the Company Commander of 'B' Company, 1st Battalion, 8th Marine Regiment as a 2nd Lieutenant (2nd Lt) and I always turned a blind eye when the Company Gunny would hang over after working hours. Sorry to it say it was not the same as my tactics or Iron Mike's. The Corps was changing.

It was not until on or about early 2003 that I went to a 1st Marine Division's birthday anniversary at the South Mesa SNCO Club at Camp Pendleton, California, when I noticed Iron Mike in the crowd. We made eye contact, and after fifty-some years we were reunited. I told him that I never got a liberty card or ID card until March 1952 when I returned from Korea. He laughed and told me that he had a purpose for doing that and he didn't want a young Marine like myself to go out in town and get in trouble—he was right.

Mike Mervosh made a lasting impression on me throughout my Marine Corps career and I will never forget him. They need to break out the mold of a SgtMaj Mervosh to bring sanity back to the Corps at this time.

If you can please furnish me some information on yourself and books you have written.

My best to Iron Mike and all he and I stand for.

Semper Fi,
Ed Garr Captain USMC (Ret)

SgtMaj Robert S. Ynacay, USMC (Retired):

Around 1974, I attended a three or four-day seminar at the University of Maryland, as a representative of the 1st Marine Division. I went with four sergeants major, and 'Iron Mike' Mervosh, the Pacific Fleet Sergeant Major, to discuss the drug problems in the Corps. There were less then ten field grade officers, including Frank Peterson, the pilot who was just selected to Colonel. A civilian expert monitored the class, and the class included Marines who had been kicked out of the Corps because of drug problems.

I remember one sergeant who was claiming his buddies in Hawaii were well organized and still holding pot parties right on the base and under the nose of the leadership. Iron Mike asked who these Marines were, but the sergeant would not say. After several questions, and not getting an answer, Iron Mike lunged across the table to grab this sergeant. Two other sergeants major had to hold him back. The civilian lost his cool. All of the Marines felt a lot pride over this action. It scared the hell out of the sergeant being questioned. Iron Mike was not about to let that Marine make a mockery of the Marine Corps and our group—he was a man of action.

In the lobby that evening, some of the college students tuned in *Hawaii Five-O* on the television. They could not believe Iron Mike was also a television star amongst their group.

Another tale of mine is about his cigar. We were out exercising and running around the track. I was huffing and puffing after a couple of miles. I looked up and here comes this guy—SgtMaj Iron Mike Mervosh, running with a *cigar* in his mouth. I still tell people about incident.

I know him and he knows me, but it is still, "Hello Marine", or "Hello Sgt Major", but never "Hello Bob." I have mimicked some of his traits while on duty. I have looked up to this guy for many years.

Your friend, SgtMaj Robert S. Ynacay

Sergeant William 'Guns' Friedlander (Veteran):

I am Bill Friedlander, veteran USMC sergeant, with active and reserve duty from 1964-1970. It is an honor to be able to make a comment or two regarding "Iron Mike".

The heart of the Marine Corps, especially in combat, is the NCO and SNCO.

Only certain special people can be efficient and set the bar, the example, and possess the leadership qualities required to lead combat Marines to win, to train and teach them, to lead by example, and to mold them into a fine fighting winning team. SgtMaj Mike Mervosh is such a man. He was a three-war Marine. He is one of those Marines who set the example, the bar, and the high standards for new generations of Marines to meet and to exceed.

While attending the Drill Instructor (DI) reunion at Marine Corps Recruit Training Depot, San Diego (MCRDSD) a few years back, "Iron Mike", along with retired 1stSgt John Anderson (awarded the Navy Cross for heroism in combat in Viet Nam), and I, visited the DI's Quarters adjacent to the 'grinder' (parade deck). Mike's dress uniform was on display in the vestibule of the building and we stopped to view and comment on the display. The duty 'fire-watch' nonchalantly challenged us, asking who were and what we were doing there. He obviously did not recognize or know whom either 'Iron Mike' or John was. Mike, with his subtle smile and dignified way, and with no sign of annoyance or being disturbed by lack of recognition, answered the young Marine saying, "I'm looking at my uniform, Marine." I then introduced both 'Iron Mike' and John Anderson to the fire-watch and then watched his startled and surprised reaction as his mouth dropped. He was unable to say anything. Mike once again had exhibited his quiet and dignified manner when dealing with junior troops and with people in general.

During this reunion, retired Marine R. Lee Ermey was a guest and together he and Mike held everyone in awe with their respectful and tasteful stories of the "old breed" at poolside late into the night. The younger Marines soaked up Mike's stories and knowledge and experience: the words of wisdom if you will. There were no highhanded mannerisms or talking down to people. All held him in awe and great respect.

He was acknowledged by the naming of the 'Iron Mike' Room at the SNCO Club at Marine Corps Base, Camp Pendleton. Part of his collection of souvenirs from his years of service and deployments decorate the room.

Mike is a warm, friendly, and extremely personable individual who is fun to be around. With perfect typecasting on a TV episode of *Hawaii Five-O* he played the part of an old sergeant major excellently and without a written script—he was just being himself.

He enjoys an occasional room temperature beer with a Dutch Masters cigar. He is a leader and a hero, although he will never label himself as such. He is a man to be emulated.

I am very lucky to be considered a friend and would follow him anywhere, anytime, under any conditions. And. as he says, "Continue To March!"

Ooorah Sergeant Major!

Respectfully,
William 'Guns' Friedlander

Joe Paulini, civilian: *Author note: Joe Paulini wrote this directly to Iron Mike Mervosh in first-person manner.*

My name is Joe Paulini, Sil Paulini's nephew. At the request of my father I have enclosed a transcript of an interview of Larry Smith, author of the book *The Few and the Proud: Marine Corps Drill Instructors in Their Own Words*. Dad thought you might get a kick out of it. I came across the interview while looking you up on the Internet. I became curious right after seeing the movie *Flags of our Fathers*. At the end of the interview Smith comments to the interviewer about who in his book he felt encompassed the Marine Spirit—I think you can guess who that may be.

As a young man I worked for a number of years for Uncle Sil, and many days when it was just Sil and I working alone he would often talk about the Marine Corps and inevitably your name would come up. Although he was proud of the fact that he fought on Iwo Jima, he only talked in vague generalities about how difficult it had been. He would usually then shift the conversation to you and talk about what an amazing guy you were. How proud he was when he would tell me (and quite frankly, anyone else) that you and he were friends.

I wished I had understood a little better then what you, he, and other men that assaulted Iwo Jima had been through. When I finished reading the book *Flags of our Fathers* I realized that I never thanked him for his service and sacrifice. But I do know that I can thank you—and I do from the bottom of my heart. Thank you for the service, sacrifice, and leadership you gave to our country. I hope that one day I have the opportunity to meet you, look you in the eye, and shake your hand to thank you personally. That would be a great honor for me.

One final note: over the Thanksgiving holiday I went to Quantico to see the new Marine Corps Museum. It is a wonderful place and does the Corps proud. I don't know if you have visited it yet, but if you decide to go, please let me extend to you a standing invitation to stay as a guest in our home and allow me the honor to take you there for a visit. We have a lot of room in our home and would love to have you as our guest. I am sure we could arrange for my dad to visit at the same time if you like, as he has not seen the museum yet.

From my family to you, we wish you a very happy holiday season and a healthy and prosperous New Year. May God bless you.

Enclosure: Except from Larry Smith (author of *The Few and the Proud):*

"Lopez (Interviewer): If we could know only one story from your book, is there one that encompasses them all?"

"Larry Smith: Iron Mike Mervosh, whose story is told in Chapter 2, was one of thirty-one men left out of a company of two hundred forty to walk off Iwo Jima under their own power after the battle had ended. He also fought in Korea and Vietnam. He retired after thirty-five years, then tried to come back to fight in the Gulf War. He served two tours as a drill instructor. At Parris Island today, they have this brutal exercise run called 'The Iron Mike'; at Camp Pendleton in California the 'Iron Mike Room' is dedicated to him at the Staff NCO Club. His parting words invariably are: "Keep charging!"

Sincerely, Joe Paulini

Author note: *It is not every day that I get a call from a Mayor of a city, but one Sunday I got a call from Mayor Jim Wood, Mayor of Oceanside, California. He had heard that I was looking for stories about Iron Mike and he wanted to know how to send me a couple of things he had. I could tell by his enthusiasm that he was a true fan of Iron Mike Mervosh. Below are two things he sent me:*

Proclamation from Jim Wood, Mayor of the City of Oceanside, California:

WHEREAS, Sergeant Major 'Iron Mike' Mervosh was born in Pittsburgh, Pennsylvania in 1923; and

WHEREAS, Sergeant Major Mervosh graduated from South High School in 1942; and

WHEREAS, Sergeant Major Mervosh began his career with the United States Marine Corps after enlisting in the Corps in 1942; and

WHEREAS, Sergeant Major Mervosh was one of the first Marines to then help form the Fourth Marine Division at Camp Pendleton, California; and

WHEREAS, Sergeant Major Mervosh was awarded two Purple Hearts for wounds sustained to his legs and stomach received on Iwo Jima during World War II; and

WHEREAS, Sergeant Major Mervosh served in five different Marine divisions prior to being sent to fight in the Korean War; and

WHEREAS, Sergeant Major Mervosh served in the Korean War with 'G' Company, 3rd Battalion, 5th Marine Regiment; and

WHEREAS, throughout the military career and retirement years of Sergeant Major Mervosh, his love of the United States Marine Corps, his nation, and his dedication to the principles of protecting individuals around the world from tyranny has never waivered.

NOW, THEREFORE, BE IT RESOLVED, that I, Jim Wood, Mayor of the City of Oceanside, California do herby proclaim **May 27, 2013 as Sergeant Major 'Iron Mike' Mervosh Day** in the City of Oceanside, and I do further wish to honor Sergeant Major Mervosh for his heroism and dedication to our nation.

Issued this 27th day of May, 2013

Jim Wood, Mayor

Jim Wood, Mayor of the City of Oceanside:

As Mayor of Oceanside I have had many encounters with Iron Mike Mervosh over the years. I never served in the military with him, but he is the type of man that always is out in front of the others. He is often asked to speak at numerous events, and his stories are something that rivets the audiences. Iron Mike is someone that you just have to admire—at the age of ninety years old he still talks about wanting to get back into the war because he feels he can still contribute! Iron Mike Mervosh is an outstanding citizen and is admired by everyone he encounters.

Barbara Hansen Harris:

I was so happy to receive your letter about writing a book about my favorite, and most respected, Marine-of-all-time.

One of my favorite memories of Iron Mike was at the 17 – 20 February 2005 Combat Veteran reunion of Iwo Jima's sixtieth anniversary at the Hilton McLean at Tyson's Corner in McLean, Virginia. Following the banquet and grand ball Iron Mike gave a private party in his room. Among the guests were Jean Fodem, Susan McConaughy who was I travelling with, and myself. He had his door wide open having no concern that he was serving alcohol and smoking a large cigar with 'no smoking' signs posted clearly throughout the hotel. We were all having a nice time and we had all joined him with drinking a beer. A hotel security person came to his door and said there was no smoking allowed in the room. Iron Mike said, "So what are you going to do—arrest me?" Iron Mike then completely ignored the security officer and that was the end of it.

For many years my father Bob Hansen, who was also an Iwo Jima veteran 1st Lieutenant, was on the reunion committee at Camp Pendleton, and was often their president. Iron Mike was a tremendous help to him, and when he was Master of Ceremonies he would dress up in his full uniform, and often was the guest speaker. He usually sat at our table at the banquet. My parents and all of my family very well respect iron Mike Mervosh.

I remember Iron Mike saying that the hat the Iwo Jima veterans wear is incorrect: they say, "Iwo Jima *Survivor*". To Iron Mike the "Japanese were the survivors—***we*** were the *'conquerors'*! Our hats should say "Iwo Jima Conqueror". He had one made for our very good friend Jim Blane, an Iwo Jima veteran from the 4th Marine Division.

Ray Dooley earned a Silver Star on Iwo Jima and he used to sell hand-made bolo ties at the 5th Marine Division reunions until he came down with Parkinson's. At that time I bought the remainder of the bolos. He told me to be sure to only give them to very special people, and of course I gave one to Iron Mike. He always wore it to Marine functions.

I have been very involved with my father's Iwo Jima reunions since 1965, and I have attended most of them. I now hold the title "Publicity Manager" of the 3rd, 4th, and 5th Marine Iwo Jima reunions at Camp Pendleton.

When I started working with Timothy Davis and Kim Blane with the Greatest Generation program I submitted Iron Mike's name to be considered for a free trip to Iwo Jima. I kept calling and emailing, and then in March 2012 Iron Mike got his free trip to Iwo Jima, Guam, Saipan, Tinian, and Hawaii. I have a photo of Iron Mike and Jim Blane on this trip both wearing their bolos I gave them, a have also enclosed the hand written thank you not I received form Iron Mike.

Susan McConaughy and I really wanted to go with him to Iwo Jima, but I am a registered nurse and Susan is a certified nurse midwife and we could not get time off from work. Iron Mike said he wanted to show us things he blew up, and he would also be very interested in having the sand on the Iwo Jima beaches analyzed for DNA—he said it had to be covered with blood from Japanese and American men. He also said, "That reminds me: I don't remember going to the bathroom on Iwo Jima. We probably just s@#t in our pants. Yes, that is probably what we did!"

There are so many Iron Mike stories, and the best ones no doubt have to do with his museum in the Iron Mike's Room at Camp Pendleton's Staff NCO Club.

Semper Fi,
Barbara Hansen Harris, his friend

Jim Blane, Veteran Marine of the 4th Marine Division:

I am pleased to know that you are doing a biography of my good friend and shipmate Marine, Iron Mike Mervosh. Barb Harris sent me a copy of her contribution, which I can use in doing my part to assist you. Iron Mike is a 'Marine's Marine', so it's not difficult to do it from the heart and with pride that I was even privileged to get to know him.

It was through Barb Harris and her help that we were fortunate to get him included in our Greatest Generation's Foundation trip to Guam, Saipan, Tinian, and Iwo Jima where we both were part of the invasion and conquest of the latter three islands, which were critical to the so-called "island hopping campaign" that included our Fourth Marine Division.

As parts of my contribution please utilize the film that was made from our tour titled "Eight Square Miles". You may have already seen it. Our CBS affiliate station in Denver made the film. You will see Iron Mike in several scenes, and some of them with me included.

Mike and I shared some great memories together during this visit even though we didn't know each other during the war. Of all the horrors of war, one in particular seems to keep me awake many nights: it was the attempt by the enemy to kill off what was left of the native Chamorro natives on Saipan at the location now called "Suicide Cliff". Mothers and their babies were forced to jump to their deaths into the pounding surf hundreds of feet below. We were helpless for the most part: our PA system was used to save some of them, but several hundred were lost. Mike and I stood together and stared at those cliffs in silence for several minutes, and I am sure he was seeing in his mind the same scene I was.

Most of our time together on this tour were happy and fun being together with others including some of the Navy guys who took us ashore and brought us back when it was over. Mike was our star and leader, and all of us old vets enjoyed being around him. He drew a crowd no matter where we were.

I look forward to reading the book when it is published.

Semper Fi,
Jim Blane

Paul W. Siverson, SgtMaj USMC (Retired):

I first met SgtMaj 'Iron Mike' Mervosh in 1993 when I was the sergeant major of 9th Communication Battalion, 1st SRIG, at Camp Pendleton, California. I had never met him before, but had heard a lot about him. I was looking for a guest of honor for our Battalion Birthday Ball and I decided to get in contact with him. After just a short while on the phone with him I got this feeling that I was talking to a legend just from the sound of his voice. I explained that our ball was going to be held in Laughlin, Nevada, and provide him all the details. As expected, he already had a busy schedule, as he was in high demand. He accepted my invitation and we arranged a meeting. Since he lived just outside the back gate of Camp Pendleton I went and visited him at his house. Iron Mike and his wife Maggie met me at the door and invited me inside. Iron Mike took me into his "Iron Mike Room", as he likes to call it, and we talked for a while. I must have seemed like I was not interested, as my eyes were wandering around the room the entire time. I kept thinking to myself what a living legend he is, and he is a grand piece of history.

Needless to say, Iron Mike was a big hit at our birthday ball, especially with the young junior Marines, but he left a lasting impression on everyone who attended. No one I have ever known could hold your attention for such a long period of time as he spoke to all of us. After that birthday ball I knew I had met one of the most admired and colorful Marines of my time. It was the beginning of a long friendship.

In 1995 I was transferred to Marine Corps Security Force Company, Bangor, Washington. I am not exactly sure whether it was 1995 or 1996, but once again I was looking for a guest of honor for our birthday ball and again I immediately thought of SgtMaj Mervosh. I called him and he accepted my invitation to attend. This was a most memorable birthday ball for me. As he started to speak every eye was intensely on him, listening to every word he said. The highlight of his remarks came as he lit up a big stogie—keep in mind that this was inside the all-ranks club that was a no smoking area. Nobody said a word to him as he continued. I was personally getting a lot of enjoyment watching all of this. Seated at the head table along with myself and my CO was a Navy captain who was the Commanding Officer of Sub Base Bangor, and also a rear admiral who was the Commander of the Submarine Force. Iron Mike gave his usual well-received remarks and was looking out over the audience. Every eye in the audience was intently fixed on Iron Mike, listening to every word spoken. He was holding his lit stogie in his hand, and I remember exactly what he did next: he said, "And remember: if we (the Corps) ever lose our customs and traditions we will become just another branch of the military like the Navy." He then took a long puff on the cigar, looked in the direction of the admiral and captain and then blew a big puff of smoke in their direction. The audience went wild when he did that, and the young Marines hollered "Ooorah" as loud as they could. Once again, Iron Mike was a hero to all, and he made a lasting impression on everyone. My Marines and sailors that attended that birthday ball got a real treat. I think everyone who attended had their picture taken with Iron Mike and they all asked to have their programs signed by him.

In 2001, while I was in San Diego at a USO conference, I made a visit to him. It was a most enjoyable visit. I have remained in contact with SgtMaj Mervosh over the years, but probably not as much as I should. SgtMaj 'Iron Mike' Mervosh is one of those Marines you never forget, and every Marine today should have the honor of meeting and talking with him.

Kevin Leahy, LtCol USMC (Retired):

I didn't have the pleasure of meeting Iron Mike Mervosh until 1999, the year I returned to Camp Pendleton from my dreaded

HQMC (Headquarters Marine Corps) tour. He was already a Marine of legend, and was long retired at that point. His achievements were the stuff of Marine Corps lore.

What a great man—even though Iron Mike was pressing eighty-years of age at the time he could work a crowd of Marines. He didn't just tell sea stories, but with motivation with what each of those Marines was up to at the time. He'd been in almost all of their positions, just decades apart. They were the students on the knee of the teacher.

This is a small point, but Mike likes a couple of Rolling Rocks when he visits. He doesn't like them ice-cold—something between refer temp and room temp. When other Marines are around I never remember that he ever had to buy one.

In 2012 my wife Lyn and I had the pleasure of hosting SgtMaj Mervosh and his wonderful daughter at the Marine Corps Ball. He was the life of the table, and a delight to all the Marines present.

I also remember him coming to the Cigar Socials that were held on the patio of the Staff Non-Commissioned Officer Club at Camp Pendleton. Those socials were always held on Monday evenings, and the cuisine was usually Mongolian barbeque. Marines and veterans would crowd about Mike and listen to his stories. A favorite memory of mine was when Iron Mike was sitting with SgtMaj Val Valentine, a retired Marine and a fellow Iwo Jima veteran. They were enjoying a nice cigar and just chatting about things. Soon the teasing started: I learned that Val was on a later amphibious wave than Mike at Iwo Jima. Iron Mike had a good time teasing Val about that, saying, "I thought I would have to get all the Japs myself before you ever got here." Val noted that he had seen the raising of the flag on Mount Suribachi. Asking Mike if he had seen it Iron Mike replied that he was otherwise occupied: "fighting and killing the enemy!"

One fond memory of mine about Mike is that I never recall Mike really cussing. What a tribute to his gentlemanly manner, especially since there were usually ladies present, but also to his calming ways that no doubt comes with the years. In fact, I think Iron Mike was always that kind of Marine who could always get the point across without cursing or profanity. There is a lesson to be learned there.

SgtMaj Michael Mervosh is a great friend. A Marine's Marine. He's an unvarnished, a straight-up kind of guy. I don't know in what part of western Pennsylvania Mike's mold is sitting, but if I were a Marine recruiter I'd find it and forge another thousand of that great man.

By Gail Chatfield: Author of "*By Dammit, We're Marines! Veterans' Stories of Heroism, Horror and Humor in World War II on the Pacific Front.*"

To know Mike is to understand what it means to be part of the "Greatest Generation." He was raised during the Great Depression and came of age during the deadliest war of the last century. Like millions of men of his generation, Mike answered the nation's call to duty and joined the military.

I interviewed Mike several years ago for the book I was writing about battles in the Pacific during World War II with an emphasis on Iwo Jima. When I asked him why he joined the Marine Corps, he offered a great observation about his life's choices as a teenager at that time. He said, "Three meals a day, a rack to sleep in and all I have to do is shoot a rifle? That's for me!" He thought the Marine Corps was the best job in the world.

I must admit I was a little intimidated when I interviewed him that first time. I read his bio: he is a veteran of three wars—World War II, Korea and Vietnam—recipient of numerous military honors, and Sergeant Major of the Fleet Marine Force Pacific, the largest field command in the USMC. More locally, Mike is quoted often in our newspapers as the go-to source for opinions and explanations about anything Marine Corps.

To meet him in person shatters any preconceived notions one might have of a retired octogenarian. He still has a commanding presence that was honed decades ago as a drill instructor. He stands up straight, doesn't suffer fools, and I suspect he could probably take on a recruit one quarter his age if necessary. We met at his room, the "Iron Mike" Room, on Camp Pendleton.

Mike has this intimidating presence but during our interview I saw that twinkle in his eye. He is a gifted and knowledgeable speaker when talking about his beloved Marine Corps as evidenced by his numerous speaking engagements throughout the year. Mike was warm, friendly and extraordinarily generous to me. Perhaps it was because I told him my father was a sergeant who fought on Iwo Jima with the 3rd Marine Division and I was eager to know what he would have experienced as a young Marine fighting on the Pacific Front. Mike had an encyclopedic knowledge of Iwo Jima and knew where the 3rd Marine Division battles were on the island and helped fill in a lot of details of those horrific encounters. And yes, I thought of him as a father figure then and continue to do so now.

Mike also, unknowingly, gave me the title of my book, *By Dammit, We're Marines!* It's a phrase he used several times to punctuate the can-do spirit of Marines as they island hopped and won the battles against the Japanese. Here in his own words is one such example as he explained what happened after the end of battle on Iwo:

"We were still eating C-rations even though the island was secure. I didn't have my real first hot meal until I got aboard ship. We lost a lot of weight, our stomachs shrunk, and we were breaking out with little infections because of the embedded ash, but that was nothing. There is always humor in battle. Coming up that cargo net was really tough because we were so weak. Sailors helped the Marines the last few feet grabbing them by the arm to get them over the railing.

A sailor got me by the arms and I said, 'Get away from me Swabby, I made it this far, I will do it on my own. I want to do it on my own, by dammit, we're Marines!' How could I not use that as a title? In fact, that same sentiment was repeated again and again by the other Marines I interviewed---they are a tough bunch and can do everything better than any other branch of service.

Writing an anthology of personal remembrances of Iwo Jima vets is a daunting task I had undertaken and Mike couldn't have been more helpful in offering ideas and information to make my book a well-rounded collection of stories. After that first interview, he invited me to attend the 4th Marine Division reunion that would be held in Atlanta in a few months and offered to introduce me to several Iwo vets to include in the book.

True to his word, I met several of his friends from the 4th Marine Division: Dominick Tutalo, Glenn Buzzard and Peter Santoro. Glenn and Dominick served with Mike in 'C' Co, 1st Bn, 24th Marines. Peter was on the same Marine Corps boxing team as Mike but in the 2nd Bn, 24th Marines. We met up in Peter's hotel room, and over bottles of Rolling Rock beer, the interviews began. These men had been friends for over six decades and were adept at finishing each other sentences, interrupting with a forgotten detail, calling out each other over exaggerations, and laughing at remembered antics the way friends do when they have spent a lot of time together.

I let the tape recorder run realizing it was more informative to just listen to them talk than to interrupt with too many questions. What seemed like perhaps thirty minutes turned out to be over two hours of long forgotten but at the same time well-remembered stories. I remember Mike telling an anecdote about his wife, Maggie, who would attend these reunions with him. She would lovingly accuse Mike of remembering these stories from long ago, yet he couldn't remember what she would have told him just a few days previously. These men had known each other for over sixty-plus years. They had been to war together and shared the bond of being Marines. It takes great effort to maintain friendships but Glenn, Dominick and Peter knew, as I would come to know: that to be Mike's friend is to be Mike's friend forever.

MGySgt Duane Siegmann, USMC (Ret) and Patti Siegmann, USMC Veteran:

My wife Patti and I lead a group of Young Marines known as "Eagle Young Marines" based at Camp Pendleton. In August 2009 the Eagle Young Marines had the pleasure of escorting Iron Mike Mervosh on a short trip to the USS Midway Museum at San Diego's harbor. Iron Mike was the guest speaker for a ceremony called "Keep '45 Alive", and the purpose of the event was to honor the military veterans and their families of the 'Greatest Generation'. During our escort trip the Eagle Young Marines rode with Iron Mike in our van and enjoyed his stories and wisdom he presented to them.

Iron Mike Mervosh has participated with our Eagle Young Marines annually at many veteran ceremonies that have included the Iwo Jima Memorial at Camp Pendleton; Memorial Day Ceremony at Fort Rosecrans in San Diego; the Memorial Ceremony at the Mount Soledad Memorial in La Jolla; the Saint Patrick's Day Parade in San Diego; and the Veteran's Day Parade in downtown San Diego, just to name a few. While the Eagle Young Marines would handle the Color Guard and carry the large ceremonial flag, Iron Mike would ride in VIP parade vehicles. Iron Mike always took time to speak to the Young Marines and told stories that inspired them. SgtMaj Mervosh has been the guest speaker at the Eagle Young Marine graduations and also at their Marine Corps Birthday Ball, where he would keep the audience at the edge of their seats with his inspiring speeches about the Marine Corps.

The past several years Patti and I have assisted Iron Mike in making his trip to the East Coast DI Association Reunion at Parris Island, South Carolina, where he was the Reviewing Officer for the recruit graduation. He was also honored for his dedicated service in every climate and place as a United States Marine.

We recently escorted Iron Mike to Hawaii, which was his last duty assignment as the Sergeant Major of the Pacific Fleet before he retired. He had not been back to Hawaii in over thirty years. The occasion for his visit was the Marine Forces Pacific Command reunion in which they were honoring Sergeant Major Iron Mike Mervosh. The current sergeant major had planned a nice reunion for Iron Mike. After meeting with the Public Affairs Marines at the Marine Corps Base Kaneohe Bay in the morning he was given a tour of the new base working and living areas in which conditions had changed a lot in thirty years. At noon our group met with SgtMaj William Stables at the dining facility, which also was an eye-opener for Iron Mike—they had a drive-through window for Marines to use! While leaving Iron Mike noticed an area outside the facility that needed some attention. When the Mess Deck Sergeant received word of Iron Mike's findings within less than a minute he had a police-call detail take corrective action. We were driven to the other side of the Oahu to Camp Smith. The Marine Forces Pacific Building was still the same, but there were many modifications done over the thirty-year period. Iron Mike still remembered his old office and it contained just a small desk with a phone and a chair. The new office area had computers, Internet, and plasma screen TVs. In the afternoon SgtMaj Stables had arranged a tour on the Pacific Fleet Admiral's boat. The boat had Marines from the Ceremonial Detail ride with Iron Mike. The boat toured the harbor areas including the USS Arizona Memorial. There was also a tour of the Pacific National Memorial Cemetery of the Pacific.

SgtMaj Iron Mike has been a great inspiration to the Eagle Young Marines. On many occasions throughout the year the Eagle Young Marines go to Iron Mike's home and spend time cleaning his yard, removing weeds and doing garage maintenance. One Eagle Young Marine that Iron Mike has truly inspired is Corporal Moreno. Cpl

Moreno has taken charge of the details and supervises the yard and maintenance work. Corporal Moreno listens attentively to everything Iron Mike teaches. Iron Mike reaches out to all levels of Marines and even the young men and woman that aspire to become Marines.

SgtMaj Bill Paxton, USMC (Ret):

While I was sergeant major of Marine Corps Base Camp Pendleton I attended the Iwo Jima Veterans annual memorial celebration and banquet. During the event we had a reenactment of the famous Iwo Jima flag raising. I sat in the audience next to SgtMaj Iron Mike Mervosh. Marines began the raising the flag just as red, white, and blue smoke grenades were popped to create an atmosphere similar to the battlefield. The lights went out and a spotlight shone on the reenactment. It was a beautiful sight. The curtain came down and two buglers played *Echo Taps*, and the audience could still see the image of the reenactment as the image faded away. The light came back on slowly. I leaned over to Iron Mike and whispered that I wished my dad could be here—he had been killed on Iwo Jima while serving with "E" Company, 2nd Battalion, 28th Marines, 5th Marine Division. SgtMaj Iron Mike leaned back and said, "Your father's here." Iron Mike also told me that five Marines and Navy Corpsman Bradley had actually raised two flags that day, and they were from the same company my dad was in.

SgtMaj Iron Mike has always volunteered to be with us in our parades, and also as an honored guest or guest speaker at events such as Marine Corps Balls and Marine Corps Mess Nights. Iron Mike is a life member of many organizations such as the West Coast Sergeants Major Association, the West Coast Drill Instructor Association, 1st Marine Division Association, 3rd Marine Division Association, 4th Marine Division Association, and many other groups.

At times Iron Mike can be very hard, but is always fair. He can still give corrective criticism effectively. He also makes the U.S. flag one of his priorities: during any reenactment of the Iwo Jima flag raising there better be a forty-eight star flag or Iron Mike will be the first to notice it. SgtMaj Iron Mike Mervosh was born on Flag Day, 14 June 1923.

Iron Mike is a hero's hero and a Marine's Marine.

Semper Fi, SgtMaj Bill Paxton.

Rob Sumowski, Ed.D Assistant Professor, Georgia College & State University

Several things have amazed me about Iron Mike. One is his amazing knowledge of warfare in both a specific and a general sense. He can speak with authority, not only on the battles in which he participated, but also on each of the battles in WWII in all of its theaters. He has a depth of understanding of battlefield tactics that is almost psychic. The man is prolific.

After a good deal of correspondence and conversation, I sent him a captured Japanese flag to sign. A buddy Marine previously had signed it. When Mike saw inscription that the other vet had written, "Iwo Jima Survivor" under his signature, Mike would have none of it. Instead he wrote succinctly, "I was not a survivor of Iwo Jima. I was a ***conqueror***. We didn't survive anything. The Marines conquered Iwo Jima." That still makes me chuckle. He's one feisty son of a gun.

Chapter 16

WRITINGS ABOUT IRON MIKE

What 'Semper Fidelis" Means to Iron Mike

S—talwart those Marines in that far off land
E—ach Leatherneck a member of an elite branch
M—anly in their bearing, these warriors so brave
P—roud of their comrades and the sacrifices they gave
E—ndowed with courage against any foe
R—ecognized throughout the world wherever they go

F—ighting men, whose valor is renowned
I—f you search the world no finer would be found
D—eadly weapons are tools of their trade
E—ach and everyone has to make the grade
L—eatherneck is the name they are proud to bear
I—t was earned because of the uniform they wear
S—alutation given to those who died, to me it was an honor to have fought at your side

A Marine

I was that which others did not want to be
I went where others fear to go and did what others failed to do
I asked nothing from those who gave nothing and reluctantly accepted the thought of eternal loneliness should I fail
I have seen the face of terror; felt the stinging cold of fear, and enjoyed the sweet taste of a moments love
I have cried, prayed, and hoped . . . but most of all, I have lived times others would say were best forgotten
At least someday I will be able to say that I was proud of what I was . . .
a Marine!

Iron Mike, the Man
Song by: Joe Paulini, ASCAP

This is a tribute to the man
The man who always said, "I can,"
A man who lived the meaning of U. S. Marines
Who had the talent to inspire
I'm proud to call the man my friend
And friend he'll be until the end
And for his country he has made a thousand scenes
From friendly skies to foreign fire
Once he was Sergeant Major Mervosh
Now he's retired, you see
And now we call him Mister Michael Mervosh
But he's still "Iron Mike" to me
He's made a million memories
And now its time to stand at ease
If anyone can make him slow down Maggie can
This is a tribute to the man
This is a tribute to the man

Hard Core Iron Mike Quotations:

"If it were easy, everybody would do it, and Marines wouldn't be needed."

"A person's true character is revealed by what he does when no one is looking."

"Being a Marine is not a job, it's a *way of life*."

"It is the duty of all Marines of all ranks to strive to be full-time Marines, the leaders, the warriors, the professionals, by being strong, tough and decisive, and by maintaining, participating, observing and preserving our fine and proud traditions, or we will just become another branch of the service and obsolete."

"Throughout the Corps' history, there have been those who have tried to have the Corps disbanded."

"We have certainly had our share of critics who say the United States Army can perform any function or mission the Marine Corps can, that there is no need for a second Army with the title of 'Marines.'"

"Whenever there is a dirty job to do and the going gets really tough, meaning when the defecation hits the ventilation, the cry will always be heard, *'land the Marines!'*"

"I liked the Marine posters. I liked that; 'The First to Fight. Kill or be killed.' I went to the Navy and they said, 'Join the Navy and see the world.' The army recruiting poster was, 'Go to the Army and learn a trade.' I went to the Marine Corps recruiter and it was: 'We offer you a rifle, pack and a hard time. If you like to kill, join our outfit.'"

"Plan your work. Work your plan."

"Life is lighter than a feather; duty is heavier than a mountain."

"Not to worry about anything, but pray for everything."

"If we don't maintain the integrity of the military awards the real ones won't mean a damn thing."

"Winners never quit, and quitters never win."

"When you are right no one remembers, but when you are wrong no one will forget."

"All gave some; some gave all."

"There is little lull in battle, but be always ready and alert."

"Little of disagreements, a lot of angel, and a whole lot of class: to a great devoted wife and daughter."

"It takes less time to do it right than to explain why you did it wrong."

"With my Marines it is always where the elite meet to eat."

"It takes a long time to get to know a friend—except in a foxhole."

"When our freedom is threatened the cry will always be heard to land the Marines . . . naturally: who else?"

"We Marines always take directions: the first to fight; the first to kill or be killed; and to win those battles with insurmountable odds and sheer guts alone."

"We Marines are always willing and capable of preserving and protecting our country and our beloved Corps."

"We Marines are always ready and first to fight regardless of the enemy's size; the challenge of being in the forefront of battle if war occurs."

"A person all wrapped up in himself makes a pretty small package."

"If you are through changing you are through."

"Do all the good you can, in all the ways you can, for all the Marines you can: while you can."

"If you are not big enough to take criticism you are too small to take praise."

"Doubt your doubts and believe your beliefs."

"Freedom does not give us the right to do as we please; but rather the ability to do as we ought."

"The rich man does wrong and boasts of it; the poor man is wronged and begs forgiveness."

"Happiness is to be found in the pursuit and possession of wisdom."

"Fool's thoughts are in their mouths; wise men's words are in their hearts."

"A man who has a habit of abusive language will never mature in character as long as he lives."

"The crown of an old man is wide experience; their glory; their fear of the Lord."

"Stumble not through a woman's beauty, nor be greedy for her wealth."

"Happy is the husband of a good wife: twice lengthened are his days."

"He or she who betrays a secret cannot be trusted; he or she will never find an intimate friend."

"A wound can be bound up and an insult forgiven, but those who betray secrets do hopeless damage."

"We Marines do our duties, not because we want to be thanked, but we are thankful; not because it is easy, but because it is hard; not because it's popular, but it is right."

"We didn't join the Marine Corps for the monetary value, nor do we look for fat paychecks. We don't seek personal gain at the expense of the Marine Corps. We Marines do not value money for any more or any less than its worth. Money is a good servant but a bad master."

"The best time to get things done is between tomorrow and yesterday."

"Marines are not 'peace keepers': they are ***peace makers.***

"In war there is no substitute for victory."

"It is fatal to enter any battle without the will to win it."

"Quitters never win, and winners never quit."

"We were trained so well: we didn't believe anything could kill us."

"One can learn more from failure than from big success."

"One way to succeed is to be a short term pessimist and a long term optimist."

Chapter 17

ESSAYS BY IRON MIKE MERVOSH

Authors Note: Iron Mike Mervosh has written a number of essays regarding his Marine Corps experiences. A few are listed in this chapter. Iron Mike received an "A" from his professor for his efforts on "Psychology for the Fighting Man".

Psychology for the Fighting Man

Presently I have the opportunity to be invited to give, or have talks to Marines of various commands. A majority of these sessions are within the Camp Pendleton area where the large infantry units are located there. Having made observations of their conversations and training I can relate my many past experiences on their behalf. I fought in three wars as an infantryman I could never overemphasize the tough training that must be endured to make a Marine suitable to encounter the many stresses under combat conditions.

There was measurable communication among these fine young men. It gave me the feeling of father to son, or teacher to student relationships. Their interest and many questions were commendable and the sessions gave me the enthusiasm to be part of their groups. I felt obligated to assist these men every possible way I could. It was a tribute to me to be accepted as part of their team to offer the timely advice that they would seek. Much was absorbed on my behalf from these discussions, ideas, questions, dialogue, etc, to prepare this report on *Psychology for the fighting man.*

It takes more than brains to make a good Marine: it takes guts. It takes endurance, the mental and physical stamina measured by the ability to stand pain, fatigue, distress, and hardship. It takes a willingness to do hard work. It takes a keen interest in doing the duties well.

Psychologists wish they could give the Marine a method of measuring these important personality assets—tests that would be as accurate and reliable as a test for measuring ability to do arithmetic or learning a radio code.

They are difficult. Some tests have been tried, and many have failed to no avail. A few were promising. One problem is that a man's personality changes in different situations. For instance: the man who is brave as a lion in the test room at a reception center may not be so brave when he gets into combat. The man who is able to make quick decisions wisely when things are quiet may go to pieces when he is distracted by machine gun or mortar fire, and he may do something that will result in his own death or the death of others. Then there are difficult situations that may be the reverse effect on some men. Those who have never distinguished themselves in training camps may become fired with new spirit when the going gets tough, astounding themselves and the other men with what they can accomplish in extreme emergencies. As the old adage implies, "when the going gets tough the tough get going".

There are tests of personality like the one in which the man tells what objects or scenes he can imagine in an inkblot, but these tests take time and require an expert psychologist to administer and interpret them. So the Marine Corps at present falls back on interviews when it wants to estimate personality. In such an interview the examiner tries to find out the Marine's interest. He goes beyond mere preferences, finding out whether or not the interests are based on the man's deep-rooted unchangeable likes and dislikes.

Everything counts in the Marine Corps just as it counts elsewhere. These things are the Marine Corps' psychological, which is just as varied as the physical material. We didn't just want one kind of aircraft or one kind of weapon. To win a war one must have the proper distribution of weapons, instruments, and a lot of other equipment. The aptitudes, abilities, and interest to drawn into the Marine Corps are its instruments, its human instruments of war. As far as the demands of war permit, they must be in the right place at the right time. The right Marine can't be put into the right job unless we know both the Marine and the job, so that we can match them up.

The Marine Corps finds out about each Marine by interviews and by tests. Every new recruit takes the General Classification Test so that his general ability and his capacity for learning new things can be found. Expert interviews can also get at some of the important characteristics of a man's personality, his deep-lying preferences and interests. Each military job has to be analyzed to see what kinds of abilities, aptitudes, and personality required. I may mention that the interests of Marine Corps comes first, as we are the nation's force in readiness, the first to fight, called upon to win the battles that seemingly cannot be won. Thus it stands the reason the primary consideration is the man with the rifle, the all-important fighting man.

During my talks with the young Marines we agreed that psychology for the fighting man was indeed a very broad field. It may involve twenty-four hours a day, seven days a week, especially when we are at war. There is a need of efficiency of the fighting man: his health and strengths, his resistance to hardships and fatigue; his alertness even when fatigued, through extreme freezing cold or exhausting heat. Toughness of mind and body is a weapon indispensable to the victory.

It's true that every man has his limit mentally, as well as psychologically. There are stresses which no man can endure, however tough-minded. Modern battle has pushed closer and closer to these final limits of man's endurance.

Grueling hardships; great fatigue; prolonged loss of sleep; lack of food and water; blistering heat; intense cold; exposure to diseases—those are some of the conditions that put a dangerous stress on the mind as well as the body. When a man must go through these things and then in addition suffers the stress of seeing his comrades killed, of being in constant peril of his own life, when dealing out death with his own hands—there may come a time when the strongest man's mind will sicken. Such as sufferer from battle shock is not a weakling—he is not a coward. He becomes a battle casualty. If given psychiatric first aid promptly he will probably recover to take his place again in a battle unit. However, if neglected he may become permanently ill, or may even seek relief from his mental wounds with death.

There is a psychological kind of deafness, which is called 'hysterical'. Because of great fear or emotional shock, a man may become genuinely unable to hear although his ears are still normally sensitive. This trouble lies in the brain. The man is not faking. He cannot cure his deafness by the act of will. He is a neurotic case and should receive medical attention as soon as possible.

Then there is the individual who no longer can concentrate. He becomes confused, which is easy in the midst of a fierce battle with a lot of men. Yet observing the expression of his face, his pulse rate, rapid breathing betrays the fierce battle going on with him. He himself may not be fully aware of the cause of the terrible sense of fear and sorrow that seems to hang over him. Yet in a way he is solving his problems. He is making himself too inefficient to continue in the fight, yet giving himself so much suffering that his conscience cannot accuse him of taking the easy way out.

Another result of unsolved mental conflict is the loss of memory; a Marine or soldiers in such a predicament may be found wandering aimlessly around. He can't remember which unit he belongs to. He may not even be able to tell his own name or respond to any orders that are given. He just doesn't understand what is happening to him, or have control of his emotions. The leader who lectures him, bawls him out or punished him for dereliction of duty is likely only to increase his problems. On the other hand, coddling or babying such men is a mistake also. What they need is understanding, help, and the assurance that comes from a firm, but friendly stiff kick in the butt may help. They need the encouragement of assurance that such situations happen to the best of men, and they can get over these problems with medical aid. It is certain that a man could not only be harmful to him, but could cause casualties among his comrades. I expected these individuals to prove themselves. These were times when a good night's sleep and a hot meal was the proper medical attention that was needed. I have experienced several cases in my own unit, and not only were they excellent combat troops later on, they also distinguished themselves beyond the call of duty. It gave me deep satisfaction that possibly I did something right and, even today I am reminded of these events during our annual reunions.

In most cases it is the first contact with the energy, the first taste of battle that is the hardest. In seasoned combat troops internal conflict diminishes. They have faced the worst and know it is not intolerable. Even troops who have to retreat are not defeated, if they have learned to conquer their source of fears. They will advance another time, having once won the battle with the inner man, and having forced the reality of battle, finding in it less terror and more opportunity for success than the green recruit could ever have believed possible.

I have indicated about personalities and a sense of humor helps morale in battle. I recall during Korea when our division was completely outnumbered and surrounded by twenty Chinese divisions. Our remarkable regimental commander, Colonel Chesty Puller, said the right thing at the right time: "We have the enemy where we want them—we not longer need to look for them. We can attack in any direction!" I can recall countless humor that happens amidst battle conditions that gave the individual Marines a psychological lift. It made a man feel his problem (perhaps a "Dear John letter") not seem so bad at all.

Even though I had discussions with my groups that lasted quite long about these personalities, it would take written pages to mention the effect it had on a fighting man. All in all, "Marine's humor can lick anything."

The use of drugs and alcohol were thoroughly discussed, and it was a problem that we did not have in World War II and Korea. It had dismal effects to the fighting man in Vietnam, and the many problems with our Armed Forces today.

Hospital visits of battle casualties were a high priority for me. The visits gave me inspiration on how these wounded men would display the great American heroes in talking of their wounds. I'll never forget a remark by a wounded sergeant: "Only a fool wants to live forever—if you must die, make your death count for something, like fighting for your country!" It's a tribute to me to have young men with so much dedication knowing how they knew that American support of the Vietnam War was not in their favor.

Regardless, it was a war against a common enemy. Wars in our past history were total wars. Total war is just what its name implies: war on all fronts with all possible weapons. There was the home front, as well as all the battlefronts. There was the military front, economic front, and the psychological front. The three kinds of warfare are all related, which make it all a total war. A military success may also be an economic victory, if it results in the capture of great quantities of enemy material or blocks important supply routes to the enemy nation. Or it can be a psychological victory if it lowers enemy morale, helps to make soldiers expect defeat, and leads the enemy people to be ready to submit.

Then there is propaganda. The goal of propaganda is always a change in the state of mind. In psychological warfare the goal is the undermining of the enemy morale, the persuading of the enemy that his cause is hopeless and that he will be better off if he gives up. When enemy morale is low, effective propaganda can make it lower. Doubt, insecurity, and frustration are the fertile soil for psychological warfare.

War is hell! Nobody likes to fight, but somebody must know how, and as Marines we certainly know how to fight and win battles. I have been there and done that, and would be willing to do it again for my Corps and country.

Hardcore Iron Mike

That tiny Pacific Island, Iwo Jima:

I'm concerned that Americans are forgetting the many bloody sacrifices made on this tiny Pacific island, as well as many battlefields like it across the world. For the first seventy-two hours Marines suffered a casualty every forty-five seconds . . . that makes Iwo Jima the bloodiest battle in the history of the world. I will never forget what I saw during the intense fighting: it was a true killing field—every square foot of it. Seventy thousand Marines hit the beach. Nearly twenty-nine thousand of us, a little less than half, were killed or wounded over the thirty-six days of nonstop intensive battles that continued without stoppage for the entire time.

Supporting us were another thirty thousand men aboard a naval armada of eight hundred eighty ships, a convoy that stretched seventy nautical miles. Before we landed on that hot beach U.S. pilots flew two thousand, seven hundred bombing sorties over Iwo Jima.

But as we hit the beach the Japanese fortified gun emplacements began blazing down with heavy artillery and mortar fire, all of it raining down on us like falling hail. Totally out in the exposed open spaces our Marines fell like flies. Young Marines were desperately trying to stuff their own guts back into their bodies. Marines were torn apart from the devastating artillery, mortar, small arms fire, and grenades that stormed down on them. The beach was drenched with red blood and was littered with the twisted bodies of the fallen Marines.

So many brave Marines fell taking that tiny island—certainly we cannot forget them! These were good Marines that fell on Iwo Jima, an island considered part of the Japanese homeland. There are six thousand, eight hundred twenty-one Marines buried on that bloody volcano.

It grieves me to say that I have seen our young people who haven't just forgotten the deeds of our Marines at Iwo Jima—they were never taught about it in the first place! Nor do these young people appreciate the debt our nation owes to our World War II veterans, and all the Americans that supported the war effort back home. The reason? It is because of our "politically correct" times. Many of our schools in the U.S. simply do not teach about World War II—the heroism and sacrifices made for our freedom.

Instead, American students are being taught a revised portion of history that more often than not paints veterans like us as the "bad guys". Some of America's finest museums in Washington D. C. proposed an exhibit portraying United States as the aggressor during WWII, and Japan as a small nation valiantly trying to preserve its culture. We know that is not the real story, and we must make sure that our next generation knows that as well.

It's not that the teachers don't want to tell our stories—it is that today's textbook publishers simply ignore or minimize our entire WWII history.

We must recognize the heroism of our WWII veterans before they all pass away. Some six hundred WWII veterans die every day now. And as each one of our veterans pass on we lose a small piece of heroic time in American history. A time in triumph and the extreme battle that was in 1945.

I never thought our nation would ignore all we accomplished; yet that is exactly what has happened. For example: the U.S. Postal Service cancelled a commemorative postage stamp that would have commemorated the bombing of Hiroshima, an act that saved the lives of thousands of Marines and soldiers, as the planned invasion of Japan surely would have resulted in millions of American and Japanese lives being lost.

What also disturbs us Iwo Jima veterans is that just a couple of years ago Japan changed the name pronunciation to "Iwoto"—maybe we shouldn't have given up the island.

We must at all times preserve our history and our stories. I want our present generation to know that seventy thousand heroic and tough Marines that fought and won the "Battle of all Battles". I want them to know all about the sneak attack on Pearl Harbor, and with our backs to the wall Americans waited in fear for the Japanese to occupy Hawaii and eventually attack our west coast. I want them to know that our American forces fought back with a strength and pride we didn't know we had.

For four long years of hell our veterans drove the Nazis back to Germany; they pushed the fanatical Japanese from the blood-drenched South Pacific islands. We lost a lot of good Marines, soldiers, sailors, and airmen . . . heroes who died in small towns across Europe and on faraway islands in the Pacific who distinguished themselves with many battle victories that eventually ended WWII.

These were brave men that helped keep our country safe. They dragged themselves through the bloody sands of Iwo Jima, the Marshall Islands, Tarawa, Saipan, Peleliu, Okinawa and many others. They also performed heroic acts in the Normandy invasion and ultimately liberated the innocent prisoners in the horrifying Nazi concentration camps. They defeated the tyranny of imperialistic Japan. They were heroes over seventy years ago, and they still are to this day.

But sadly, many Americans don't know the first thing about WWII or our proud veterans that made the sacrifices in preserving our precious freedom that we all cherish. They don't know what "Iwo Jima", "Okinawa", or even "Omaha Beach" mean.

Our veterans could tell them . . . if only someone would give them a chance. For me, I would be delighted to comply.

Marine Lingo Sliding Down Cracks in 'Deck'

During this time of year, we Marines seem to pay a little more attention to Marine Corps traditions, mainly due to the celebration of the birthday of the Marine Corps. And although the birthday of our Corps is certainly one of the most prized traditions, I feel we are losing many others. One of the traditions we seem to be losing is Marine talk and terminology. The Marines of today go through "doors" instead of hatches. They hang things on a "wall" instead of a bulkhead. They walk on "floors", not decks, and the go to the "bathroom" instead of the head. And the list goes on. How many Marines today know what a "field scarf" is, or a "housewife"? I don't even hear the term "pogie bait" used anymore. This may sound like a trivial matter, but it starts a trend towards forgetting our history, traditions, and customs.

What sets us apart as Marines from the other military services are our way of doing things. Our traditions and customs are what the Marine Corps spirit lives on. Traditions are not learned from books, they must be practiced, preserved, and handed down from one generation to the next. That is what makes them traditions and daily events.

Traditions are shown in many forms: traditions of devotion to duty, self-sacrifice, versatility and dependability; traditions of loyalty to God, country and Corps; traditions of uniform, insignia and equipment; traditions to *Honor, Courage, and Commitment.* Traditions are as much a part of each Marine as his rifle and equipment. One term that really bothers me the most is how our Marines have become known as "customers". Since when are we customers? We don't graduate "customers" from recruit training—we graduate *Marines*; we don't take care of "customers"—we take care of *Marines*. The bottom line is: we don't call Marines "customers": we call them ***Marines***.

We have many symbols of our traditions: the eagle, globe and anchor, perhaps our most sacred: our motto "Semper Fidelis"; our Mameluke and NCO swords; our uniforms and personal appearance; our physical fitness; our discipline and courtesies.

The list goes on. If we start forgetting any one of these traditions, such as Marine talk and terminology, then what comes next?

We must preserve all our traditions and customs and we must practice them on a daily basis. Even more, we must demand our youngest Marines practice them on to their next generation. "Aye, Aye, Sir!"

Being a Marine is not just a job, but a way of life

A new term has invaded the sacred vocabulary of the Marine Corps. Its one which I have yet to figure out or where I came from. I can only assume it is a prodigy of "Generation-X".

The term I am referring to is "comp-time". More and more these days I hear Marines requesting comp-time off because they missed a day off on a holiday, or because they had to stand duty, or because they had come in on a weekend to perform some mission. When I joined the Marine Corps it was for twenty-four hour day, seven days a week, fifty-two weeks a year. There is nothing on any of the nine enlistments or reenlistment contracts that I have signed promising me any compensation. As far as I can tell, this has not changed. What has changed, I fear, is our level of commitment to being a Marine. It seems to me that these days, Marines look for more excuses for not coming to work than they do for coming to work. Personal things that could easily be taken care of on one's own time always seem to be taken care of during duty hours. This is not commitment. When we all signed that contract, we committed ourselves to the finest military organization in the world—the United States Marine Corps. If you are not truly one-hundred percent committed to that fact, then you need to seek employment elsewhere, perhaps someplace where they authorize you comp-time when you are hired. Good luck! Granted, there are emergencies that arise from time to time that need and require immediate attention. But these should be exceptions rather than the norm. Commitment is one of our Corps Values. It is one of the things that makes us different and separates us from the other branches of armed services. We must remember that the Marine Corps is not a nine-to-five, Monday-to-Friday job, but a way of life, chosen only by those who want to be associated with the very best.

Can you look yourself in the mirror each day and honestly say you have that level of commitment required to be a Marine full time, or do you only have the part-time commitment? Perhaps you can go to your CO and request some "comp-time" to figure it out.

Courage: desired leadership trait

What do you think of when you hear the Core Value term "Courage"? According to the Core Value Charter, "Courage" is that value that gives you the moral and mental strength to do what is right with confidence and resolutions, even in the face of temptation or adversity.

Are you a leader of courage, or do you just go along with the program, salute and go along to get along? Do you have the courage to speak up and offer constructive recommendations that at times may go against the grain? Or, are you more apt to imitate that old dog statue we're used to seeing in the back of automobiles that just stay there and shook its head up and down. The "yes man" syndrome is all around us, and many in senior leadership billets. Is that what our young Marines of today need to emulate: leader without intestinal fortitude who are afraid for their own careers, rather than stand up for what is right for the Corps and their Marines?

I encounter these types of individuals on a daily basis, both in the officer and enlisted leadership structure. In the Core Value Charter, it states "I will make decisions and act in the best interest of the Department of the Navy and the nations, without regard to personal consequences."

Those who fail to offer constructive recommendations because they are more afraid for their own careers are not doing the Marine Corps or their Marines justice. I doubt very much if our great leaders of the past, leaders like Chesty Puller, Dan Daly, John Basilone, or Smedley Butler were ever "yes men." They put the welfare of their Marines first, ahead of their own careers.

The careerism sickness we have today is surely not what our great leaders of the past envisioned the Marine Corp would become what it is today.

Those who shove their integrity aside and their willingness to stand tall and be heard are violating their oath of office to defend America, not their careers. The Corps prides itself on its rich and illustrious history, heritage and traditions. If we are to continue to be the finest military organization in the world, we need not be afraid to stand tall, speak and be heard for what we know to be right and just for the Corps and our Marines.

If you get your toes stepped on along the way, then so be it. Your Marines will have far more respect for you and our Core Values if you stand up for them and not only for yourselves. In closing "Non sivi se patri" . . . "Not for yourselves, but for the country."

Lead by example: avoid double standards

SgtMaj Houle's article in *The Globe* highlighted some very interesting points. What he addresses is a matter of basic leadership. However, I would like to expound on his article one step further. As

SgtMaj Houle points out, all Marines, by virtue of their enlistment, agree to abide by a set of rules "according to regulations and the Uniform Code of Military Justice." Sound familiar? All enlisted Marines signed this upon enlistment. Officers swear (or affirm) to "faithfully discharge the duties of the office." Do we all abide by this as leaders?

We have something in the Marine Corps today I like to refer to as "selective enforcement of regulations." We have all seen some of our senior leadership, enlisted and officers, violate rules and regulations because it doesn't suit their desires. This example of negative leadership enhances the double standard image we have in the Corps. Some examples that immediately come to mind are:

Chewing gum while in uniform.

The wearing of unauthorized sun glasses in uniform.

The wearing of pagers in uniform, not authorized by the commander as organizational property.

There are many more but these are a few of the most common. When our junior Marines see these violations they assume it's all right for them also.

We have all heard that the Marines of today are smarter than the Marines of yesterday. This must be why in days gone by, when you told a Marines to do something, he or she did it without hesitation. Today, you hear, "Why," or "Show me where it says that." And it's not just from the enlisted Marines. Not too long ago I approached a captain who was chewing gum in uniform and in a tactful way, as tactful as a sergeant major can be, explained that it was wrong to chew gum in uniform, especially when talking to Marines. His response: "Where does it say I can't chew gum in uniform?"—This from a captain! ALMAR 299/97 (Marine Corps Uniform Meeting Nr 193 Issue) addresses a very interesting new policy change to the Uniform Regulations.

"Marines are known not just for their battlefield prowess, but for their unparalleled standards of professionalism and uncompromising personal conduct and appearance. It is a Marine's duty and personal obligation to maintain a professional and neat appearance of a Marine. The use of chewing gum, chewing tobacco, cigarettes, or the consumption of food while walking in uniform, are examples of activities that detract from the appearance expected of a United States Marine."

Now I ask this question: How much selective enforcement of this regulation do you think you are going to see? There are many already who say this is an upcoming change not in effect yet. Read paragraph 3 of the ALMAR—it states "Per CMC direction." To me that says it's in effect now. This is going to be one of the most interesting and challenging regulations to enforce because it will be the greatest example of selective enforcement to come in a long time. I wouldn't be surprised if this word hasn't even filtered down to the junior Marines yet even though the ALMAR is dated 11 September.

Does this sound familiar—"And this appointee is to observe and follow such orders and directions as may be given from time to time by superiors acting to the rules and articles governing the discipline of the Armed Forces of the United Stats of America." It appears on all promotion warrants, from private first class to sergeant major. To follow such orders and directions means to obey and enforce all orders and directions. This pertains to all rules and regulations, not just the ones we like or desire to obey and enforce because it suits our needs and personal desires.

This does not apply to all Marine leaders. However, as leaders we have our ten percent also. If you feel uncomfortable reading this you're probably one of the ten percent. As SgtMaj Houle states in his article, it takes a complete focus of all Marines to make sure our image remains untarnished. As Marine leaders we make recommendations, not policy, whether we like it or not. We are, however, tasked with enforcing policy, whether we like it or not. Our mission is to support the commander and carry on—Aye, Aye, Sir!

Our young Marines today are our leaders of tomorrow. They will carry on what they see and what they are taught. Let's see to it they carry on properly and in the highest traditions of the United States Marine Corps.

My thoughts of Iwo Jima

Iwo Jima is eight square miles of black volcanic ash and rock. We landed on that hellhole 19 February 1945, but it would be the end of March before intensive and bitter fighting would find the island secured.

To those who say that can be taken cheaply without those two atomic bombs I say, "Tell that to the Marines!"

One needs first hand accounts of Marines to recall their battle and it always seems unreal. It seems unreal that Marines that endure the fatigue, the terror, the filth, the horror and bitter fighting and then come out of it sane and sound. Thus Marines who look so ordinary are giants who fought across the Pacific and defeated the hated enemy. There's toughness about these Marines that age cannot weaken. A fearlessness that only those who walk and talk with death can attain.

One has to be there to know what battle is like. We can seek out survivors, talk to them, admire them, but we can never know what it was like.

Combat creates a true brotherhood in battle. But for the entire blessing, being alive and not suffer the wounds, the pains, and the terror is the fact we have contributed toward our Marine Corps history.

But as Marines who fought on Iwo Jima and those other horrific battles will not fade from history. One day, if the rest of us are remembered at all, it will be as people who lived the time the battle of Iwo Jima was fought. That's why we Marines are proud, as it should be.

Marines extremely honorable

Remarks by the Assistant Secretary of the Army, Sara Lister, suggesting we are "extreme and not connected with society" indicates either she doesn't know her job or she is yet another example of forces at work to decimate the Marines.

If we Marines were connected to society then there ethical and moral standards would certainly decline.

In a world today, a Marine boot is trained to defend his country, but his character is tested to the limit. The move to the Marine Corps from public life is a huge step from gangs, drugs, and sex to the core values system of honor, courage, and commitment. I say that's really being extreme, isn't it?

Yes, we Marines are extremists! We are extremely proud; extremely trained; extremely ready; extremely good fighters; extremely professional; and extremely squared away. So many can say we are "extremists'. I recall when we Marines were out in the field, which was most of the time. At our tent camp each Marine Company had a canvas bag filled with water that was supported by a tripod. The bag had several spigots to pour the water. I also recall the nomenclature of the water bag—it was "Lister Bag". It could not be more appropriate in naming two bags as "Lister". Yes, Ms. Sara Lister, we are proud to be "extremists"!

"Fortitude" is admirable under any flag

We had unhappy moments fighting in a defensive position; and felt our best in the offensive, always pushing forward aggressively.

The one emotion that showed a deep pride in our combat teams, and other combat teams, was to see if the mission is accomplished.

There are many ways to describe the terrors of war, its filth, loneliness, comradeship, humor, and heroism. Believe it or not, we Marines prided ourselves with training in misery so we can endure the hardships, rigors, and miseries of battle, as we experienced and endured the many battles that we fought and won during the island hopping in the Pacific while fighting and holding the hated enemy.

There were only three phases in a front-line Marine: relief, wounds, and death. A Marine grave marker in battle summarized the period between:

And when he gets to heaven
To Saint Peter he will tell
One more Marine reporting, Sir!
I've served my time in Hell

Those of us who survived left with our own thoughts and a great many dead comrades. It may take a long time to know a friend—except in battlefields.

Remembrances

How well I remembered feeling tough and indestructible when I joined the Marine Corps. After a period of intense training I was then shipped overseas to fight for my country. The sacrifices were many with our Marines departing from our loved ones; but time heals that. The tough part was fighting the enemy that was suicidal and fanatical. We then had the hard task of enduring the elements and also having to fight many diseases such as malaria, dengue fever, tropical ulcers, coral cuts, etc. We had deprivation of food and water. Along with fighting the enemy we also had to fight off mosquitoes, land crabs, tarantulas, poisonous snakes, etc. I often wondered: "If the elements are this bad, hell—let the Japs have the damned island!"

While in the foxholes I had thoughts of the bugles that blew to declare reveille in boot camp. Reveille started at "zero-dark thirty"! Then there was the chow call, call to morning colors, call to quarters, Taps, and 2200 lights out. It was a mournful call to lull us into a deep sleep after a very tiring day of physical training and close order drill. The drill instructors were on our butts, constantly yelling in our ears and rapping our knuckles with their swagger sticks and a swift kick in the ass.

Paycall! Wow, thirty bucks a month and we were always paid in *cash*. Most of us boots sent the money home during that depression era. We lined up in two lines alphabetically with 'A' through 'M' in one column and 'N' through 'Z' in the other. Those of us with names starting with 'M' were always the last ones paid.

Back in the barracks it was good old regimentation. We had lots of inspections: weapons inspections every morning. We also had physical drill under arms. We had a daily routine of spit-shining our shoes until we could see ourselves it the reflection. Our bunks had to be made up so that it was so tight you could bounce a quarter on it. Our rifles were slung under our bunks. We had footlockers and inside we kept our shorts, shirts, socks, and everything had to be folded real neat.

I remember a 0200 short-arm inspection (and inspection in which a male must squeeze his penis to see if there are any signs of venereal disease. All the guys had to watch. We had to list all the pro-stations and how to take one. With all those scare tactics I didn't even want to meet a pretty girl. Being a boxer my boxing coach told me he'd take care of the girls for me.

Back in the barracks we didn't need locks for our personal gear while we were shaving or taking a shower. Wallets and packs of cigarettes were left open on a bunk. When a Marine returned to his bunk his wallet was untouched and maybe a cigarette or two was missing.

We were out in the field a week or two conducting our rigorous training, and the long hike back to our barracks covering thirty-miles with full transport packs and our service weapons. After the long march during the previous night the word 'hike' was written and then the word became 'march' instead. Boy Scouts and civilians call it a hike—Marines refer to it as a march. It makes good sense to refer to it as a force march in lieu of a force hike.

After the long march back to our barracks we unloaded those heavy packs. We shaved and took a pleasant hot shower. We then donned our freshly pressed uniforms and filed out in formation in front of the barracks ready for personal and weapons inspection. If we passed our inspection we obtained our liberty card from the Duty NCO.

Heading for liberty we got out of the bus at the main gate and formed three ranks, and then the MPs would hold inspection on us. In our company it was a very rare thing that the MPs could scrutinize and find any discrepancies. If a Marine did not pass the MP inspection he would be sent back to his unit.

On rare occasions an individual in the Corps would be drummed out. The bad ass had to stand at attention in front of the formation while the first sergeant read the dishonorable discharge. He then stripped the man's uniform of any rank insignia and past awards, and then gave him a swift kick in is rear end. A sentry then escorted the man out of the gate into his cruel world.

Why I cannot hear?

I left my hearing on Iwo Jima
Caused by an artillery shell blast
And I left my nerves in that big foxhole
Where I was sure I would die at last
Now the machine gun's bullets were everywhere
Attempting to puncture and tear
But the blast from an artillery shell
I'm here to tell you

It's really hell!
Oh, you say, that was sixty-nine years ago
When you were early twenty!
Yes it was, but I still can hear
Now that I am ninety
I was mighty glad it was over
In the spring of forty-five
Mighty glad to leave that Hellhole
While some of us were still alive.

My final objective areas and inspection

And when he goes to Heaven
To St. Peter he'll tell
"Another Marine reporting, Sir
I've served my time in Hell!"

That empty chair that appears on the stage.
A ceremony symbolizes our missing and fallen comrades:

Author Note: There is a small dinner table on stage with seating for one. The table has a bible, a place setting for one, and a Purple Heart medal. SgtMaj Iron Mike Mervosh will give the speech below and describe to the audience the symbolism of the table items.

A good many of us were very young when we willingly went into combat. However, all Americans should never forget the brave Marines who answered our nation's call to the cause of freedom in a very special way.

The empty chair and the items on the table symbolize our missing and fallen comrades as the Purple Heart is displayed as a medal of valor.

The Bible represents the strength gained through faith sustained by our country, which was founded as "one nation, under God" . . . no exceptions.

The glass is empty to remind us of those who have gone before. Only the dead have seen the end of war. The glass is inverted to symbolize their inability to share a toast.

So let us pay tribute and honor our fallen comrades, as they have given all their tomorrows for our today and give a thought and a prayer to our silent and unseen comrades. They wanted to live and fight the enemy, but were not afraid to die.

They asked so little yet they gave so much in making the ultimate sacrifice in preserving our precious freedom that we all cherish, as well as our democracy and making this commemorative event possible for us.

The United States has entombed the "Unknown Soldier". The Marines do not entomb an "Unknown Marine" . . . All of our Marines are known.

Let us raise our glasses in a toast to all our fallen comrades and our "Known Marines".

Six random thoughts:

1. The Japanese fought below the ground and we fought above it. We made them pay for every square inch of ground and we also paid a huge price, but we still beat their asses.
2. We are living in this country full of unfounded villains and unrewarded heroes.
3. There are three classes of people: those that make things happen; those that have no idea of what is happening. In an organization you often see a small group that make things happen and leads the group to real service. Then there are those that are bystanders, and there is a large fringe that knows nothing of what is accomplished.
4. The supreme quality for a leader is unquestionably in looking out for his Marines. Be firm but fair. Without it no success is possible whether it's during field training or on the battlefield. If a Marine's subordinates find him guilty of phoniness, or if they find out that he lacks forthright integrity, he will fail. His leadership teaching and actions must be square with each other.
5. With all the poisonous snakes and mosquitoes in those jungle-infested islands I would jokingly tell Marines, "Snake bites Marine, snake dies. Mosquito bites Marine, mosquito gets drunk. Woman bites a Marine, Oh boy!"
6. A ninety-year old retired Marine sent in a sexual riddle from his youth.

Question: What is the difference between a diplomat and a lady?
Answer: When a diplomat says, "yes", he means "perhaps". When he says, "Perhaps", he means "no". When he says, "No", he's no diplomat. When a lady says, "No", she means "perhaps". When a lady says, "perhaps", she means, "yes". When a lady says, "Yes"—she's no lady!

More Random Thoughts

Gun Control: Hit the target.

Marine Rifleman: The enemy can run, but he will die tired once hit by a bullet.

Carpenters hammer nails; plumbers fix pipes; Marines kill the enemies.

Mental toughness: Starts in boot camp.

Iron Mike's Medals and Decorations

Bronze Star with Combat Distinguishing Device
Purple Heart with two Gold Stars
Meritorious Service Medal
Navy Commendation Medal with Combat Distinguishing Device with two Stars
Combat Action Ribbon
Presidential Unit Citation with four Stars
Navy Unit Commendation with one Star
Meritorious Unit Commendation with two Stars
Good Conduct Medal with ten Stars
American Campaign Medal
Asiatic-Pacific Campaign Medal with four Stars
World War II Victory Medal
Navy Occupation Service Medal with three Stars
Vietnam Service Medal with five Stars
Korean Presidential Unit Citation

Republic of Vietnam Meritorious Unit
Citation with Cross of Gallantry
Republic of Vietnam Honor Medal
Republic of Vietnam Meritorious Unit Citation
Civil Action Medal
United Nations Medal
Republic of Vietnam Campaign

Chapter 18

AN INTERVIEW WITH IRON MIKE MERVOSH

Author note: Some of the written materials that Iron Mike has in his possession cannot be used in this book because the publisher has a requirement that all materials must have a release by the author providing permission to include in the book. Some of the authors of the materials have long since passed away or there is no record of their whereabouts in order to obtain their permissions. As a result it was necessary to interview Iron Mike about these stories and letters in order to extract the essence of the stories about him. Iron Mike has several bookcases chock full of albums that contain letters, speeches, photos and other materials that he has saved over the years.

Author: Sergeant Major, you have lots of albums in those bookcases. Can you describe some of the contents in them?

Iron Mike: Sure I can. Let's see: here is a letter from a Sergeant Dominic D. Dipierri. This is a special one for me because it told me exactly what happened to my brother Milan in Korea. He talks about enlisting in the Marines after high school just as the Korean War started. After boot camp he was sent to Korea and was with "I" Company, 3rd Battalion, 7th Marine Regiment. Almost immediately they were engaged in combat. He and his two buddies from Fresno were all wounded. My younger brother Milan was a corporal doing a sergeant's job and he wanted them to set up 60mm mortar as quickly as possible, but he wrote how the tree line made it impossible to set up the mortars in firing positions. Milan located a rock outcropping that the mortars could be set up on. Milan volunteered to go out as a forward observer and planned on sending back information to register the guns properly. When Milan finally assured the unit that the guns were properly set Dominic wrote that all hell broke loose, and then the phones went dead. He said they were told to fire the guns for effect and sometimes had the mortars in prone positions. They stopped the enemy attack, but were very exposed to enemy fire the entire time. When everything settled down a stretcher with a Marine covered by a poncho was carried by their position—he found out later it my brother Milan who had been killed in the action. It was the first time I ever knew exactly what happened. You can see why this letter is important to me!

Dan DiPierri also wrote a poem about me—it was titled Iron Mike Mervosh, SgtMaj, USMC (Ret). He was a very talented man. His poem highlighted my life—it included everything from my Serbian upbringing to the death of my brother Milan in Korea.

Author: You have so many letters there. What else do you want to share?

Iron Mike: I have a lot letters that come from Marines that I served with when I first entered the Marines. Here is one from a guy we all called "Doodle"—his real name was Donald Marston and he died in 1984. He wrote about his illness, but he really wanted to let me know that he truly felt that I was a leader of men and would make it big in the Marines. Doodle was a great guy and a good Marine.

Author: Iron Mike, do you only keep letters from Marines?

Iron Mike: No, I have lots of letters from civilians. Here is one from a guy named Vincent Gutierrez. He wrote that he never served in the military, but he was always in awe of military men who fought the wars that preserved our freedom. We met in San Antonia, Texas, on Armed Forces Day, and he was apparently elated to have met me—so much so he wrote this letter. Our meeting was something that he held in the highest regard and in his letter he said, "The respect and admiration I feel for your sacrifice is impossible to measure, and that I, as an American citizen, respect you, honor you, and I am forever grateful of your service." It's nice to know that I had that kind of impact on people.

Author: You seem to have that kind of impact on Marines too.

Iron Mike: Here is a letter written to me by a very good Marine buddy, Al B. Kolar. We knew each other since I was a PFC at Camp Lejeune, North Carolina in 1942. We were both in Charlie Company, 1st Battalion and our unit became 24th Marines in the 4rh Marine Division. We made landings together at places like Roi-Namur, Saipan, Tinian, and Iwo Jima. He writes here that to him I seemed like I *was* the Marine Corps because I must have lived and breathed the Marines all the time in the two and a half years we spent together. But he wrote this letter to remind me of how I saved his life.

Author: How did you save his life?

Iron Mike: His letter reminded me how we landed on Iwo Jima. Mount Suribachi was on our left and we had to proceed against heavy gunfire. We had managed to progress about one hundred yards when we came across a large Japanese blockhouse, and in order to take it we had a lot of casualties. One night we ended up spending the night in a Japanese cemetery, but at the time we didn't know it—he reminds me in the letter that we found out when I ordered them to dig foxholes and we started coming up with bones of the dead Japanese.

We kept moving forward on the island, and it was really tough going with extremely rough terrain. He wrote that it was like a miniature Grand Canyon and there were bushes and trees that were just blown apart with a lot of debris lying on the ground. There were large sandstone rocks, and the Japanese had built tunnels everywhere, and the caves and tunnels were perfect cover for the Japanese. We were heading toward the beach and were pushing the Japanese who were ahead of us. We decided to isolate the Japanese. Corporal Kolar was ordered to take a squad of Marines and make a clockwise circle around the Japanese. If he pulled that off we would have the Japs isolated and we could keep them from scattering. The other squad was going in a counter-clockwise direction with the same mission. He wrote how hard it was to move in the rough terrain and debris. He called his squad to a halt and tried to see where the other squad was. But while he was standing he was hit just above the ankle by a Japanese sniper and he started to fall—while falling he saw the three Japanese that had shot him and they were about ten yards in front of him and appeared to be in a cave entrance. One Jap was sighting in on him and within seconds he was hit again, this time in the left leg by the ankle again. Corporal Kolar fell backwards over a fallen tree and his legs were on one side of the tree and his head and body on the other side. He dropped his rifle when he fell so he tried reaching his .45 pistol, but in the fall his cartridge belt got twisted around and his body was lying on the weapon. Kolar shouted for a corpsman, but the corpsman and Marines could not get close enough to help him because the Japanese could easily shoot them. He wrote that the corpsman asked how he was doing and he yelled back that he was getting cold and numb, so the corpsman tossed a small bottle of brandy to him. Within minutes Corporal Kolar was getting cold again so the corpsman tossed another bottle of brandy, but most of the little bottles fell to the ground. The Japanese then started to shoot at the corpsmen.

About forty-five minutes went by and he wrote that he heard a loud voice yell out, "Kolar!" He immediately knew it was my voice. He told me where the Japanese were. I told Kolar to hold on and I would set a smoke screen so the Japanese couldn't see us try to rescue Kolar. We set off three 60mm mortar rounds and I yelled out, "We got 'em!" Corporal Kolar had enough energy left to rise high enough to pull his .45 out to get ready for an attack. However, we were the ones approaching him. He wrote how excited he was to see his Marine buddies coming in to save him. Part of his letter was to let me know that on that day he did not have an opportunity to thank me. He felt that what I did was just for him, but in the letter he said, "I know that Mike is an all-Marine and would do it for any other Marine . . . I am proud to know Mike, the best Marine!"

Author: You mentioned earlier that you had participated in a seminar called the "Pacific Panel" along with some other veterans of WWII. What did they have to say?

Iron Mike: I was invited to participate in the panel discussion along with some other veterans of different services. The audience was a group of students and they were there to learn about what we went through in WWII. The moderator was a teacher by the name of Linda Dudik. After the session was over she and her students wrote to me about the impact they got from the session. I talked about my experience on Iwo Jima. Linda wrote to me about some of the phrases

I used in describing that battle: "Courage was taken for granted", "A perfect battle on a perfect battlefield—a landscape similar to the moon"; and "fighting man against fighting man".

Author: I see the students wrote to you also. What did they have to say?

Iron Mike: The students wrote about their impressions of what I had said to the group. Ted Nestman wrote that he liked my jovial attitude and was impressed with how I was able to stand there with "sheer presence" and talk calmly about my experiences as though nothing bad had occurred. He felt like I was telling a story around a campfire—I was cool and collected to him.

Another student, Kimberly Chandler, wrote how she felt the whole night was amazing. She liked how the vets on the panel had camaraderie amongst themselves. She also enjoyed the rivalry between the Marines and the Navy men on the panel. Kimberly said hearing our experiences was better than reading a book—it was more realistic.

Kyle Wheeler described how he was fascinated with my thirty-five years in the Corps and how I had been in WWII, Korea, and Vietnam. He was even more impressed that I had volunteered to return to active duty during Desert Storm in 1992. He asked me if I would do it again and my answer was a strong, "Yes!"

Liz Wells was impressed with the way I told my stories. She liked the pride I had for my time with the Marines.

Author: They all seem to see the same qualities in you.

Iron Mike: I think these young people like the way I just speak my mind and I am not trying to be politically correct. Here's another letter, this one is from Laudenke Gallegos: "My choice of Iron Mike being my favorite speaker was simple: he was a very outspoken man. It's no mystery why Iron Mike is so recognized among Marines—he is a combat soldier due to his attitude."

Arthur McCann wrote: "Mike 'Combat Crazy' Mervosh was an exciting, energetic, and commanding person who made me crack up laughing. He would be a perfect recruiter for the Marine Corps because he makes his experience in the service feel like anyone can do what he and his buddies did . . ."

Interviewer: It is obvious that the crowd was impressed by your command presence and the manner in which you tell your stories. What other correspondence do you have in your books?

Iron Mike: Well, here is a letter from Marine Dan Dans who was the Commandant of Marine Corps League #942. I spoke at their meeting and he wrote to thank me. He said, "I wish there was more time allotted for you as a speaker—your stories and retrospect's are absolutely incredible. Your history and service in the Marines Corps is above reprise. The love and loyalty you still have to this day is so commendable: you, my friend, *are* the Marine Corps!"

Author: Iron Mike leafs through his array of binders that hold his cherished letters and written memorabilia. He stops at a piece that was written by a Marine, Sergeant Cindy Fisher.

Iron Mike: Here is an article written by Sergeant Cindy Fisher, USMC. I gave a speech at the SNCO club at Camp Pendleton and she taped my speech and then wrote about the speech in an article for the base publication *Scout*.

Author: It must be important since you kept it. What did she have to say?

Iron Mike: Well, she started off describing me by saying I looked like a grizzled sergeant major—I must give people that impression. But she relates how I stand tall with my shoulders back and ready to take on the world. My nameplate that night simply said, "Iron Mike" and she made mention of that too. She commented on my Korean War boots I was wearing and how shiny they were. She said my face was wrinkled like an old road map from previous battles I fought in.

Author: I am looking at what she wrote here and she seems to be complimenting you with a good description.

Iron Mike: Grinning, Iron Mike said, "I guess I still have it!"

Author: What was this event about when you gave this speech?

Iron Mike: It was a Field Mess Night for officers and staff non-commissioned officers of the 1st Marine Regiment of the 1st Marine Division, and I had been asked to be their guest of honor that night. She wrote that I had been in the 4th Marine Division in World War II, serving with them during their entire existence from inception to ending.

Author: It looks to me like she did a lot of background research on you—she mentions the medals of valor you received.

Iron Mike: Well, she must have because I don't talk about my medals in my speeches. She did mention my Bronze Star and second Navy Commendation Medal that I received while serving with the 5th Marine Regiment, 1st Marine Division while in Korea. She slipped in medals from Vietnam too, but I never mentioned those in the speech.

Author: I see here that she also noted how the younger Marines flock around you. Why do you think they are drawn to you in such a notable manner?

Iron Mike: Well, I think they just want to be around someone who has seen a lot of action. They see me as an "icon", and they want to get their pictures taken with me. Sometimes it baffles me, but I go along with it. A lot of them take "selfies" with me.

Author: That is understandable, and you certainly must recall that day in the MCRD Command Museum conference room when I was interviewing you and a Chief Warrant Officer gunner came in to ask directions—once I told him who you were he immediately asked if he could have me take a photo of you and him together. He was really excited to meet you live and in person.

Iron Mike: Sergeant Fisher mentions here that I have time for everybody and that "Semper Fidelis" might as well be tattooed on my chest. She says that I never stopped being a Marine, and proudly talked about the Marine Corps' past as well as the future. She quoted me when I said, "Iwo Jima is recorded as the bloodiest battle in the history of the Marine Corps. There were so many unselfish and unrelenting acts of bravery, courage, and heroism that occurred routinely on a daily basis that it was taken for granted, and most of it was unaccounted for. Which brought forth that inspiring message that would live on forever by Admiral Nimitz: 'that among those that fought at Iwo Jima, uncommon valor was a common virtue.'"

Author: Iron Mike, I have heard you say those things many times. What else did you say in your speech?

Iron Mike: Well, Sergeant Fisher pointed out that I reminded the audience "we joined the Corps for life, not for a fat pay check or perks, but because we wanted to serve our country and fight its battles. If it were easy, everyone would do it, and Marines wouldn't be needed. Being a Marine is not a job; it's a way of life. It is the duty of all Marines of all ranks to strive to be full-time Marines—the leaders, the warriors, the professionals—by being strong, tough, and decisive, and by maintaining, participating, observing, and preserving our fine and proud traditions, or we will just become another branch of the service and will be obsolete."

Author: I see here that you summed up your speech with, "Whenever there is a dirty job to do and the going gets really tough, meaning when the defecations hits the ventilation, the cry will always be heard: "Land the Marines!" I can only imaging how the group of Marines you were addressing reacted.

Iron Mike: Well, they were all pretty motivated, that is for sure!

Author: You have a letter from Joe Paulini. What is that one about?

Iron Mike: Joe wrote a letter to me on behalf of his uncle Sil Paulini, a Marine that served with me on Iwo Jima. Joe had read done some research about me on the Internet and he ran across an interview between myself and author Larry Smith who wrote The Few and the Proud: Marine Corps Drill Instructors in Their Own Words. Joe used to work with Sil and Sil would talk about Iwo and what we did, but according to Sil he used to talk a lot about me, and Sil was obviously very proud that he and I were friends and would let everyone he knew know that he knew me.

Author: I see that he included an enclosure—what's it that?

Iron Mike: It is an excerpt from an interview between a person named Lopez and author Larry Smith. Lopez asked Larry Smith if there was one story from his book The Few and the Proud that seemed to encompass all the other stories in the book. Larry Allen quickly said, "Iron Mike Mervosh, whose story is told in Chapter 2, was one of the thirty-one men left out a company of two hundred forty-two to walk off Iwo Jima under their own power after the battle had ended. He also fought in Korea and Vietnam. He retired after thirty-five years, then tried to come back to fight in the Gulf War. He served two tours as a drill instructor. At Parris Island today they have this brutal exercise run called 'The Iron Mike'; at Camp Pendleton in California the 'Iron Mike Room' is dedicated to him at the Staff NCO Club. His parting words invariably are: 'Keep charging'!"

Author: Iron Mike, when I read Larry Smith's book I too was impressed with your chapter. The irony of his book is that I am now the biography author of books about two of his subjects—you and Sergeant Major 'Ooorah' Paxton. Larry Smith wrote me a letter and he urged me to push hard to get your Iwo Jima stories into this book.

Iron Mike: Well, Larry Smith is a great author and we have become good friends since he wrote the books.

Author: You mentioned that you have saved some of your favorite speeches by various military leaders. What is your favorite one?

Iron Mike: I am glad you asked. To be honest, my favorite speech was by Navy Rear Admiral J. Stark. He was obviously very fond of Marines and what they stood for. He started his speech by talking about the numerous things he particularly liked about Marines. He cited for example: the way Marines March; how they do basic training; how they cultivate an ethos conducive of producing hard people in a soft age; that they only have one boss—their Commandant; that Marines are stubborn; they obey orders; they make the most of the press; and their professionalism.

Admiral Stark then described all the military services by comparing each to a specific breed of dog and explained why:

He felt the Air Force was like a poodle—always looking perfect and bit pampered and that they travel first class, but then agreed that poodles started out as hunting dogs and could become dangerous.

He then described the Army by likening them to a St. Bernard dog—big, heavy and clumsy, but also powerful with lots of stamina.

He felt the Navy was a lot like a Golden Retriever—good-natured and always good around the house. Everybody, including kids, love them, that their hair is sometimes too long, they go wandering off for long periods, and they love the water.

For the Marines he said he felt they were like two breeds: Rottweiler's and Dobermans—he felt that those two breeds described us perfectly—big and mean and skinny and mean. Marines have short hair and they go for the throat.

The Admiral said that "first to fight" is not just the Marine's motto, but also our way of life. He reviewed some of our historical battles dating back from Tun Tavern to modern times. He stated that Marines have distinguished themselves by their bravery, stubbornness, and aggressive spirit, sacrifice, love of country, and a strong loyalty to one another. He went on to say that Marines have done what they have done for you and I, and the country they love so strongly. They ask nothing more than the honor of being a United States Marines.

He ended his speech with this quote: "That's why I like Marines."

Author: The admiral certainly paints a pretty accurate picture of Marines! I see you have another scrapbook there—what have you come up with now?

Iron Mike: I received a copy of an essay titled A Hero Made of Iron written by Lindsey Watson. She had been in the audience of one of my many talks I have given over the years and she was so taken by what I said and represented that she wrote this essay about me. Here—read it and see what I mean.

Author: After reading this I can see a big pattern in all the writings about you—everyone sees the same qualities in you and report basically the same thing—they see you as a strong leader. She went to the trouble of researching your decorations, and she cited most of your battles and wars.

Iron Mike: Yes, she did a lot of research after my speech. But I love her last line the best: "He is truly a hero made of iron".

Author: On 7 June 2009 you participated in a two-part interview that appeared on C-Span. They questioned you about your combat experiences starting with your participation with the 4th Marine Division and taking you all the way up to the Vietnam War. The stories you told there are the same stories that you tell all the time. They never seem to vary.

Iron Mike: Well, the stories don't change because I tell the same stories about what really happened. Those stories are just as vivid to me today as they were on Iwo Jima in 1945. So it is not hard to tell the story the same way every time.

Author: A lot of people have told me they have seen those C-Span interviews. It is a valuable way to preserve our history. I understand you also gave a similar interview to the MCRD Command Museum staff so they could also preserve your history. Was that interview similar to C-Span's?

Iron Mike: To me one interview is like the next. They ask me a question and I try and answer it directly without clouding it with a lot of BS. I am comfortable with getting interviewed—I have had a lot of interviews you know.

Author: I certainly can understand that—I have done quite a few interviews with you myself. You make a good subject to interview because you never hesitate to answer all the questions. You have such a great memory of events that happened so long ago—that helps a lot.

Chapter 19

PHOTOS OF IRON MIKE

Part One: The Early Days

Iron Mike Mervosh before he became "Iron Mike". This is his boot camp picture when he was just a private. His face shows his happiness in realizing his dream of becoming a Marine. At the time he had no idea where the journey would take him over the next thirty-five years.

By the time Iron Mike out posted from boot camp and went on to infantry training at New River, North Carolina (later renamed "Camp Lejeune") he had been promoted to Private First Class (PFC). His leadership and rapidly accumulated knowledge of weapons allowed him to assist with weapon instructions. In the photo PFC Mervosh is kneeling beside the tents they were billeted in.

Not all the time spent in the Pacific front was engaging the enemy—unless you can consider the opponents of this baseball game "enemy".

The Fourth Marine Division had returned to Maui from their initial tour at the Marshall Island and the Marines were given a chance to relax. Iron Mike is at bat and his athletic abilities are easy to detect. Between Iron Mike and the catcher is PFC Thomas whose arm is bandaged—he had been hit with a machine gun burst on the Marshall Islands.

Iron Mike was a great athletic specimen. He was a superb boxer and is shown here preparing for a middleweight boxing bout. Iron Mike eventually became the Fourth Marine Division's Middleweight Boxing Champion. It was felt that Iron Mike could have turned professional, but wounds he received in his many battles in the Pacific ended that possibility. Iron Mike was fearless in the ring—just like he was in combat!

The Fourth Marine Division was pounded as they landed on the black volcanic sands of Iwo Jima. There was no place to hide or duck for cover—everyone was exposed to heavy fire from everything from light weapons fire all the way up to heavy artillery fire. The attrition rate was horrendous with heavy casualties. All the Marines could do was to inch their way forward and try to keep as low to the sands as possible. Mount Suribachi looms in the background partially obscured by the smoke from the gunfire.

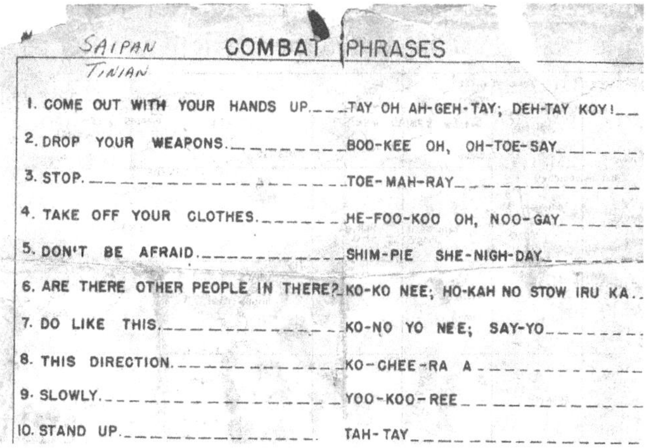

SAIPAN
TINIAN

COMBAT PHRASES

1. COME OUT WITH YOUR HANDS UP	TAY OH AH-GEH-TAY; DEH-TAY KOY!
2. DROP YOUR WEAPONS	BOO-KEE OH, OH-TOE-SAY
3. STOP	TOE-MAH-RAY
4. TAKE OFF YOUR CLOTHES	HE-FOO-KOO OH, NOO-GAY
5. DON'T BE AFRAID	SHIM-PIE SHE-NIGH-DAY
6. ARE THERE OTHER PEOPLE IN THERE?	KO-KO NEE; HO-KAH NO STOW IRU KA..
7. DO LIKE THIS	KO-NO YO NEE; SAY-YO
8. THIS DIRECTION	KO-CHEE-RA A
9. SLOWLY	YOO-KOO-REE
10. STAND UP	TAH-TAY

On each mission the Marines were all given a cheat-sheet that phonetically spelled out certain Japanese commands so they could communicate at the most basic level just in case they took any prisoners into custody. Iron Mike saved one of his cheat sheets from Tinian and Saipan. The sheet was of little value to most of the Marines since prisoners were not taken with any degree of frequency.

This photo is one of Iron Mike's favorites—it represents the "walking wounded", the thirty-one Marines that were left out of his original company strength of two-hundred forty-two that were part of the invasion of Iwo Jima. Iron Mike is shown in the top with an arrow pointing at him. When the photo was taken he was the acting company commander, as he was the senior man left out of the group—all the senior men had been either killed or were severely wounded and had to be medically evacuated. On the far right another arrow shows his future brother-in-law. Many of those in the photo are wounded including Iron Mike. To Iron Mike Mervosh this photo symbolizes the "perfect battle on a perfect battlefield". The Marines proudly display two Japanese Flags they captured on the island.

Following the fighting at Iwo Jima Iron Mike is shown sporting his gunnery sergeant stripes. His sleeve proudly displays his Fourth Marine Division patch. It is obvious that Iron Mike is grinning because he is happy to be alive after what he went through in battles across the Pacific.

After WWII was over Iron Mike was sent to the Second Marine Division and began doing Med-tours in the Mediterranean. He stands in front of the St. Peter's Cathedral at Vatican City in 1951. Iron Mike carries a Billy club, but said he was there to help his fellow Marines in case they got in trouble. Iron Mike loved these tours, as the liberty was great at all the ports.

The day finally came—thirty-fives years after starting his career in the Marines Iron Mike finally retired from the Marine Corps. His career was a stellar one and at the time of retirement he was the senior-most enlisted man in all of the armed forces. He stands outside of the tented area where his reception was held. Sergeant Major Iron Mike Mervosh wanted his career to end at Pearl Harbor because it was the attack on Pearl Harbor that initially motivated him to join the Marine Corps. But like all Marines before him, his retirement did not mean he was no longer a Marine—he continues the tradition of "once a Marine, always a Marine!"

Part Two: Famous People Meet a Famous Marine

Iron Mike Mervosh was a big draw for Hollywood and TV movie starts. Here Iron Mike stands with actor Lee Marvin. Lee Marvin was special to Iron Mike—they both shared fighting in the South Pacific. Lee Marvin was in the battle of Saipan, but was wounded and had to be Medivac'd out.

Iron Mike stands next to his beautiful wife Maggie along with television and movie star Robert Stack. Robert Stack had been a naval gunnery instructor during WWII and held a common bond with Iron Mike.

Hugh O'Brien was a movie and TV star, but also was the youngest drill instructor in the history of the Marine Corps—he had just turned eighteen years old before graduating as Honor Man of his platoon and he was asked to step in a help train recruits during the early phase of

WWII. Following his Marine Corps career he became an actor and had starring roles in both movies and TV—his most famous role was that of "Wyatt Earp" on TV. He stands at a western-themed affair with Iron Mike and Maggie.

Part Three: Second Career—Retirement

Not many people have their own personal parking space—Iron Mike has his at the Staff NCO Club at Camp Pendleton. Iron Mike stands proudly next to his sign—nobody dares park there either.

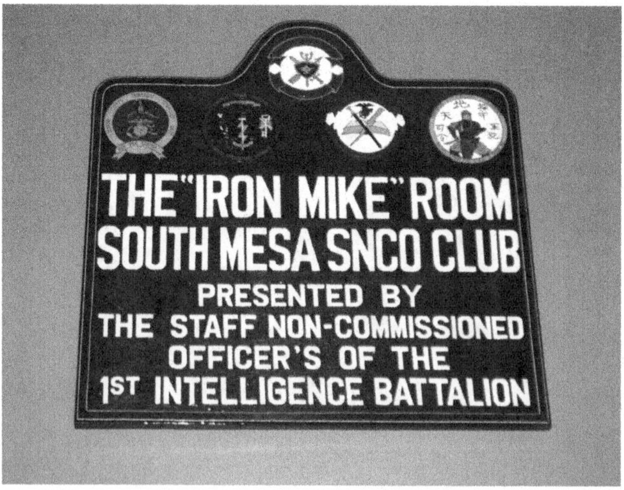

This sign hangs on the wall at the Camp Pendleton Staff NCO Club. It is self-explanatory—Iron Mike has his own dedicated room there. It is *the* place to go.

The "Iron Mike Room" comes complete with standing rules. The stakes can be high if someone breaks the rules.

The Chosin Reservoir was not a battle that Iron Mike fought while in Korea, but the significance of that battle was so historic that he feels a great affinity for those that fought in the battle. The Korean War was a personal war for Iron Mike, as he lost his younger brother Milan in that conflict.

A fellow Marine presented this special forty-eight star American flag to Iron Mike and it hangs proudly on the wall of the Iron Mike Room at the SNCO Club at Camp Pendleton. The forty-eight star flag is very special to Iron Mike—it was the flag that represented America during World War II and also the Korean War. If SgtMaj Mervosh sees a flag that has been desecrated, or if he finds an Iwo Jima statue that has a modern fifty-star flag he will go off like a Roman candle. The flag is personal to Iron Mike—he put his life on the line for it, and he lost a lot of buddies who fought with him to protect what the flag stands for.

A special museum room is part of the Iron Mike Room. There are rows of glassed-in shelves that display mementos Iron Mike has saved over his entire life.

This display case shows the various patches and insignia used by the Marine units prior to the Commandant's order in 1948 to cease wearing the patches and insignia. After 1948 the Marines only had the Eagle, Globe, and Anchor as the sole symbol of what the Marine Corps stands for.

On well over one hundred-plus occasions Iron Mike has been asked to be a guest speaker or a guest of honor at an event. He has travelled all over the U.S. to cover these requests, and he has built up a national following. He always gets a plaque or something to commemorate the occasion. This one is for being the Guest of Honor at the 2008 Marine Corps Birthday Ball held by the Security Battalion.

One of the trophies Iron Mike is most proud of is his Fourth Marine Division Middleweight Boxing Championship Trophy. This is displayed in his Iron Mike Room inside the museum room.

The trophy displays of Iron Mike's boxing exploits are proudly displayed in the museum room.

The most iconic and famous image ever made that reflects winning the battle is the image of raising our flag on top of Mount Suribachi during the first few days of battle on the island of Iwo Jima. Iron Mike was fighting on the black sand beaches below Mount Suribachi when it occurred. He rose with his binoculars to take a peak at what all the ships offshore were honking their horns about—just the fact that he had a pair of binoculars gave the Japanese a clue that Iron Mike was a leader and they immediately fired many rounds at him, one of which hit his belt. He dropped back down and continued his fighting.

The Iron Mike Room museum contains many artifacts of his thirty-five years of Marine Corps service.

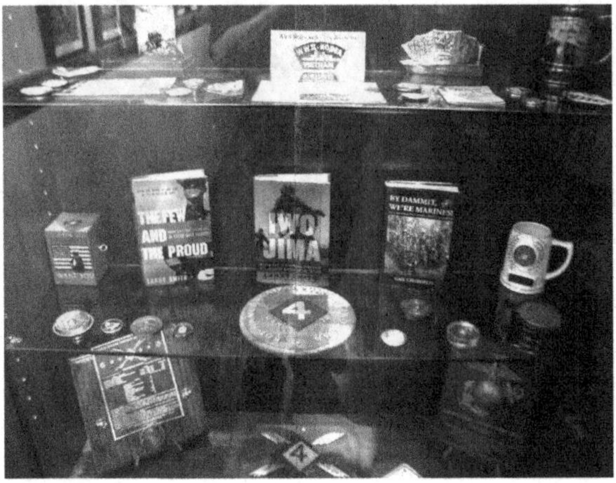

Three books are displayed on the shelves of his museum room: *The Few and the Proud* by Larry Smith; *Iwo Jima* also by Larry Smith; and *By Dammit, We're Marines* by Gail Chatfield. Those books all contain stories about Iron Mike. Soon *Hardcore Iron Mike* will sit next to the others.

Iron Mike is shown in the center picture with President Gerald Ford.

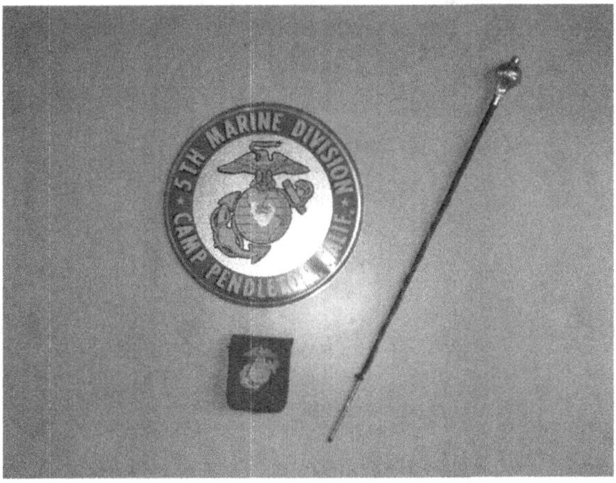

The Iron Mike Room has a number of mementos of the various divisions and commands that Iron Mike was with—here is a memento to the Fifth Marine Division.

Chesty Puller is one of Iron Mike's Marine Corps heroes—as for that matter Chesty is a hero to just about every Marine! Iron Mike had the privilege of sitting with Major General Puller and he got the following advice: "Mike, before I leave I want you to have a smoke, drink a beer, take a chew, and take a chance!" Iron Mike took that to be a direct order.

The display in the Iron Mike Room would not be complete without a copy of Joe Rosenthal's iconic image of the raising of the Flag over Mount Suribachi—Marines who were on the island at the same time Iron Mike was there signed the photo. This is priceless.

Most Marines keep their old uniforms in a seabag—Iron Mike keeps his in this glass case in his museum room. He wears it on special occasions, and not many Marines can say they can still fit into their uniform after being out of the Marines for thirty-eight years!

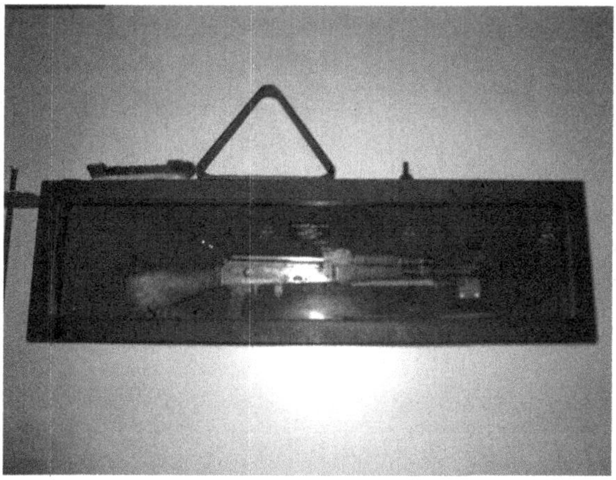

A Marine friend gave this Russian AK-47 rifle to Iron Mike. This was the weapon used by the communist during the Vietnam War—it is currently one rifle that represents about twenty-three percent of all rifles in the world and is used by almost all of our enemies at the present time.

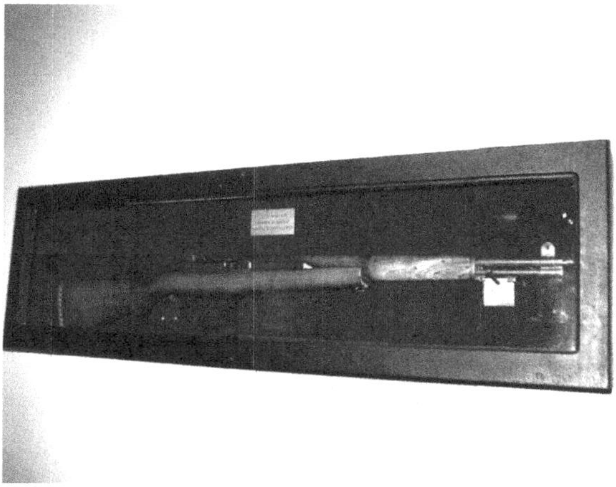

The same Marine friend who offered the AK-47 to Iron Mike also presented this M-1 Garand. This rifle was the same type used by Iron Mike in both WWII and the Korean War and is Iron Mike's favorite rifle.

This plaque reflects all of the current Marine Corps Staff NCO rank insignia. Iron Mike held every pay grade rank that the Marine Corps offered, but the Marine Corps had not yet introduced the Lance Corporal (E-3) ranking until Iron Mike was already a sergeant major.

Part Four: The Best 'Marine' Room—Ever!

Iron Mike has the absolute best Marine's room ever! Just about every square inch of his den is full of his memorabilia, nick-knacks, and photos of his entire Marine Corps career.

One item of interest is this montage of photos and articles covering his retirement and factors like his nineteen and one-half year's of time-in-grade as a sergeant major.

When the Greatest Generation Foundations sent Iron Mike, and a select few other WWII veterans involved in the Pacific theaters, on a trip back to their old battle fields such as Tinian, Saipan, and Iwo Jima, his trip and history was written about and appeared on the front page of *Page One*. The men involved were offered this free trip back to their battlegrounds and were provided first-class treatment the entire trip. Iron Mike is shown standing on top of Mount Suribachi. The beach he landed on in 1945 is shown right behind him in the photo. So many years had passed and the island's plants and flora had come back—it looked very different than he last saw it in 1945. He said it was nice to stand there and not be shot at. Iron Mike was upset that a Japanese flag was flying at the peak of Mount Suribachi—he felt an American flag should fly to honor all of the men killed and wounded in the taking of the island.

Korean War veterans were offered a free trip back to Korea in honor of their military service in the Korean War. This photo is of a nameplate that spells Iron Mike's name in the Korean language.

This shot is of the east wall of Iron Mike's den. All the other walls are similar and filled with his memories.

This shot is of the north wall in his museum-like den.

This is the west wall of his den. Most Marines would die to have a room like this. Not only is his den wallpapered with his memories, his garage is the same way!

Here is an example of how Sergeant Major Mervosh's house is decorated outside of his den.

Part Five: Special Events

Iron Mike Mervosh was the guest speaker at the 50th Anniversary of the Iwo Jima invasion. He is wearing his dress blues that he keeps in the glass locker in the museum room in the Iron Mike Room in the SNCO Club at Camp Pendleton. He recently attended the 70th Anniversary of the Iwo Jima invasion but a photo was not available.

Iron Mike stands with his Marine buddy Jim Blane—both are showing off their handmade Bolo ties that were presented to them.

In a museum Iron Mike eyes the Korean War cold weather gear. The gear brought back a lot of memories of the extreme cold he faced in Korea and how his feet were frostbitten so bad that his toenails no longer grow. It was tough time for everyone involved in that war. Iron Mike feels that Korea was the last war the U.S. fought in which there were no "rules of engagement" to inhibit the way Marines engaged the enemy. In the Korean War the Marines could take out the enemy whenever and wherever they found them.

One hat that Iron Mike likes to wear is his cap with all three wars he fought in: WWII, Korea, and Vietnam.

Korean War veterans from Tacoma, Washington held a 50th anniversary of the Korean War and invited Iron Mike to be their guest speaker. He poses here with one of their members.

Iron Mike holds an informal party at his hotel room with friends. He ignores the "no smoking" signs in the room and continues to smoke his big cigar. Barbara Hansen Harris is giving Iron Mike a big hug. The event was for the Combat Veteran Reunion of Iwo Jima's sixtieth anniversary at the Hilton McLean at Tyson's Corner in McLean, Virginia.

Iron Mike was invited to be the Parade Reviewing Officer at a recruit graduation at Parris Island, South Carolina. Here he is arriving at the parade deck prior to the parade starting.

Iron Mike stands tall at the position of 'attention' and salutes the passing platoons in his ever-so-sharp Marine Corps manner. Prior to the parade the narrator read his bio to the visitors—he was a big draw after the parade was over as the recruits and families united. Many came up to him just to meet him and shake his hand, and that included the young DIs in the event. Iron Mike is the name of the recruit's motivation run and they were awed to meet the man the run was named after.

Immediately following the parade the Depot Chief of Staff, Colonel Ricky Tabowski turned to Iron Mike and saluted him to the surprise of the enlisted DIs observing this—it was a keen showing of the ultimate respect this officer had for Iron Mike's legacy. The Parris Island Depot Sergeant Major, SgtMaj Gary Buck stands with Iron Mike and one of the senior drill instructors while Iron Mike is presented with a plaque reflecting their appreciation.

Iron Mike Mervosh standing with Parris Island's Depot Sergeant Major, SgtMaj Gary Buck on the right, Col Ricky Tabowski, Chief of Staff on the far left, and his flame thrower buddy from Iwo Jima, Dominic Tutalo.

Larry Smith, author of *Iwo Jima* and *The Few and the Proud*, and former editor of *Parade Magazine*, sits with Iron Mike at the East Coast DI Association reunion banquet at Parris Island. The author is very proud to know Iron Mike and wrote a great chapter in his book *The Few and the Proud* about Iron Mike's storied Marine Corps career.

Iron Mike is signing his autograph on books while the book author Larry Smith looks on. Iron Mike is a big draw and everyone wants a piece of his history.

The line of Marines wanting their books autographed was somewhat endless.

Iron Mike in front of the Iwo Jima display at MCRD San Diego Command Museum. Mount Suribachi rises in the background. SgtMaj Mervosh spent the most harrowing thirty-six days of his life fighting Japanese there. It was the "perfect battle on a perfect battlefield" according to SgtMaj Mervosh.

I had invited SgtMaj Iron Mike Mervosh to attend the MCRD recruit's training day #56 tour of the San Diego Command Museum. Their tour lasts two hours and they spend twenty minutes in each of the six primary galleries. On this day I had Iron Mike stay in the WWII Gallery and he stood by the Iwo Jima display. When each platoon of recruits came into the room I introduced him and then let him talk to the recruits—he blew them away with his stories of the hardships they faced on Iwo Jima, yet inspired them beyond belief with his motivating style. He was the hit of the day and every recruit that passed through will no doubt remember this icon and their opportunity to meet him.

When I had my first book signing for my first book *The Yellow Footprints To Hell And Back* SgtMaj Iron Mike came. I was thrilled he was there and I gave him an autographed copy of my book. I had no idea that I would eventually write his book as well. I am very proud of my association with this man and he has inspired me to be more than I thought I could be. Everyone should as lucky as me . . .

Chapter 20

GLOSSARY OF MARINE CORPS TERMS

Alignment: The left-to-right straightness of rows in formations

Amtrac: Tracked amphibious tractor vehicle used to transport the first waves of the invasion on Iwo Jima. Called an LVT, it eight feet wide, nine feet all, and twenty-seen feet long.

As you were: Resume what you were doing

Assholes and elbows: In a hurry; quickly

AWOL: Absent without leave

Banzai: Usually a suicidal infantry assault in which the commander of the Japanese forces refused to employ on Iwo Jima when the Marines initially landed on the beaches. Ironically, had he ordered one the first night of the invasion, it may very well have succeeded because the landing forces were so disorganized.

BAR: Browning Automatic Rifle. This was the principal automatic rapid-fire weapon for a squad. It was a gas-operated 30-06 caliber, and could be fired via tripod or standing up. Basically it was a "walking machine gun," and its twenty round magazine could be emptied in three seconds. Each BAR man had an assistant who carried ammunition for it.

Barracks: The living quarters building that houses Marines or other military men and women

Barracks cover: Marine dress uniform cover

Bazooka: Common name for the tubular 2.68 rocket launcher, fired over the shoulder. It was used against tanks or fortified positions. Each platoon had at least two. The assistant inserted the shell from the back, and then tapped the gunner on the shoulder. Effective range was about one hundred meters.

Bed: Bunk, sack, rack

Bends and thrusts: The most hated exercise recruits get; often used for incentive training PT; sometimes referred to as "Bends and MF's"

Betty: Japanese light bomber

Billet: Assignment of job; place of residence

Blouse: noun: Jacket; verb: to tuck in; secure

Blousing bands: Elastic bands used to secure utility trouser cuffs on boots

Boondocks: Rough terrain, gung ho

Boondockers: Marine field shoes, usually worn with canvas leggings

Boot: Recruit; also refers to high top leather footwear

Boot camp: The training place for Marine recruits; a place of endearment to young Marines.

Brain housing group: The brain or mind

Brother: A fellow Marine (always capitalized)

Brown bagger: A married Marine

Brig: Jail

Brig rat: A person in jail

Bulkhead: Wall

Butt: The target mechanism used to hold the targets at the rifle range

Butts: The target area at the rifle range

Civvies: Civilian clothes

Bucket issue: Initial issue of all items a recruit will need to start boot camp.

By your leave: A request of an enlisted man to pass an officer; a request of a recruit to pass a drill instructor or officer

By-the-numbers: In sequence

C-2/C-4: A putty-like plastic explosive that could be molded by hand. It was favored for use in satchel charges. A fuse set off a blasting cap, which caused the C-2/C-4 to explode.

Cammies: Camouflage uniform (see Camos)

Camos: Camouflage utility uniform

Camp Matthews: An old rifle marksmanship training range used by the Marines. It is now the University of California, San Diego at La Jolla (UCSD).

Campaign cover: The drill instructor hat; Smokey-the-bear hat; the Hat

Cannon: large heavy artillery of four basic calibers: the 37-millimeter, which could be dragged up to the line of combat by hand. It could fire ten rounds a minute, and it employed mostly canister, small bullets in one shell that spread out like shotgun pellets, but with more lethal range; the 75-millimeter pack howitzer, which could be broken down and then carried by several Marines; and finally the 105's and 155's.

Carry on: Continue what you were doing: as you were

Cattle car: A trailer used for hauling military personnel and their gear; looks like a trailer used for hauling cattle

Ceiling: Overhead

CG: Commanding General

Chit: An authorization

Chow: Food

Chow hall: Mess hall

CINCPAC: The sort of acronym loved by the military. This one stood for Commander-in-Chief, Pacific Campaign

Civilian: Anyone other than a military person

CO: Commanding officer; conscientious objector

Colors: The flag; a ceremony of raising or lowering of the flag

Company: Composed of several platoons; one of several units in a battalion

C-rations: Canned field rations (also known as "C-rats")

Cruise: A tour of duty on a ship that requires four years of enlistment time.

C-2/C-4: Plastic explosives, forms like hard putty

Corky's: The worst eatery anywhere; found around the corner from the Los Angeles Military Processing Center

Corpsman: A Navy medic that serves with the Marines in the Fleet Marine Force

Corsair: A single-engine Marine fighter plane

Cover: noun: A hat; verb: alignment of one person behind another

Choke yourself: A suggestion to a recruit, that he take the hand of his drill instructor, and use it to choke himself as a disciplinary measure—not allowed by the SOP

Crew chief: The man in charge of a helicopter flight crew

Crucible: The final event of recruit training that brings recruits together as a team. After the multi-day event is over the recruits are issued an Eagle, Globe and Anchor emblem (EGA) and they are considered Marines from that point on.

CP: Command post

D-Day: Debarkation (invasion) Day

Deck: The ground or floor

Defecation hits the ventilation: when all hell breaks loose; not a pretty thing

DI: Short for "drill instructor"

DI's grass: Any dirt around the barracks or Quonset hut and is considered sacred and belongs to the DI exclusively—until incentive training is ordered and then it becomes "the pit".

Ditty bag: A small cloth bag with a drawstring used to hold dirty clothes

Ditty bop: A certain swagger; an attitude of walk

Doggie or Dog Face: A soldier in the Army

Draftee: A person that was inducted into the military by the Selective Service

Drill instructor: The trainer of recruits; DI; a God-like figure; the object of nightmares to recruits

DUKW: Manned by black soldiers—not Marines. This amphibious vehicle known as the "Duck" was fifteen feet by eighteen feet, with four-wheel drive, rubber tires, and a propeller that drove it through the water. One company of DUKWs was assigned to each Marine Division on Iwo Jima.

Duty: Time required being on the job; in charge; job assignment

Duty Hut: A drill instructor's Quonset hut; a duty office

Duty Office: A drill instructors office

Duty NCO: The non-commissioned officer in-charge at each unit every day

Ear-banger: Someone who seeks to curry favor with a superior

Edson Range: Rifle range for rifle marksmanship training located at Camp Pendleton California

Enlistee: A person that voluntarily joined the military

E-vac: Medical evacuation

Eyeball: To scrutinize; to gaze at

Fartsack: A mattress cover

Field day: A general or thorough cleaning of a barracks; an athletic competition

Field Day: An athletic competition between units; a thorough cleansing of a barracks

Field strip: To disassemble; take apart

First Phase: The first phase of recruit training

First sergeant: Senior man of a company or small units

First shirt: See First Sergeant

Flame-thrower: A portable weapon carried by hand or fired from a tank (Zippo), projecting an incendiary fuel such as jellied gasoline, or a mixture of high-octane gas and diesel fuel. The hand-carried version weighed seventy-two pounds and held five gallons, which could be burned up in about seven seconds.

Footlocker: The wooden box each Marine has under his rack to store his gear

Frags: Fragmentation grenade

Frogs: French soldier

Gang way: Step aside; make room

Gas chamber: A small building that is used to demonstrate the affects of tear-gas on recruits and other trainees; a place that causes horrible consequences for users.

Gear: Equipment

Geek dunk: Ice cream

GI can: A trash can; sometimes highly polished in recruit barracks

Gook: Asian enemy (politically incorrect)

Grab-ass: Horseplay; goofing off; playing around

Grinder: Parade deck

Guide: The man in front of the platoon formation that carries the Gideon; the recruit in charge of the platoon in the drill instructors absence

Guideon: A pennant attached to a staff that gives the unit designation; carried by the Guide

Gung Ho: Based on a China proverb that means to work together. It was adopted by the Marines to describe an overly zealous member of the Corps.

Gunner: A warrant officer in charge of a weapons related unit

Gunney: A gunnery sergeant

Gyrene: slang term for Marine and is despised by Iron Mike along with "Jarhead"—"By Dammit, We're Marines!"

H-Hour: The hour at which an operation begins

Hall: Passageway

Hand grenades: There were three types: fragmentation, incendiary, and smoke. After pulling the pin (by hand, never by the teeth) there are three to five seconds prior till the explosion once the lever was released. It was customary to let two seconds go by before throwing it so that it could not be flung back by the enemy. The effective radius was about ten yards. The Japanese version resembled a potato masher, which was activated by rapping on one's helmet. At times on Iwo Jima it seemed that more grenades were thrown than bullets were fired.

Hat: Drill Instructor (most commonly used at Parris Island); cover

Hatch: Door

Head: Toilet

Head-call: A trip to the toilet

Higgins Boat: Overall name of the flat-bottomed landing craft devised by Andrew Higgins for the Normandy invasion in June, 1944. Various types included the LCI (Landing Craft Infantry); LCT (Landing Craft Tank); LCVP (Landing Craft Vehicles and Personnel); and the LCM (Landing Craft Medium). The LVT was the amphibious tracked ship-to-shore vehicles known as the 'Amtrac'.

Hooch: a makeshift shanty or bunker used by Marines as living quarters in Vietnam

House apes: children

House Mouse: The drill instructor's maid or go-fer

Honcho: Boss; man in charge

HQ: Headquarters

"I": A term a recruit cannot ever call himself or herself

In-your-face: The act of getting up-close and yelling directly at the recruit, and often entails the DIs cover brim up against the bridge of the recruits nose

Incentive training: Extra physical training imposed for infractions or lack of motivation; also known as "IT"

Irish Pennant: A loose string on a uniform; any loose item such as sheets protruding from under a rack

"Iron Mike" Mervosh: A crusty sergeant major who at one time was the senior most man in all the military services. A man revered by all.

He epitomizes what being a Marine is all about. Served all thirty-six fighting days on Iwo Jima—Ooorah!

IT: See incentive training

ITR: Infantry Training Regiment (Now known as "School of Infantry")

Jap: A slang term for Japanese soldier or Japanese enemy during WWII (politically incorrect)

Jarhead: A Marine

Junior drill instructor: drill instructor junior to the platoon commander or senior drill instructor

Junk-on-the-bunk: An inspection requiring all of a Marines' gear to be laid out on a bunk in a formal layout

KaBar: A solid six-inch fixed blade knife carried by virtually every Marine, primarily for combat, but also useful for opening K-rations

KIA: Killed in action

Landing zone: A place where a helicopter lands to drop off Marines in a combat situation; sometimes referred to as "LZ"

Leave: An authorized absence over twenty-four hours

Liberty: Time off less than 24 hours

Lifer: A Marine that is in for life or career

Line of departure: A suitably marked offshore line intended to coordinate landing craft so they could land on designated beaches according to predetermined schedules.

Lock and load: Arm and ready your weapon; get ready

Low quarters: Marine dress shoe

LP: Listening post

LZ: see Landing Zone

Machine gun: There were two basic types: the first was a .30 caliber, air-cooled version that could be fired standing up or on a ten-pound tripod. Its webbed belt carried 250 rounds. Each gunner had an assistant. The second was a heavy version, which was water-cooled, and rested on a fifty-one pound tripod. It was brought up at night for perimeter defense. A squad leader, gunner, assistant gunner were assisted by six ammo humpers. Two machine guns were assigned to each platoon. The water-cooled gun weighed ninety-one pounds.

Maggie's drawers: A red flag flown over a target when the shooter has missed the target completely

Manual-of-arms: Drill movements involving the rifle; rifle movements

Medivac: The medical evacuation of a wounded person; see E-vac

Mess hall: An eating facility; chow hall

M-1 Carbine: A .30 caliber carbine with a fifteen round magazine that lacked the stopping power of the M-1 Garand

M-1 Garand: The infantryman's favorite weapon. It was a gas-operated .30-06 caliber semiautomatic rifle with an eight-shot clip. Unlike the bolt-action Springfield '03, the M-1 could be fired repeatedly by just pulling the trigger. With its eighteen-inch bayonet attached it weighed almost ten pounds. The bayonet was snapped onto the end of the muzzle when the Marine landed on the beach, and also put it on when snooping around caves, or any time in which the enemy might engage in close-in fighting.

M-14: Standard rifle issue during the initial phase o f the Vietnam era. Also a gas-operated semiautomatic rifle but had the option of having a selector switch attached that would convert it to full automatic fire. Use a 7.62 X 57mm NATO round (.308 Caliber).

Marine Unit: A division included twenty-thousand men and consisted of the following: four regiments; engineers; pioneer; tank; service; motor transport; medical; amphibian tractor battalions; a signal; laundry company; war dog platoon; observation squadron; and two replacement battalions. A regiment consisted of three thousand, three hundred men broking into three battalions. A battalion numbers one thousand men, or three companies. A company was made up to two hundred fifty men and a rifle platoon that held forty-five Marines and two Navy corpsmen. Mortar platoons were smaller, usually eighteen to twenty, and machine gun platoons held up to fifty-six men.

MCRD: Marine Corps Recruit Depot, one in San Diego, California and the other at Parris Island, South Carolina. San Diego has jets, Parris Island has fleas.

Military time: Twenty-four hour clock: starts at 0001 and runs through 2400 each day; does not require the use of AM or PM to identify morning and afternoon

Mortar: A short smoothbore gun for firing shells at high angles. Six Marines manned the 60-millimeter mortar: the gunner, his assistant, and four carriers. It was muzzle-loaded and could be elevated to forty-five degrees. It was very accurate from three hundred to seven hundred yards, and would reach as far as one thousand, eight hundred yards. There was also an 81-millimeter mortar.

MOS: Military occupational specialty

Motivation Platoon: A platoon previously used in recruit training for incorrigible recruits or those in need of attitude adjustments.

Moto-run: A five-mile run by graduating recruit companies the day before graduation and is the first viewing by families of their graduating member at the beginning and end of the run.

Mountain climbers: An exercise in which a recruit gets into a push-up position with arms fully extended, and then in alternating movements drives his knees to his chest in a rapid manner; derogatory term: "Mount Motherf*ckers"

Mustang: An officer that was a former enlisted man

Nambu: Japanese light machine gun

NCO: Non-commissioned officer

NCOIC: Non-commissioned officer-in-charge

Noncom: Noncommissioned officers are the enlisted men, especially gunnery sergeants and the like, who really enable the Marine Corps to function.

Non-qual: A Marine that fails to qualify with the weapon at the rifle range

Office pogue: A desk-bound Marine

Officer-of-the-day: The duty officer each day at all commands

OIC: Officer-in-charge

Ooorah: Outstanding; gung-ho shout of many Marines: SgtMaj Bill Paxton's favorite term

Outstanding: Job well done; exceptional

Overhead: Ceiling

Overlap: The overlapping of schedules of graduating platoons and incoming platoons

Over-the-hill: Unauthorized absence

Parade deck: The grinder; used for marching and ceremonies

Parris Island: Island in South Carolina that MCRD is located at; a haven for sand fleas

Passageway: A corridor or hallway

Perimeter: The guarded edge of a position

PI: Parris Island

Pit: The designated location for doing incentive training PT

Physical training: Exercising activity; PT

Platoon: Made up of four squads; eighty-five to ninety men (Vietnam era)

Platoon commander: The senior drill instructor; wears a shiny black leather duty belt, now referred to as "senior drill instructor".

Pogey bait: Candy or sweets; taboo for any recruit

Police call: The time allocated to clean up an area

Police-up: To clean up

Post Traumatic Stress Disorder: A debilitating disorder caused by stress from a traumatic incident such as combat or other trauma; also known as PTSD.

PT: Physical training

PTSD: See Post Traumatic Stress Disorder

Pugil stick: A heavily padded pole used in hand-to-hand combat training to simulate rifle and bayonet fighting

Quonset hut: A metal building with a round non-stop roof; used for recruit billeting during the Vietnam War era

Quarters: Living space

Rack: Bunk; bed

Receiving Barracks: The place recruits initially start at when arriving at MCRD

Red lead: Ketchup

Reveille: Time to get up in the morning

Rifle grenade: An adaptor on a rifle muzzle that could launch shoot a grenade up to one hundred fifty yards, whereas thirty yards was about the maximum for one thrown by hand.

Rifle range: The place where Marines learn to shoot their weapons; a shooting range for qualifying or practicing with the weapons.

Round: Cartridge or bullet

RTBn: Recruit Training Battalion

RTR: Recruit Training Regiment

Salt: A Marine who has been in the Corps a long time; an old hand

Saltpeter: a substance recruits believe is put in their chow during boot camp to squelch their manly urges.

Salty: Having an attitude; opinionated

Sand flea: A small flea that creates a living hell for Parris Island recruits

Satchel charge: A hand-carried charge of dynamite or C-2 or C-4 plastic explosive that could be thrown once a flame-thrower had been used to blast the occupants in a cave into retreat.

Scuttlebutt: Drinking fountain; gossip or rumor

Sea bag: A duffel bag used to carry one's possessions

Sea lawyer: a person who thinks he has all the answers; know-it-all

Sea story: A big story; an exaggeration

Second Phase: Second phase of recruit training; time at the rifle range; period for mess and maintenance week

Secure: to put things in their place; to tie something down; to stop doing something

Sergeant Major: Senior enlisted man of a battalion, regiment, or other large unit

Series: Four platoons that proceed through boot camp as a unit (Vietnam era)

Series Gunny: The gunnery sergeant in a recruit series that is in charge

Series Officer: The officer of a recruit series

782 gear: Field equipment; canvas gear issue

Shit bird: A screw-up; a messy or undisciplined person

Short timer: A Marine with a short time left on their enlistment

Sickbay: A medical clinic or hospital

Sick bay commando: A person that goes to sickbay frequently

Side ammo: Salt, pepper, and condiments

Sighting-in: Adjusting the sights of the rifle to hit the target at various distances

Skipper: A captain; commanding officer

Skivvies: Underwear

Slop chute: Enlisted men's club

Smoke flares: Flares that give off different colored smoke

Smoke grenade: A grenade that releases colored smoke for signaling or to conceal movement

Smoking lamp: The authority to smoke when it is lit

Snapping-in: Practicing shooting the rifle without rounds; practicing trigger-squeeze

SOP: Standard Operating Procedure; a standard set of rules for handling recruits that covers all situations

Spit-shine: Super-glossy shines on boots, shoes, or leather gear caused by hours of meticulous applications of shoe polish

Springfield '03: The principal combat rifle used before the M-1 Garand came along. It was a .30 caliber bolt-action rifle, which meant each shell had to be ejected manually. The Springfield had a five-round clip. Extremely accurate at extreme distances.

Squad: One row of the three to four rows that each platoon was made up of

Squad bay: Barracks interior

Squad leader: The person in charge of the squad; stands at the front of the platoon with other squad leaders, behind the guide

Squadron: Consisted of two or more groupings of aircraft or divisions of ships

Squared away: Neat; organized; orderly; one who has his act in together; dependable

Stand by: Prepare

Standby: Waiting status

Starchies: Starched utility uniform

Survey: Dispose of; eliminate; turning in used equipment for new gear, worn-out clothing; also used to describe a Marine being discharged: "Surveyed out of the Corps".

Swab: Mop

Swabby: A sailor (see Swab-Jockey)

Swab-Jockey: Any sailor, squid, or anchor clanker (see Swabby)

Taps: The time lights go out; time for bed

Tet: Vietnamese New Year

Tet Offensive: The Tet Offensive was a surprise military campaign conducted between 30 January and 23 September 1968, by forces of the Viet Cong.

The Island: could be used to describe any island, but most often to describe Guadalcanal

Third Phase: Final phase of training

Thompson submachine gun: This was a hand-held .45 caliber rifle with a drum magazine that could hold fifty rounds, or a magazine that could hold twenty rounds. It was useful in close combat at point blank range, otherwise not much good. Tankers and artillerymen favored it. Made famous by gangsters in the late 1920's.

Thumping: Touching a recruit; maltreatment; violation of the SOP (Standard Operating Procedures for recruit training)

Tojo: Single-seat single engine aircraft used to intercept B-29 bombers. With its poor visibility on the ground, weak armament, and high landing speed, pilots generally disliked it. This was the type of plane shot down by Lt. Robert Merklein. Tojo was also the name of Japan's Prime Minister during the war.

Top: Short name for master sergeant; first sergeant; master gunnery sergeant or sergeant major: it stems from being the top sergeant of the command unit. According to Iron Mike there are no "tops" in the Marine Corps: a "top' is a round object with a piece of string around it to spin on the surface.

Topside: Above; upstairs

Tracer: Bullet with a phosphorous coating, designed to burn in flight to provide a visual indication of trajectory

Turn to: Begin work

Twentynine Palms: Marine Corps Base located at Twentynine Palms, California.

Twentynine Stumps: See Twentynine Palms

UA: Unauthorized absence

Uglier than a barrel full of assholes: Pretty damned ugly!

Uglier than a seabag full of rear-ends: See 'Uglier than a barrel full of assholes."

Utilities: Olive drab or camouflaged field uniform

Weapons Carrier: A three-quarter ton vehicle, manufactured by Dodge that looked like an oversized pickup truck. It was designed to carry mortars or machine guns and their crews.

Weasel: Small tracked vehicle used for towing .37-millimeter cannon, among other things.

White sidewalls: A high and tight Marine haircut

WIA: Wounded in action

Willie Peter: White phosphorous rounds that explode into a mushroom cloud that used for targeting and inflicting casualties.

WW: Walking wounded

Yellow footprints: Painted yellow footprints that mark the spot recruit's first stand on after exiting the bus upon arrival at MCRD; the starting point of boot camp; the beginning of hell for a period of time; footprints etched in the minds of every Marine

"You": A term a recruit can never call a drill instructor

Zeke: A Japanese fighter-bomber, larger than a Zero

Zero: A single-engine Japanese fighter plane that was light, fast, and very maneuverable

Zero-dark-thirty: Very early in the morning; before sunrise

CREDITS

It is with great thanks that the people listed below took the time and effort to call, write, or submit information that made this book possible. Credit is also given to people or entities mentioned in this book.

Larry Smith: Author of *The Few and the Proud.* Former editor of Parade Magazine and New York Times; author of *Beyond Glory; Medal of Honor Heroes in Their Own Words*

Gail Chatfield: Author, *"By Dammit, We're Marines! Veterans' Stories of Heroism, Horror and Humor in World War II on the Pacific Front."*

C-Span: *Mike Mervosh Oral History Interview, Parts 1 and 2*

Hawaii Five-O: *Bones of Contention:* Directed by Douglas Green; Creator Leonard Freeman; Written by: Alvin Sapinsley

Jim Cerenelli: Marine veteran who served with Iron Mike Mervosh in the Fleet Marine Force Pacific.

Brett Dingerson: Marine veteran who served with Iron Mike Mervosh in the Fleet Marine Force Pacific.

Gene Fioretti PLLC, Chemical Engineer, B.S., M.S., a good friend of Iron Mike.

Al B. Kolar, Marine Corps Veteran who served with Iron Mike Mervosh with the Fourth Marine Division.

Vincent T. Gutierrez, civilian, a dedicated Iron Mike follower.

Sergeant Dominic D. Dipierri (USMC veteran): who wrote Iron Mike a letter about 'Iron Mike's brother who died in action in the Korean War. Wrote a poem about Iron Mike.

Donald "Doodle" Marston: a long-time Marine buddy of SgtMaj Mervosh.

Captain Ed Garr, USMC Retired, who served as a PFC under Tech Sergeant Iron Mike Mervosh at Camp Lejeune, North Carolina.

SgtMaj Robert S. Ynacay, USMC (Retired): a long time friend of Iron Mike Mervosh and recently deceased.

Sergeant William 'Guns' Friedlander (USMC veteran): a friend of Iron Mike.

Joe Paulini, civilian: an admirer of Iron Mike Mervosh, and nephew of Sil Paulini who served with Iron Mike in the 4th Marine Division.

Jim Wood, Mayor of the City of Oceanside, California who proclaimed 27 May 2013 as "Sergeant Major Iron Mike Mervosh Day" in the City of Oceanside.

Linda Dudik, historian/teacher who narrated "Pacific Panel" in which Iron Mike participated as a panelist.

Ted Nestman, civilian, for a review he wrote to Mike Mervosh after he was a student attending 'Pacific Panel'.

Kimberly Chandler, civilian who wrote to Mike Mervosh after attending 'Pacific Panel'.

Kyle Wheeler, civilian, for a review he wrote to Mike Mervosh after he was a student attending 'Pacific Panel'.

Liz Wells, civilian, for a review she wrote to Mike Mervosh after she was a student attending 'Pacific Panel'.

Kyle Shields, civilian, for a review he wrote to Mike Mervosh after he was a student attending 'Pacific Panel'.

Laudenke Gallegos, civilian, for a review he wrote to Mike Mervosh after he was a student attending 'Pacific Panel'.

Arthur McCann, civilian, for a review he wrote to Mike Mervosh after he was a student attending 'Pacific Panel'.

Merlin H. Hamburg: a veteran Marine and good friend of Mike Mervosh.

Barbara Hansen Harris, civilian, a friend of Iron Mike Mervosh.

Jim Blane, Veteran Marine of the 4th Marine Division, a friend of Iron Mike Mervosh who shared similar experiences in the Pacific Campaign with the Fourth Marine Division.

Paul W. Siverson, SgtMaj USMC (Retired): friend of Iron Mike Mervosh.

Kevin Leahy, LtCol USMC (Retired): a good friend of Iron Mike Mervosh.

Marine Dan Dans, Commandant of Marine Corps League #942: an admirer of Iron Mike Mervosh and all of his accomplishments.

Sergeant Cindy Fisher, USMC, admirer of Iron Mike Mervosh.

MGySgt Duane Siegmann, USMC (Ret) and Patti Siegmann, USMC Veteran: friends of Iron Mike.

SgtMaj Bill Paxton, USMC (Ret): friend of Iron Mike Mervosh.

Rob Sumowski, Ed.D Assistant Professor, Georgia College & State University, and admirer of Iron Mike Mervosh.

Printed in the United States
By Bookmasters